THE PRESIDENT OF GOOD & EVIL

TAKING GEORGE W. BUSH SERIOUSLY

PETER SINGER

Granta Books
London

Granta Publications, 2/3 Hanover Yard, Noel Road, London N1 8BE

First published in Great Britain by Granta Books 2004
First published in the US by Dutton 2004

A CIP catalogue record for this book is available from the British Library.

1 3 5 7 9 10 8 6 4 2

Printed and bound in Great Britain
by Bookmarque Limited, Croydon, Surrey

Contents

Chapter 1

Introduction

We are in a conflict between good and evil, and America will call evil by its name.

—George W. Bush, United States Military Academy, West Point, June 1, 2002

George W. Bush is not only America's president, but also its most prominent moralist. No other president in living memory has spoken so often about good and evil, right and wrong. His inaugural address was a call to build "a single nation of justice and opportunity." A year later, he famously proclaimed North Korea, Iran, and Iraq to be an "axis of evil," and in contrast, he called the United States "a moral nation." He defends his tax policy in moral terms, saying that it is fair, and gives back to taxpayers what is rightfully theirs. The case he makes for free trade is "not just monetary, but moral." Open trade is a "moral imperative." Another "moral imperative," he says, is alleviating hunger and poverty throughout the world. He has said that "America's greatest economic need is higher ethical standards." In setting out the "Bush Doctrine," which defends preemptive strikes against those who might threaten America with weapons of mass destruction, he asserted: "Moral truth is the same in every culture, in every time, and in every place." But in what moral truths does the president believe? Considering how much the president says about ethics, it is surprising how little serious discussion there has been of the moral philosophy of George W. Bush.

Bush's tendency to see the world in terms of good and evil is especially striking. He has spoken about evil in 319 separate speeches, or about 30 percent of all the speeches he gave between the time he took office and June 16, 2003. In these speeches he uses the word "evil" as a noun far more often than he uses it as an adjective—914 noun uses as against 182 adjectival uses. Only twenty-four times, in all these occasions on which Bush talks of evil, does he use it as an adjective to describe what people do—that is, to judge acts or deeds. This suggests that Bush is not thinking about evil deeds, or even evil people, nearly as often as he is thinking about evil as a *thing,* or a force, something that has a real existence apart from the cruel, callous, brutal, and selfish acts of which human beings are capable. His readiness to talk about evil in this manner raises the question of what meaning evil can have in a secular modern world.

My professional interest in the president's ethics dates from his intervention in my own field, bioethics, in his first special prime-time televised address to the nation as president on August 9, 2001. The speech was devoted to the ethical questions raised by stem-cell research. I was preparing to teach a graduate seminar on bioethics when I learned that Bush was going to speak to the nation on that topic. Issues about the moral status of human embryos were part of the syllabus for my course, and I thought it might be interesting for my students to read and discuss what the president had to say. As an educational tool, that worked well, for the speech provides a clear example of an unargued assumption that is very common in the debate about abortion and early human life. Following the events of September 11, 2001, the nation turned from its discussion of stem cells to terrorism and how to respond to it. But once Bush's ethics had caught my attention in one field, I paid more attention to all the other issues that he saw in moral terms. To what extent, I asked myself, does the president have a coherent moral philosophy? Is there a clear moral view lying behind the particular views he expresses, and if so, what is it?

This book expounds George W. Bush's ethic as it is found in his speeches, writings, and other comments, as well as in the decisions he has made as an elected official. It does not attempt the impossible task of covering everything he has said and done, or even every major issue of his presidency, but instead focuses on those issues that most sharply raise fundamental ethical principles and hence reveal the president's views about right and wrong.

Once we are clear on what Bush's ethic is, the question arises: how sound is it? Or at least, that question arises for everyone who believes that there is a role for reason and argument in ethics. Some think that all we can ever do in ethics is state our own position, and if others hold different views, we can no more argue against them than we can argue over matters of taste. Bush rejects this skepticism about morality. Speaking at the inauguration of his second term as governor of Texas, he said that our children must be educated not only in reading and writing, but also in right and wrong, adding: "Some people think it's inappropriate to make moral judgments anymore. Not me." Well, not me either, so that is one view about morality on which the president and I agree. If reason and argument were of no use in reaching ethical judgments, we would not be educating our children in right and wrong, we would be indoctrinating them in the views our society holds, or the views we hold, without giving them reasons for thinking those views to be true. I'll assume that when Bush said that our children should be educated in right and wrong, he did not mean that we should be indoctrinating them. So he must think, as I do, that we can usefully discuss different possible ethical views, and judge which of them are more defensible. In the course of this book I argue that Bush's own moral positions are often not defensible. If I succeed in persuading you of this, I will have established that Bush is at least correct when he asserts that it is possible to educate people in right and wrong.

As we have already seen, Bush's readiness to talk about right and wrong goes back long before September 11, 2001, before his election as president, and before his campaign for that office focused on the idea that (in what everyone understood to be a contrast to Bill Clinton) he would bring "honor and dignity" to the White House. Bush begins his preelection memoir, *A Charge to Keep,* by saying that one of the defining moments in his life came during the prayer service just before he was to take the oath of office for his second term as governor of Texas. As Bush tells the story, Pastor Mark Craig said that people are "starved for leaders who have ethical and moral courage . . . leaders who have the moral courage to do what is right for the right reason." Bush tells us that this sermon spoke directly to "my heart and my life," challenging him to do more than he had done in his first four years as governor. He resolved, it seems, to be the kind of leader for which, as Pastor Craig had said, the people are starved.

But despite Bush's assertion that Craig's speech was one of those moments "that forever change you . . . that set you on a different course," it seems that he was on that course already. Morality was center stage in his inaugural speech for his second term as governor, which he had obviously prepared before he heard Craig's sermon. After saying that our children need to be educated in right and wrong, he went on to say: "They must learn to say yes to responsibility, yes to family, yes to honesty and work . . . and no to drugs, no to violence, no to promiscuity or having babies out of wedlock." Precisely at what point Bush decided to make ethics a central theme of his public life is difficult to say. Perhaps it was during a summer weekend in 1985, when Bush had joined his parents and other family members at the Bush summer residence in Kennebunkport, Maine. The evangelist Billy Graham was invited to join the family, and as Bush walked along the beach, Graham reportedly asked him if he was "right with God." Bush replied that he wasn't sure, but the conversation started him thinking about it. In *A Charge to Keep* he pinpoints this as the moment when "Reverend Billy Graham planted a mustard seed in my soul" that led him to "recommit my heart to Jesus Christ" and become a regular reader of the Bible. Certainly Bush's Christian beliefs play an important role in his moral thinking.

The fact that George W. Bush is the president of the world's only superpower is reason enough for wanting to understand his moral views. But it is not the only reason. Bush represents a distinctively American moral outlook—not, of course, one shared by all Americans, but nevertheless one that plays a more central role in American public life than it plays anywhere else. Having lived most of my life outside the United States, I am frequently struck by how differently Americans think from Europeans, Australians, and even Canadians about social, political, and ethical issues. Bush and I are of the same generation—indeed, we were born on the same day, July 6, 1946—and yet in some ways we live in different ethical universes. To understand Bush better is to understand one strand in the complex set of ideas that makes America different. So this book is not only a study of the ethics of one United States president, but also an outsider's look at a major strand of American thinking—the way of thinking that currently guides the policies of the world's dominant nation, and that openly espouses the aim of making the twenty-first century "the American century."

Given the global significance of Bush's views of right and wrong, it may seem surprising that philosophers have paid little attention to his ethics. One likely reason for this is that philosophers consider him unworthy of their attention. When I have told friends and colleagues that I am working on a book about "Bush's ethics," some of them quip that the phrase is an oxymoron, or that it must be a very short book. Don't I realize, they ask in incredulous tones, that Bush is just another politician who says whatever he thinks will get him elected, or reelected? He doesn't even have the attention span, they tell me, let alone the brainpower, to think out a coherent philosophy. Instead of wasting my time by taking his remarks on ethics seriously, they suggest, I should expose the hypocrisy of all his talk about morality. I should show that what he actually does is always in the interests of his Texan friends in the oil industry, or of the big corporations and wealthy individual donors who contribute so heavily to his campaign coffers.

There are times during this book when I do ask whether what Bush does is consistent with what he says he believes, and after I have done that, I will ask whether the cynical view my friends have taken is correct. Obviously Bush is a politician, and subject to the same pressures as any politician, but I think the truth is more complex than my skeptical friends suggest. Even if they are right about the president's motives, however, that doesn't drain all the interest from the moral philosophy that he defends. Tens of millions of Americans believe that he is sincere, and share the views that he puts forward on a wide range of moral issues. They also accept unquestioningly the bright, positive image of America and its unique goodness that shines through his speeches. Those who think I am naive about Bush's own views may therefore see what follows as an examination and critique of a set of beliefs widely shared by the American public, no matter whether the chief spokesperson for the position really believes what he is saying. So in the pages that follow my starting point is to take what Bush says at face value, and inquire how defensible the positions that he espouses are.

PART I

BUSH'S AMERICA

Chapter 2

A Single Nation of Justice and Opportunity

We will carry a message of hope and renewal to every community in this country. We will tell every American, "The dream is for you." Tell forgotten children in failed schools, "The dream is for you." Tell families, from the barrios of L.A. to the Rio Grande Valley: "El sueno americano es para ti." Tell men and women in our decaying cities, "The dream is for you." Tell confused young people, starved of ideals, "The dream is for you."

—George W. Bush, Indianapolis, Indiana, July 22, 1999

While many of our citizens prosper, others doubt the promise—even the justice—of our own country. Sometimes our differences run so deep, it seems we share a continent, but not a country. We do not accept this, and we will not allow it. Our unity, our union, is the serious work of leaders and citizens in every generation. And this is my solemn pledge: I will work to build a single nation of justice and opportunity.

—George W. Bush, Inaugural Address, January 20, 2001

It's your money.

—George W. Bush, Tax Family Event, Kirkwood Community Center, St. Louis, Missouri, February 20, 2001

Hope, Justice, and a Tax Cut

The first of the three previous quotations are from Bush's "Duty of Hope" campaign speech, an inspiring address that offered hope to every American, and the key text for his philosophy of "compassionate conservatism." Standing next to Bush as he delivered the speech was Indianapolis mayor Steven Goldsmith, a Republican lauded by conservatives for working with faith-based organizations to provide community services. Goldsmith subsequently became President Bush's special advisor on faith-based and not-for-profit initiatives. The theme of the speech is that economic prosperity is not enough. Referring to Adam Smith's famous "invisible hand," that free competition in the marketplace makes the self-interested strivings of individuals contribute to the common good, Bush says the invisible hand can work many miracles, "but it cannot touch the human heart." Noting that America's prison population has tripled over the last fifteen years, Bush talks about the estimated 1.3 million "forgotten children" who have one or both parents in jail and are almost six times more likely than other children to go to prison themselves. He pledges that his administration will bring help and hope to these and other innocent victims of crime, leaving no one behind. In an important statement of his philosophy of government, he rejects the idea that the proper response to all these problems is for the government to get out of the way and leave people alone. No, he insists, the American national character "shines in our compassion" and we have "a vision of the common good beyond profit and loss. . . . Americans will never write the epitaph of idealism."

The second quotation shows Bush carrying this spirit of idealism into the inauguration of his presidency. In a pair of statements that epitomizes the social philosophy of compassionate conservatism, he said, "America, at its best, is compassionate" and "America, at its best, is a place where personal responsibility is valued and expected." His pledge to "build a single nation of justice and opportunity" links justice to the key American ideal of giving every individual the opportunity to succeed. As in his campaign speeches, he spoke of children at risk, and suggested that whatever our view of the causes of this situation, we can all agree that the children are not at fault. And again he urged that this is not a problem that can be simply left alone: "In the quiet of American conscience, we know that deep, persistent poverty is unworthy of our nation's promise. . . . Where there is suffering, there is duty."

The third quotation could have come from any of a large number of Bush's speeches. As a candidate, in campaign speeches, and as president, when pressing Congress to enact the tax cut he wanted, he told Americans that "It's your money." His message was that when governments tax their subjects, they take money that belongs to the taxpayers and spend it—instead of letting the taxpayers decide for themselves how they want to spend it. Thus he turned the tax issue into a vote for or against "big government." Here's an example:

> It's your money. [My proposed tax cut] will give you a chance to set your priorities for your family. It says that we in the federal government have a fundamental trust in the people of America, and that's where our faith should be—in the people. The best government is that which trusts America, and there's no better way to make that trust explicit than to share your money with you.

On another occasion, Bush told Americans that they pay more in federal, state, and local taxes than they spend for food, clothing, and housing, and added, "This isn't right, folks. We ought to send some of your money back to the people who pay the bills." When addressing Congress about the tax cut, he told the representatives that the existence of a budget surplus showed that the American people had been "overcharged" and, on behalf of the American people, he was "asking for a refund." Although some might want to use the money on "more and bigger government," this was, in Bush's view, the wrong choice. His preferred option was "to let the American people spend their own money to meet their own needs."

It doesn't take a great deal of reflection to appreciate that the line of thought expressed in the third quotation pushes against that expressed in the first two. To help children with parents in prison will take money, whether the assistance is given by a government agency, or by faith-based and other community charities assisted by government resources. Much more money will be needed to end "deep, persistent poverty" in America and "build a single nation of justice and opportunity," no matter how it is done. Some of this money may come from private charity, but realistically, most of it will have to come from taxes. If the money raised from taxes is "your money," and needs to be refunded to the American people, from where is the money needed to fight poverty and achieve justice going to come?

Bush's Moral Case for a Tax Cut

If it were not for the events of September 11, 2001, the Bush presidency might have been most notable for its sharp tax cuts. A big cut in personal taxation was one of Bush's central campaign planks. He argued that it was not just an economically sound thing to do, but the right thing, the fair thing, to do. As a candidate, Bush said that he would cut taxes by $1.6 trillion over ten years. He favored both a cut in income tax rates and an end to the estate tax. At the outset of his presidency, he urged Congress to pass his tax cut, and the outcome was the Economic Growth and Tax Relief Reconciliation Act of 2001, which cut income tax rates and abolished the estate tax, for a total tax cut of $1.35 trillion over ten years. Less than two years later, he urged Congress to cut taxes by a further $726 billion over ten years. The Senate insisted on reducing the size of the cut, but nevertheless the outcome was another major tax cut of $320 billion over ten years. Since that figure depends on some artificial "sunset clauses," putting time limits on cuts that later Congresses will be under great pressure to maintain, the total impact of the second round of cuts could, over ten years, equal or even exceed what Bush asked for—one estimate is that it will cost $800 billion. Enacting so large a tax cut when the budget surplus had already been replaced by a deficit shocked many economic commentators. The conservative and usually staid London *Financial Times* commented: "On the management of fiscal policy, the lunatics are now in charge of the asylum." Whatever the cynics may say about politicians' promises, tax cuts is one on which Bush delivered.

It is here, in Bush's ideas about taxation, that his distinctively American philosophy of government emerges most clearly. European, Canadian, or Australian politicians may also want to cut taxes, but it is hard to imagine them making a moral argument for a tax cut in the way that Bush argued for his initial tax cut. Bush's language seems to echo the libertarian view that all taxation is theft, for if "it's your money," then isn't it theft for the government to demand your money from you, under pain of fines or imprisonment if you refuse to hand it over? Indeed, Bush's speechwriter on economic issues, David Frum, has referred to Bush's use of "It's your money!" as "folk libertarianism." The best-known recent defense of the libertarian view of the legitimate function of the state was put forward by the late Harvard professor of philosophy Robert Nozick. In Nozick's view, unless there are historical injustices to correct, the state should be limited to the "night watchman" functions of defending the nation from outside enemies, and providing law and order within it. But Bush does not want so minimal a state. In his inaugural address, after referring to the duty to relieve suffering, Bush said: "Americans in need are not strangers, they are citizens; not problems, but priorities." He also supports federal spending on education, insisting only that schools receiving federal dollars should be tested to show that they are educating their students. So helping Americans in need and providing education for all children appear to be among his priorities. The proportion of the taxes you pay that go toward meeting these priorities, then, is presumably not "your money" but the government's money. So the government should give the taxpayers back only the money that is left over after the government has met "priorities" or "needs."

But how is this line between "your money" and "the government's money" to be drawn? In arguing for his initial tax cut, Bush pointed out that the government was running a surplus. So one plausible interpretation of his position is that when the priorities or needs have been met, and there is still a surplus, then the government should remember that the money was yours in the first place, and return it to the people from whom it came. But the surplus that the

United States government was running in 2000 was not a surplus *after* all needs and priorities acknowledged by Bush had been met, for he also talked about the unmet needs of, for example, disadvantaged children. If the government had spent more on ways of giving these children a greater opportunity to achieve the American dream and on other programs to overcome deep, persistent poverty, there would have been no surplus. There may have been a deficit, requiring a substantial tax rise to cover it.

Bush's argument for a tax cut is therefore caught in a dilemma. If he is not taking the extreme view that the government has no right to tax at all, and if he also rejects the minimalist state view that the government is entitled to tax only to the extent necessary to keep the peace at home and abroad, then his frequent appeal to the idea that "it's your money" is deceptive. For what this approach says is: "It's your money, but the government can and should take your money to meet needs or priorities." Thus if the budget is in surplus, whether the surplus should be used for a tax cut, or for meeting additional needs or priorities, is a matter of judgment, of weighing the pros and cons. It is that judgment, not the simple slogan "It's your money," that decides whether there should or should not be a tax cut. The slogan presents a view of the problem so oversimplified as to be deceptive.

Is it really *your money?*

When Bush told American taxpayers that the budgetary surpluses accumulated in recent years was "your money," most of them would have taken that as a truism. Of course it was their money—where else did the government get its money from, but by taxing the money they earned? Yet this assumption rests on what New York University Law School professors Liam Murphy and Thomas Nagel—among the few philosophers who have paid attention to any of Bush's ethical prounouncements—have called "the myth of ownership." Ownership is not a natural relationship between a person and a thing. It is a social convention, and in societies with a legal system, it is defined by the law.

Take a simple example. If I collect berries in the forest, do I own the berries I collect? Today, it may depend on who owns the forest. If I own it, I own the berries. If you own it, and you did not permit me to collect anything from it, then I have stolen your berries. What if the forest is in public ownership? Then laws and customs may determine ownership of forest products. Suppose that the use of the forest has been regulated by ancient customs, interpreted when necessary by a council of representatives of all the surrounding villages. Then my claim to the berries depends on the customs. The custom might be that all the berries should be picked together, and then divided equally among the villagers. In that case, I would not own the berries I collect. Alternatively, the gatherers of berries might be able to keep what they pick, after giving a percentage to the council, which uses the proceeds to pay the wages of foresters. The foresters ensure that the paths I use are not overgrown, and they protect honest villagers against brigands who would otherwise rob them of their pickings.

Suppose that the custom is for the council to receive one basket of berries in every ten gathered, but some pickers think that the council could provide the necessary services quite adequately if it received only one basket in twenty. Last Sunday I gathered twenty baskets of berries. Would an opponent of the "every tenth basket is for the council" custom be justified in pointing to my twenty baskets of berries and telling me: "They're your berries!"? No. If the council had not paid the wages of the foresters, I may not have been able to get through the forest to the places where the berries grow. Had I managed to achieve that, I may still not have been able to avoid the brigands and return with the berries I picked. Even if the council takes more than it needs, there is no sense in which the berries I picked are *all* mine.

The seventeenth-century philosopher John Locke—a major influence on early American political thought—argued that we gain a right to property by "mixing our labor" with natural objects, as long as we leave "enough and as good" for others. If I have carved a piece of wood into a chair, tilled the land, or gathered berries, they become mine—provided there is still wood, land, and berries for others to do the same. But why does mixing my labor with something that was not mine make the entire object mine? Might not mixing what is mine with something that is not mine just as easily mean that I lose what is mine? (If I own some salt, and put it into a lake, I don't make all the water in the lake mine.) There is no good answer to this challenge to Locke, or at least none that shows the existence of a natural right to property. Nor is the requirement that when we appropriate objects from nature, we leave enough for others, one that can be satisfied today. The best justification of a right to private property is that we will all be better off if we recognize such a right. But if it is the common good that justifies the recognition of a right to private property, then the common good can also set limits to that right.

Now consider a modern society based on private property and free enterprise. Instead of gathering berries, I work for a large corporation that makes automobiles, much appreciated all over the world by those who can afford them. The corporation's stock is listed on the national stock exchange, and it financed its modern factory by issuing bonds. For my labor, the corporation pays me a wage, on which I pay taxes. Let's say my wages are $1,000 a week, and from that I pay $200 in taxes. If an opponent of this rate of tax were to point to the $1,000 check and say "It's your money!" that claim would be even more difficult to defend than the parallel claim about the berries. For the corporation could not make its cars without a legal system that fosters and protects mining rights, private ownership of land, an accepted currency, systems of transport, the production and sale of energy, the existence of an educated labor force, corporate oversight, the protection of patents and the prevention of monopolies, judicial resolution of disputes, national defense, and the protection of trading routes. Even if it could make them, without security and at least a moderate degree of prosperity, few people would buy them. In other words, without taxes, and the system of regulation that could not exist without taxes, the corporation would not be able to pay me $1,000 a week—and if, somehow, I did get paid, the money would be of little value because I could not be secure in my ownership of anything I bought with it.

Herbert Simon, a Nobel Prize–winning economist, has estimated the proportion of income in wealthy countries that is the result of social capital—including technology and organizational and governmental skills—rather than individual effort. Given the enormous differences between average incomes in rich and poor countries that cannot be explained by differences in effort, he suggests that social capital is probably responsible for at least 90 percent of income in wealthy societies like the United States. So for affluent countries, he argues, "On moral grounds, then, we could argue for a flat income tax of 90 percent to return that wealth to its real owners." This moral argument does not make allowance for the effects of such a tax on incentives. That, Simon thinks, is a question to be settled by experimentation and observation, not by philosophical debate. But the argument that people in rich countries earn only a small proportion of their gross income by individual productivity, unaided by social capital, and that it may be legitimate to impose very high rates of tax, remains.

The conclusion to draw is that if we put aside utopian fantasies that have no relevance to the real world, it makes no sense to talk of the money you would have if the government did not levy taxes. A system of government is conceptually prior to property rights—and a system of government requires taxation. Oliver Wendell Holmes, the great Supreme Court justice, is often quoted as saying, "Taxes are the price we pay for civilization." And without civilization, he might have added, you would have no money. Especially in a complex modern society, there is no way of sorting out what your property entitlements might be if there were no government and no taxes. Bush's tagline, "It's your money," rests, as Murphy and Nagel point out, on a notion of a pretax distribution of resources that is "deeply incoherent."

Fairness in Taxation?

In addition to asserting that cutting taxes is the right thing to do because the government surplus is the taxpayers' money, Bush also argued that the specific tax cuts he proposed were fair. As a candidate, there were two elements of the tax cuts on which he focused: a cut in income tax rates, and the abolition of what he called "the death tax." Later, he also argued that it was unfair to tax dividends from corporations that had already been taxed.

Bush insisted that everyone should get a tax cut—the wealthy as well as those who were struggling financially. Moreover, he wanted marginal income tax rates dropped by a similar number of percentage points for all those who pay income tax. So the highest marginal income tax rate, of 39.6 percent, was cut to 35 percent, and the lowest rate from 15 percent to 10 percent. When Bush proposed this cut, Vice President Al Gore pointed out that Bush's tax plan gives the greatest benefits to the wealthiest 1 percent of Americans. In the final presidential debate, Jim Lehrer asked Bush about that claim and received this reply:

> LEHRER: What do you say specifically to what the vice president said tonight? He's said it many times, that your tax cut benefits the top 1 percent of the wealthiest Americans.
> BUSH: Of course it does. If you pay taxes, you're going to get a benefit. People who pay taxes will get tax relief.

Bush's response was not truthful. Tens of millions of low-income Americans pay no income tax, but everyone who buys anything affected by sales tax is a taxpayer. These taxpayers get no tax relief under his plan. Because of the way Lehrer phrased his question, Bush was able to evade Gore's real charge, which is not that his tax plan simply "benefits" the top 1 percent of the wealthiest Americans, but that *most* of the benefits go to them. Even cutting the lowest marginal tax rate would benefit the wealthy, because they pay that rate on a part of their income. So why cut the higher marginal tax rates as well?

After he was elected, Bush continued to defend the fairness of his planned cut in this misleading manner. In February 2001, he said: "My plan . . . doesn't single out some Americans for relief, while leaving others out. It's tax relief for everybody who pays taxes. That's what the times and basic fairness demand." Two days later, he reiterated that it was fair that "everybody who pays taxes should receive relief. And that's why we drop all rates. We drop the top rate and we drop the bottom rate." A Bush spokesperson said that under the president's "fair, responsible tax-relief plan, the typical American family will get to keep $1,600 more of their hard-earned money." It isn't clear who is supposed to be "typical," but for the four out of five income tax payers earning less than $73,000 a year in 2001, what they got, on average, is $350, and over the next ten years, their yearly savings won't rise much from that figure, generally staying below $500. On the other hand, by 2010 the plan would allow the richest 1 percent to keep, on average, another $45,000 of "their money," which may or may not have been hard-earned. By that year, 52 percent of the total tax cuts will go to the richest 1 percent. Of the total reduction of tax revenues in that year of $234 billion, the richest 1.4 million taxpayers will divide up $121 billion, while the remaining $113 billion will have to be shared between the rest of the 139 million American income tax payers. That will give the richest 1.4 million taxpayers, on average, more than one hundred times the tax savings that the rest get.

The 2003 tax cut also gives the greatest benefits to the rich. In 2005, a married couple with two children earning $41,000 a year will be paying $323 less in taxes than they would have if the 2003 tax cut had not been passed. A similar couple earning $530,000 will save $12,772. So the richer couple, earning more than twelve times as much as the couple on a lower income, saves nearly forty times as much in taxes. For most taxpayers, the cut will mean a rise in after-tax income of less than 1 percent; but for those earning over a million dollars a year, the rise will be 4.4 percent. This is not an even-handed reduction of the tax burden for all taxpayers.

Bush apparently thinks that a fair tax cut is one that cuts marginal income tax rates by roughly the same number of percentage points at the top and at the bottom of the income scales. But cutting marginal income tax rates by roughly the same number of percentage points at the top and the bottom of the income scales does not contribute toward reducing those differences between Americans that he so movingly described in his inaugural address—the differences that "run so deep, it seems we share a continent, but not a country." In fact, it increases those differences by widening income inequalities, both in absolute dollars and in percentage terms. By denying the state the resources needed to reduce inequality, it also makes it less likely that those differences will be overcome in the foreseeable future. Why then does Bush think such a cut is fair? Since his exposition of fairness in taxation never goes beyond a few short phrases, we can only attempt a reconstruction that seems consistent with other things he has said about taxation.

If we were to take the "It's your money" line seriously, we might think of fairness in taxation as something akin to the distribution of a stash that has been recovered from a thief. Suppose the thief stole $10,000, in varying sums, from many people, but before being caught he spent most of it, and the stash contains only $1,000. We might then think that the fair thing to do is to give each of the thief's victims 10 percent of the money he or she lost. Similarly, if Bush believes that the government has taken money it should not have taken, perhaps he thinks that government should return the money to those from whom it was taken, on a basis that is proportionate to how much was taken in the first place. That is not exactly what his tax cut does, but it seems to be what his language implies should be done.

If this is the intuitive notion of fairness that Bush is appealing to when he says that a fair tax cut is one that cuts all tax rates by a similar amount, it cannot be sustained. In returning the thief's ill-gotten gains, we may feel that it is not our role to inquire into the needs of the thief's victims, and on that basis, we may simply decide to give everyone the same percentage of what they lost. This may be a fair procedure to adopt if we lack the information we would need to bring about a more substantively fair outcome. Suppose, however, that we know that the $200 the thief stole from Angela means that she is facing eviction and homelessness because, through no fault of her own, she is $100 short with her rent. On the other hand, the $1,000 that was taken from Barbara is less than she spends each week shopping for stylish clothes at expensive boutiques. Bush's idea that we should return the money to everyone from whom it was taken, in some way proportional to what was taken from them, would mean that we should return $100 to Barbara and only $20 to Angela. Everyone benefits from this distribution, it is true, but is it fair that as a result of the thefts, Angela will be homeless, whereas Barbara may, at worst, have to do without that stunning little handbag she saw in a Soho boutique? There is no inherent reason why giving back the same proportion of the money stolen is any fairer than trying to undo, as far as possible, the harms caused by the thefts, with the greater harms having priority over the lesser ones. If we choose the latter principle, we will make sure that Angela can pay her rent before we contribute anything toward Barbara's penchant for wearing designer clothes.

There is more to be said about the fairness of Bush's tax cuts, but first we need to look at another aspect of his view about unfair taxation.

The "Death Tax" and Equality of Opportunity

Bush campaigned on the elimination of the estate tax, which he usually refers to as "the death tax." The estate tax is effectively a tax on inherited wealth—and in America, it targets only the estates of those who die seriously wealthy. In 1999, tax was only payable on the top 1 percent of estates by value. Because the tax is progressive, with the rate rising as the value of the estate rises, more than half of the total revenue raised by the estate tax was collected from estates not merely in the top 1 percent, but in the even more rarefied strata of wealth to which only one American in 700 belongs—estates worth at least $5 million. As Princeton University professor of economics Paul Krugman says, "Tales of family farms and businesses broken up to pay the estate tax are basically rural legends; hardly any real examples have been found, despite diligent searching." Despite this, during the presidential debates Gore proposed amending the estate tax to exempt even more family farms and family businesses. But Bush insisted, on the grounds of fairness, that this was not enough: "Eliminate the death tax completely," he said, "because people shouldn't be taxed twice on their assets. It's either unfair for some or unfair for all."

Again, Bush's intuitive moral judgments are not self-evidently right. The objection to "being taxed twice on their assets" presumably refers to the idea that people have been taxed on their income, and then they are taxed again on their accumulated wealth, built up from their after-tax income, when they die. But if dead people don't talk, they don't pay taxes either. Legally, the "death tax" is a tax on the estates of people who have died. In effect, it is a tax on the heirs of the person who died. They are not being taxed twice on the assets they are receiving. One could, of course, imagine a system in which there is no estate tax, but money gained by inheritance is treated as income for tax purposes. But for many taxpayers that would be worse than an estate tax, because inheriting even an estate of moderate size would put them in a high tax bracket for the year in which they inherited it.

In any case, even if the "death tax" did tax people twice, there is no moral rule that says no one may be taxed more than once. Bush used the same argument about double taxation to promote his 2003 proposal for a tax exemption for dividends, arguing that the corporations that paid dividends had already paid corporate taxes on their profits. (This was another tax cut that favored the rich, for 85 percent of stocks and bonds, by value, are held by people in the top 10 percent of the income spectrum. In the end Congress reduced the tax on dividends for most taxpayers to 15 percent, but did not abolish it entirely.) There are many taxes that tax people twice, or to be more precise, tax a particular stream of income twice. When people buy goods or services, the money they are spending is what was left to them after paying income tax, so a sales tax also "taxes people twice." Few people object to it for that reason. If it is not wrong to tax people on what they spend when they are alive, even though they have already paid income tax on the money they are spending, why should it be wrong to tax what people leave when they die?

Bush's inaugural address holds out exactly the image of a just society that provides a moral foundation for the estate tax—the idea of "a single nation of justice and opportunity." He was right to say that the differences between prosperous and poor Americans "run deep." They run much deeper than they do in other developed nations, and they have become deeper over the past twenty years. Although America is one of the world's richest nations, the proportion of the adult population living in relative poverty is more than twice as high in the United States as it is in France, Germany, or

Italy—19 percent as against about 8 percent. American children do even worse—fully one-quarter of them live in poverty, compared with about a tenth or less in the major nations of continental Western Europe. Nor is this only because the wealthy United States has a higher benchmark below which people count as poor—on the contrary, those in the poorest 10 percent of the American population are worse off, in absolute terms, than are those in the poorest tenth of the populations of Austria, Belgium, Denmark, Finland, France, Germany, Italy, Japan, the Netherlands, Norway, Sweden, and Switzerland. A Swedish family with children that is at the threshold of that poorest 10 percent will have an income that is 60 percent higher than a similar family at the threshold of the poorest 10 percent of Americans. The Swedish family will also have the security of a safety net of income support and free health-care services that far surpasses anything available to the poor in America. The public provision of such services has long been taken for granted in all the nations of Western Europe.

Not coincidentally, Americans have the lowest life expectancy at birth of any major industrialized nation, being expected to have lives that are nearly three years shorter than those of Swedes, two years shorter than Canadians, and shorter, too, than those of the Japanese, Germans, French, British, Dutch, and Italians. Matched against the European table, American life expectancy would fall somewhere between that of Greece and Portugal.

At the other end of the scale, the richest 1 percent of Americans hold more than 38 percent of the nation's wealth, a concentration unmatched in any other developed nation. And the gap between the rich and the rest of society is growing wider. The Congressional Budget Office has reported that between 1979 and 1997, the after-tax income of the top 1 percent of Americans rose 157 percent, while the income of those in the middle-income range rose by only 5 percent, and that of the poorest fifth of the population actually fell. U.S. census data show an increasing share of income going to the top 20 percent of the population, and especially to the top 5 percent. In 1970, according to *Fortune* magazine, the average annual compensation of the top one hundred chief executives was thirty-nine times the pay of an ordinary worker. By 1999, it had risen to more than 1,000 times the pay of ordinary workers.

Such deep differences in income and wealth raise, as Bush correctly noted, a serious doubt about whether America is a just society. Indeed, for those who support an egalitarian ethic—one that says that people should be equal in wealth—it is evident that America is very far from being a just society. But equality of wealth has never been prominent among American values. Instead, the distinctively American form of equality has been equality of opportunity. Bush paid tribute to this idea in his inaugural address, when he proclaimed that the grandest of all American ideals is "an unfolding American promise that everyone belongs, that everyone deserves a chance." In other contexts he has said that equal opportunity is "what America is all about" and that "every child must have an equal place at the starting line." According to the American ideal, what matters is that everyone should have an equal opportunity to be successful, whether that means becoming rich, or being elected president. Given equal opportunity, the fact that one person is rich and another is poor is not itself a sign of injustice. Some choose to work hard and save what they earn in order to get on, while others are less industrious, or spend what they earn as soon as they get it. Advocates of equality of opportunity generally think it right that those who work and save should be rewarded for their effort and for curbing their spending. But if the person who is poor did not have the same opportunity to succeed as the person who is rich, then the society is unjust.

Although the ideal of equal opportunity enjoys wide support among Americans, all the evidence suggests that even by this standard, the nation is a grossly unjust society. After all, a nation with a particularly high percentage of its children living in relative poverty will have great difficulty providing every child with "an equal place at the starting line." Some children have plenty of nutritious food, a warm place to sleep in the winter, and air-conditioning in summer. From their early years of schooling, they have their own room, desk and Internet-linked computer. Others have none of these advantages. How can children living in such different circumstances have an equal start in life?

America has always prided itself on providing education to all of its citizens. Giving extra funds to schools in disadvantaged neighborhoods would help, though even that would not overcome differences in the home environment. In contrast to most developed nations, which fund schools from national or at least state taxes, school funding in the United States is usually local and tied to property taxes. This means that schools in wealthy districts receive more, per child, than schools in poor districts—precisely the reverse of what would be needed to give each child an equal place at the starting line. There are, admittedly, some federal and state funding programs that mitigate the effects of this "the more you have, the more you get" funding system, but the federal government would need to spend much more on elementary and high school education to overcome the disadvantage for children living in poor areas.

To take advantage of the best economic and career opportunities available today, a college degree is virtually essential. In 1994, the last year for which figures are available, a student aged 18–24 from a family with earnings in the top quarter of the population was ten times more likely to gain a degree by the age of twenty-four than a student from a family with earnings in the bottom quarter. Worse still, this ten-to-one ratio had climbed sharply since 1979, when it was only four-to-one. America must yield to countries like Canada, Germany, the Netherlands, Sweden, and the United Kingdom in terms of the likelihood of a poor person rising out of poverty in any given year. Moreover those members of the poor in America who do manage to escape poverty are more likely to fall back into it within five years than their counterparts in those countries.

Real equality of opportunity is extraordinarily difficult to achieve in any society with sharp inequalities of wealth, because rich, educated, well-connected parents can always give their children advantages that the children of poor, uneducated parents will lack. Nevertheless, if we want to enhance equality of opportunity, it is hard to think of a better way to start than with a tax on inherited wealth. Such a tax makes society fairer because it taxes people who are receiving a benefit that they have done nothing to deserve. An inheritance is a windfall, something that is just as likely to come to the idle as to the hardworking. Conservatives who worry about the disincentive effects of welfare on the poor should have no difficulty in accepting that a similar effect can follow from receiving what Warren Buffett has called "a lifetime of food stamps based on coming out of the right womb." Several studies suggest that people who grow up knowing that they will never need to earn their own living consume more and work less—in plain old-fashioned language, they are more idle and wasteful—than those who do not have such an assurance. But even if that is not the case, as long as people can pass great wealth on to their children, there can never be real equality of opportunity.

Some of America's wealthiest people oppose the abolition of the estate tax. An organization called Responsible Wealth has initiated a petition for its retention. Launched by William Gates, Sr., father of the world's wealthiest person, the petition was signed by 120 millionaires and billionaires, including Gates, Sr., the investor and philanthropist George Soros, CNN founder Ted Turner, Steven C. Rockefeller and other members of the Rockefeller family, Ben Cohen of Ben & Jerry's, and heirs of the Roosevelt family. Warren Buffett, the world's fourth-richest person, was not a signatory, but he has supported the idea, telling *The New York Times* that the estate tax played a critical role in promoting economic growth by helping to create a society in which success is based on merit rather than inheritance. Repealing the estate tax, he said, would be equivalent to "choosing the 2020 Olympic team by picking the eldest sons of the gold medal winners in the 2000 Olympics." Gates, Sr., told a Senate Finance Committee hearing on the estate tax, "While we may not be able to ensure that all children start their lives on a level playing field, that is something we should strive for and the estate tax keeps us closer to that ideal." Evidently, the sense of justice of these wealthy individuals is more powerful than their desire to pass on their own wealth intact to their heirs. One can only wonder why this sense of justice is not shared by the president, who spoke so eloquently about justice and opportunity in his inaugural address.

Bush's Choice

Bush's conception of "a single nation of justice and opportunity" cannot be reconciled with his opposition to taxes on a small number of especially high-value estates and on dividends, nor with his support for giving most of the budget surplus that existed when he was elected to the presidency back to taxpayers who are not in need, nor with his continued support for tax cuts favorable to the rich after that surplus disappeared. If we "do not accept" and "will not allow" the deep inequalities between Americans that Bush described in his inaugural address, we should have seen the budget surplus—when there was one—as a result not of too much taxation, but of too little spending. It is impossible to achieve the priorities that Bush himself speaks about—priorities like ensuring that every American child has an equal place at the starting line—without resources.

To this, Bush and his supporters will no doubt respond that to imagine that one can fight poverty or bring about equal opportunity by more government spending is to repeat the mistakes of earlier generations. In his foreword to Melvin Olasky's *Compassionate Conservatism,* Bush said that it was a mistake to think that compassion means government "spending large sums of money and building an immense bureaucracy to help the poor." The result of this spending was that "we hurt the very people we meant to help." That, however, is a myth. Studies of national tax and spending policies have shown that socicties in which governments tax more, as a proportion of gross domestic product, are also societies with lower income inequality. Higher welfare spending does reduce inequality. And since among the richer nations (for example, the twenty-three higher-income members of the Organization for Economic Development and Cooperation) the more equal ones have, on average, a higher income per capita, more redistribution by the state leads to a lower rate of absolute poverty, as well as to greater equality and a lower rate of relative poverty. In any case, more government spending on fighting poverty and promoting equal opportunity does not necessarily mean programs delivered by the government. If fighting poverty and helping every child to get an equal start is better done by faith-based and private charities than by the government, then that is where the money should go.

Since Olasky has been the dominant influence on Bush in this area, it is worth looking at the book to which Bush wrote the foreword. Much of *Compassionate Conservatism* is a kind of travelogue through poverty in America. Traveling with his son Daniel, Olasky visits faith-based and other nonprofit organizations fighting poverty in run-down urban areas. Recounting his journey, he is able to provide the reader with inspirational stories of the work of heroic people fighting against violence, drugs, and a general feeling of hopelessness. These people really do make a difference—but as Olasky himself points out, their limited resources mean that the difference they make is very small compared with what needs to be done.

Here are some examples. Melvin and Daniel Olasky visit the Fair Park Friendship Center in South Dallas, run by the Reverend Stephan Broden. Its "summer education and evangelism program" for elementary school-age children is "doing wonderful but limited service, as thousands of children roam the streets." In West Dallas, Kathy Dudley, a dedicated and hardworking Christian community leader, "has a yearning to do more, and she knows that more resources are needed." Another "legendary poverty fighter" from Dallas is Ben Beltzer, head of the Interfaith Housing Coalition. The efforts of Beltzer and those like him need government money, Olasky writes, but without red tape that hamstrings their work.

Then father and son go to Indianapolis, to see the impact of Mayor Goldsmith's efforts to provide government support for faith-based charities. Goldsmith's "Front Porch Alliance" gets praise for helping to cut government red tape, but there is still not enough money to do what needs to be done. A program run by the "seemingly tireless" Reverend Jay Height at his Shepherd Community Center only reaches a small number of people. This leads Olasky to raise the question of "using taxpayer funds to expand good programs that could reach many more." Heading for the nation's capital, Olasky mentions that there are 129 different faith-based organizations focusing on youth in Washington, D.C., and asks, "Imagine what could happen if the government learned how to help, not hinder, such groups."

Once in Washington, Melvin and Daniel meet Hannah Hawkins, who helps abandoned children. She won't accept government money because then she couldn't pray with the children, which prompts Olasky to say that if only the government officials would give Hawkins funds without strings attached, her kids could have "new play equipment, new books, help with utilities, and so forth. . . ." In other words, the need for more resources, and the idea that governments would be able to provide these resources if only they weren't so inhibited about funding faith-based organizations, is a constant refrain in the pages of the book that Bush describes, in his foreword, as a clear summary of the principles of compassionate conservativism by its leading thinker.

One might think, then, that the highest priority of the new compassionate administration pledged to build a single nation of justice and opportunity would be to provide very substantial additional funds for faith-based and other nonprofit charities. Since the budget was in surplus when Bush took office, these funds were available even without tax increases. Instead, the tax cut was a higher priority. When told, seven months after he took office, that the surplus was rapidly dwindling, Bush said that this was "incredibly positive news" because it would create "a fiscal straitjacket" for Congress and prevent the growth of the federal government. That statement suggests that cutting the size of the federal government was a higher priority for Bush than building a single nation of justice and opportunity. But cutting the size of government is not, in itself, a good thing. If the section of the government cut back was doing something desirable that cannot be done except by the government, it is a bad thing. Education, for example, was one of Bush's priorities, and one on which he got swift legislation through Congress. Yet after the surplus disappeared, Bush said he had to cut back on spending, and would spend only $22 billion of the $28 billion that the legislation had authorized to be spent on education in 2002. Another specific measure that Bush pledged to take if elected was to allow taxpayers who do not itemize their deductions to deduct contributions to charity. Usually, those with high incomes claim each specific contribution, but those with lower incomes take a set deduction without listing what they have given. People on lower incomes therefore do not reduce their taxes by giving to charity. Bush sought to change this, and thus encourage more charitable giving. But as *The Washington Post* reported, his tax cut limited his ability to deliver on his own campaign promises. Because the tax cut had already reduced expected tax revenue, the deduction had to be limited. For most of the households affected, the maximum savings on next year's taxes was $7.50. By 2010, this would rise to a savings of $30 a year. That isn't going to provide many of the resources that, as Olasky saw, the charitable organizations need. Indeed, the very modest increase in charitable giving that this change may achieve is likely to be overwhelmed by the much greater decrease that results from the abolition of the estate tax. John J. DiIulio, Jr., the man Bush appointed to direct the most tangible of his compassionate conservatism initiatives, the White House Office of Faith-Based and Community Initiatives, made this point very bluntly: "Repeal [of the estate tax] could undercut another administration priority: encouraging private contributions to charities, religious and nonreligious alike, that help the poor."

In his foreword to *Compassionate Conservatism,* Bush urges us to "share our resources—both material and spiritual—with those who need them most." How much sharing of our material resources it would take to get really serious about creating a single nation of justice and opportunity is anyone's guess, but it seems reasonable to suppose that it would have taken all of the budget surplus that existed in 2000, and more. That surplus was a substantial material resource that could have been shared with those who need such resources most. It could have been used to rally Americans to the cause of compassion, and to give faith-based and other nonprofit charities the support they need to fight poverty effectively. It could have paid for initiatives sufficient to give the forgotten children in failed schools, the families from the barrios of L.A., and the men and women in America's decaying cities, reason to believe the president who told them: "The dream is for you." Instead, Bush chose a tax cut that only accentuated the economic inequality that had already been growing so rapidly in America since the 1970s. The number of Americans living in poverty rose in 2001 and increased again in 2002.

Worse was to come. In 2003, when it was clear that the budget surplus had turned into a substantial deficit, and that more spending was needed for the war with Iraq, Bush nevertheless successfully pushed Congress to pass another huge tax cut. Now, with no surplus, Bush could not so easily argue that "It's your money." Instead, he promoted his tax cut as a means of helping to speed up economic recovery and create more jobs. In his 2003 State of the Union address, Bush said, "The economy grows when Americans have more money to spend and invest; and the best and fairest way to make sure Americans have that money is not to tax it away in the first place." But as of this writing, despite all the tax cuts, it seems probable that there will be fewer Americans on the payroll when Bush finishes his first term of office than there were when he began it. The last time that happened during any presidential term was during Herbert Hoover's presidency, from 1929 to 1933—and Hoover faced a much more serious economic downturn than Bush has. Bush's response to this situation is: "If Congress is really interested in job creation, they will make every one of the tax relief measures we passed permanent." The tax cuts still have, under the existing legislation, several years to run. It is difficult to see how making them permanent will help Americans who are out of work now.

Bush might have done more to create jobs if, instead of cutting taxes, he had stimulated the economy by increasing government spending. Since the poor will almost certainly spend their money rather than save it, increasing the various kinds of benefits they receive is more likely to give a quick boost to the economy than tax cuts that go mostly to the rich. It would therefore have been both better and fairer than the tax cuts Bush proposed. In any case, two weeks later, Federal Reserve Chairman Alan Greenspan sharply disagreed with the president's economic argument for a tax cut, suggesting that "There should be little disagreement about the need to reestablish budget discipline," and warning that anything that exacerbated the budget deficit was poor economic policy. Greenspan's stellar economic credentials, and doubts about the wisdom of Bush's actions among many other leading economists, and even some of his own party members, did not cause Bush to hesitate in touring the nation to promote his further tax cut—and in rejecting a compromise proposal from the Senate as a "little bitty" one. Running a large deficit is ethically dubious because it is like one generation having a party and leaving the mess for another to clean up. The fact that the next generation will consist of a smaller proportion of taxpayers supporting a higher proportion of elderly people makes the situation even worse. George Akerlof, a professor of economics at the University of California, Berkeley, and the 2001 Nobel Laureate in economics, has described the current deficit as "a form of looting" and warned that in the future, if America is to avoid the threat of bankruptcy, Medicare and Social Security will have to be cut back heavily.

Why was Bush still arguing for a large tax cut after the surplus had disappeared and against the economic advice of Greenspan and many others? If the ethical justification he offered for his 2001 tax cut—when the budget was in surplus—was inadequate, an ethical justification for his 2003 tax cut seems totally absent. Unless, as the *Financial Times* speculated, the real agenda was deliberately to bring about what Akerlof has warned is likely to happen: a fiscal crisis that would provide a justification for slashing federal spending on popular social programs such as Medicaid, Medicare, and Social Security. If that speculation turns out to be true, "compassionate conservatism" will have turned into its very opposite: a conservatism that increases the power and affluence of the rich, and is prepared to be utterly heartless to the poor and elderly.

A Concluding Note: Is Equal Opportunity Enough?

Although the purpose of this chapter has been to demonstrate the inconsistency between Bush's tax policy and his support for equal opportunity, it would be a mistake to believe that the ideal of equality of opportunity offers an adequate conception of a just society. Even if every child did have an equal place at the starting line, that would not make the society just. The metaphor of the starting line suggests that life is a race. In any athletic competition, natural differences in ability and temperament will play a major role in deciding the winner. I am quite sure that I could never have been a successful football player, no matter how hard I trained, and I very much doubt that I could have made it as a concert pianist, either. I might, perhaps, have been more successful in a profession requiring some mathematical ability, or language skills—areas that some with more sporting or musical talent than me might not have done well in. We no more deserve our natural abilities than we deserve to inherit the wealth of our parents. Our society rewards people who are good at sport, or financial analysis, or who are beautiful and can act or sing well, but gives very little to those who have nothing to sell in the marketplace except their physical labor—and even less to those incapable of labor. There is nothing inherently just about this arrangement. Recognizing that the rewards people get are significantly influenced by the good fortune of inherited abilities should lead us to look beyond equality of opportunity. Even in a society in which everyone does start with an equal opportunity to prosper as far as their natural abilities allow them to, it may be just to relieve the distress of those who end up at the bottom. By this measure, too, most developed nations, including the nations of the European Union, Canada, and Australia, are closer to being just societies than is the United States. The policies Bush is pursuing will broaden the "justice gap" between these different societies, and take the United States further still from Bush's own announced goal of becoming "a single nation of justice and opportunity."

Chapter 3

The Culture of Life

I worry about a culture that devalues life, and believe as your President I have an important obligation to foster and encourage respect for life in America and throughout the world.

—George W. Bush, remarks by the president on stem-cell research, August 9, 2001

Life before Birth

After George W. Bush's inauguration as president, it took more than six months before an issue arose important enough for him to make a prime-time television address to the American public. That issue was whether the federal government should fund research into stem cells derived from human embryos—a question that, he told Americans, was "one of the most profound of our time." To provide background for the speech, the White House issued a "Fact Sheet on Stem Cells," which stated that many scientists believe that stem cells have the potential to offer new ways of treating a wide range of diseases that affect approximately 128 million Americans. These new therapies could, according to the fact sheet, lead to cures for Parkinson's disease, juvenile diabetes, Alzheimer's, spinal cord injuries, and heart disease. To conduct research into these potential therapies, stem cells need to be grown and propagated in laboratories. Only stem cells derived from human embryos have been shown to possess the ability to develop into virtually all the tissues of the human body. These are therefore the ones that scientists believe to hold the most promise of cures for major diseases. Once a cell has been taken from a human embryo, it can be maintained in the laboratory, and will produce more cells, which will in turn produce further cells, and so on, until there are millions of cells available for research. This creates a line of cells that are all descended from the original cell taken from an embryo. Scientists speak of "cell lines" to refer to the entire group of cells, past and present, that have this kind of relationship to a particular original cell, much as we might speak of a "line of descent" from an ancestor. Cell lines can grow indefinitely, but they all start with an original cell taken from an embryo. The embryo does not survive the removal of the stem cells. That is why the use of stem cells is ethically dubious for those who think that a human being has a right to life from the moment of conception.

In his speech to the nation, President Bush pointed out that as a result of the widespread use of in vitro fertilization (IVF), there are already many human embryos frozen in laboratories and not wanted by the couple from whom the egg and sperm came. This happens because women undergoing IVF are usually given drugs to induce them to produce several eggs. All of these eggs will be collected, and sperm will be added to each of them, in order to ensure that there are enough viable embryos to transfer to the uterus to achieve a pregnancy. But to transfer more than three embryos at the same time is not good medical practice, because of the risk of triplets or a higher multiple birth. Usually the surplus embryos are frozen, in case the woman does not become pregnant. Then she can use them later, without having to repeat the procedure for collecting her eggs. If, however, she succeeds in becoming pregnant the first time, and the couple does not wish to have any more children, what is to be done with the frozen embryos? Bush mentioned that some frozen embryos are destroyed or donated to science, while a few have been implanted in an adoptive mother and developed into healthy children.

In thinking through the ethical issue of whether to allow federal funds to be used for research into stem-cell lines taken from frozen embryos, Bush told Americans, he "kept returning to two fundamental questions." The first of these is: "Are these frozen embryos human life, and therefore, something precious to be protected?" The second is: "If these embryos are going to be destroyed anyway, shouldn't they be used for a greater good, for research that has the potential to save and improve other lives?" Bush gives the first question an affirmative answer. He quotes the view of a scientist who says that the five-day-old cluster of cells is a "pre-embryo," not yet an embryo, an entity that has the potential for life, but is not yet "a life." But—perhaps to dramatize how he himself has gone back and forth on the issue—Bush then cites an ethicist who claims that thinking of the early cluster of cells as a "pre-embryo" is a callous rationalization. This ethicist contends that we all started our lives as embryos. That is the foundation of Bush's decision that the federal government will not fund stem-cell research in a way that encourages the destruction of human embryos.

In the remainder of his speech, Bush said that he would allow federal funds to be used for research with stem-cell colonies that had already been derived from embryos prior to his speech. As a result of private research, he said, "more than sixty genetically diverse stem-cell lines already exist." Since for these cell lines, "the life and death decision has already been made," he said that the federal government could fund research exploring the potential of stem cells without "crossing a fundamental moral line by providing taxpayer funding that would sanction or encourage further destruction of human embryos that have at least the potential for life." The National Institutes of Health subsequently claimed that there were seventy-eight stem-cell lines that could be used, in accordance with the president's policy. Scientists wanting to use them have found, however, that many of these lines are not suitable for research use, or are subject to proprietary claims that prevent them from being made available to other scientists, and in April 2003 *The New York Times* reported that there were only eleven useful lines available for researchers. This number was subsequently confirmed by Dr. Elias Zerhouni, director of the National Institutes of Health, in testimony to a congressional subcommittee. These cell lines, according to Dr. Irving Weissberg of Stanford University, all had "the genetics of people who go to in vitro fertility clinics—the white, the rich and the infertile." Another expert was quoted as saying that between one-hundred and 1,000 different human cell lines might eventually be needed, to provide good matches with the American population. Several scientists told the congressional subcommittee that frustrating negotiations over the terms on which the cell lines could be used had prevented them from getting to work, or greatly increased the costs of their research. Dr. George Daley, a Boston scientist investigating the use of stem cells to cure the immune deficiency known as "bubble boy disease," said that the Bush policy "threatens to starve the field at a time when greater nourishment is critical." Another researcher, Dr. Gerald Schatten of the University of Pittsburgh, said, "If we're going to do this, let's do it. We didn't go to the moon and decide to come back one-third of the way."

Worse still, all stem-cell lines in existence before August 9, 2001, were grown on irradiated mouse tissue, which makes them unsafe for clinical use. For this reason, Art Caplan, one of America's leading bioethicists, has said that although Bush presented his decision as a compromise between those for and against a complete ban on research using stem cells derived from human embryos, the decision is "in fact nothing more than a ban." The same consideration led Arlen Specter, a widely respected Republican senator from Pennsylvania, to send Bush a letter asking him to "expand" his 2001 decision, and allow federal funds to be used for research on a wider range of cell lines.

Putting these factual questions aside, however, what should we think about the moral argument that Bush was making? I accept his claim that the early embryo is "human life." Embryos formed from the sperm and eggs of human beings are certainly human, no matter how early in their development they may be. They are of the species *Homo sapiens*, and not of any other species. We can tell when they are alive, and when they have died. So as long as they are alive, they are human life.

The real problem with Bush's argument lies in his assumption that if the embryos in question are human life, they are "therefore something precious to be protected." Why does the fact that something is human life mean that it is something precious that we should protect?

Every year in the United States, millions of embryos die. Each of them had the unique genetic potential of an individual human being. These embryos do not die in laboratories, nor in abortion clinics, nor after women have taken RU486, the "abortion pill." They die as part of a natural process that has, as far as we know, been going on as long as there have been human beings. Some scientists estimate that for every embryo that becomes a child, four fertilized eggs fail to make it. Others think that the ratio is closer to one lost fertilized egg for every child born. Even on the lower estimate, more than three million embryos die annually in the United States from natural causes. These are embryos that have failed to implant in the woman's uterus. They are released with her menstrual bleeding. In most cases the woman never even knows that she conceived.

Should we feel that this loss of embryos is a terrible thing, a kind of ongoing holocaust? If each human embryo is "something precious to be protected," then surely that is how we should feel. Perhaps the president should consider the use of federal funds for research designed to understand why these embryos are so frequently lost, and to find ways of giving them the protection that their precious nature requires? Bush may be unaware of the number of human embryos that die in this way. But he has appointed a Council on Bioethics to advise him. The council is chaired by the prominent University of Chicago bioethicist Leon Kass, and its members include scientists who know the relevant facts. Will the council advise the president about this huge, constant loss of precious embryos, and inquire into what can be done to stop it? That seems unlikely. No one, not even the staunchest opponents of research on human embryos in Congress, is planning to fund such a research program. The truth is, politics aside, virtually no one except couples who want to have a child really cares about the loss of embryos. And even couples seeking to conceive only care about whether they will be able to have a child. They don't really care for the particular embryo that was lost. More often than not, they aren't even aware it ever happened.

Bush tells us that every embryo is unique, "like a snowflake." He is right: both embryos and snowflakes are unique. But the fact that something is unique is not in itself a reason for trying to preserve it. (We don't try to preserve snowflakes.) Bush needs to tell us why the uniqueness of each human embryo is a reason for preserving it. Since he doesn't do so, we can only speculate. Does he think that it is good for more unique human beings to be born? But since every human being, identical twins aside, is genetically unique, all we would have to do to achieve that goal is encourage people to have more children. Yet in his speeches on social issues Bush commonly exhorts young people not to become single parents—which suggests that the production of more unique children is not a sufficiently high priority with the president. At least, it is not enough of a priority with him to outweigh the social problems that he sees such children as causing. Why, then, should producing more unique children outweigh the value of research that could save or dramatically improve the lives of tens of millions of Americans?

Let's try again. Perhaps Bush's real reason for opposing the destruction of human embryos is not that more unique children are a good thing, but that once a human life exists, we should protect it. If so, there is still a gap in the argument. Bush's move from "the embryo is human life" to "the embryo is precious and to be protected" rests on the unargued assumption that has made the abortion debate in America so intractable: the idea that to be a member of the species *Homo sapiens* is sufficient to make a being's life precious. We need to be told why this should be so—why, for example, the life of a member of the species *Homo sapiens* has a greater claim to protection than the life of a member of the species *Pan troglodytes*, the chimpanzee. Bush has not proposed a ban on the use of federal funds for the destruction of chimpanzee embryos—or even, for that matter, for the deliberate infliction of lethal diseases on adult chimpanzees.

Why does Bush think that all human life is precious and to be protected? Here, obviously, we are entering into a question that is fundamental to the whole outlook he refers to as promoting the "culture of life"—not only to his decision on embryos, but also to his opposition to abortion, from which flow many other actions his government has taken. (On his first day in office, he reinstated President Reagan's order barring health-care organizations all over the world from receiving American funding if they perform abortions—even when these services are separately financed—or if they even offer women advice about abortion. Subsequently, for the same reason, he froze millions of dollars of American assistance for the World Health Organization and United Nations Population Fund programs to advance reproductive health.) One reason for Bush's view that all human life is precious is evidently his religious beliefs—as he tells us, plainly enough, in his August 2001 speech, when he says, "I also believe human life is a sacred gift from our Creator." Bush's religion and the role it plays—and should play—in his decisions as president is the subject of Chapter 5. But before we explore that question, we need to consider whether there are not other, nonreligious, grounds on which one could defend the argument that all human life is precious and to be protected. Can't it be defended on secular grounds?

Bush does give another, apparently nonreligious, argument for respecting human life. He is concerned, as we have seen, about "a culture that devalues life," and believes that it is his obligation, as president, "to foster and encourage respect for life." Later in this chapter we will see how well Bush lives up to this important obligation. First, though, we should note that when Bush talks about "respect for life" in these contexts, he means "respect for human life." He presides over a government that funds research that kills millions of nonhuman animals every year, ranging from mice and rats to hamsters, cats, dogs, baboons, and chimpanzees. Bush has never questioned this funding or suggested that it raises a profound ethical issue. There are boundaries around the kind of life for which he wants to encourage respect. If you are on one side of the boundary, your life must be respected and protected from destruction, even if that means hindering research that could save many more lives. If you are on the other side of the boundary, your life does not have to be respected, and you can be harmed or killed for almost any reason whatsoever, including the testing of a new kind of food coloring. Here, of course, Bush shares the standard view that human life is special, held by the overwhelming majority of Americans and people all over the world. Even so, if we really want to understand the ethical issues at stake, we need to ask why Bush or anyone else would oppose the destruction of early human embryos for research while supporting the destruction of other forms of life for similar purposes.

One possible ground for drawing the line between the human and the chimpanzee is that *we* are human and so we should protect all members of *our* own species, but we have no duty to protect members of *other* species. That's a bad answer, because it rests on a simple, unargued preference for "our own." If we rely on the bare claim that we are human and so should protect our own kind, we have no comeback against racists who maintain that they ought to protect their own kind—by which they mean members of their own race, but not members of other races.

A better answer is that humans are more precious than other animals because human beings have mental capacities that make it possible for them to live in ways that, as far as we can tell, cats, dogs, baboons, and even chimpanzees, cannot. Only human beings have sufficient awareness of the future to plan their lives, with careful deliberation, not for a day or a week, but for years ahead. Only humans can think through their moral choices and be held morally responsible for what they do. This answer avoids the generalized selfishness of "my duty is to my group just because it is *my* group." Instead it points to characteristics of human beings that can plausibly be held to have some moral significance. Of course, it is we human beings who judge these particular characteristics to be especially valuable, and we might be biased in selecting just the characteristics I have mentioned. If, for example, we valued beings who could fly or run well, we might think that hawks and cheetahs are particularly precious and to be protected. Yet choosing the characteristics that depend on our higher mental capacities as the basis of special value, or of a stronger claim to protection, does not seem arbitrary. Our mental capacities, when they are working properly, make our lives markedly different from those of other animals. We share with many other animals the capacity to feel pain, and also to feel emotions like love and fear, but perhaps not—except for a few species, of which chimpanzees would be the best-documented case—the capacity to understand that we have a past and a future. Perhaps that capacity to see our own life as extended over time, and therefore to have future-oriented desires, may provide grounds for holding death to be a greater tragedy when it befalls beings like us than when it befalls beings lacking that capacity.

Bush, as we have seen, argued that if the embryos are human life, they are precious and to be protected. We can now see what is wrong with this argument. If human life is more precious than nonhuman life, it is because humans possess higher mental capacities that nonhuman animals lack. Embryos, however, are utterly lacking in such higher mental capacities. Hence if it is the possession of higher mental capacities that marks the line between beings whose lives need to be protected and beings whose lives do not need to be protected, then human embryos—and fetuses, for that matter—fall on the wrong side of the line. None of them plans ahead, deliberates over choices, or can be held morally responsible. Bush's position requires a morally relevant line of demarcation that human embryos pass, but all nonhuman animals fail. The plausible line of demarcation we have been discussing won't do that job.

Admittedly, the idea that only beings who can plan ahead, deliberate over choices, or be held morally responsible are precious and should be protected has implications that go far beyond the status of early human embryos. Newborn human infants don't have those capacities either. But almost all human infants are loved and wanted by their parents, and that is enough reason to consider them precious and to protect them. Since the law needs clear lines, and birth provides a clearer, more evident line than any other point that we might take to mark the moment when a right to life begins, there are grounds for making birth the point at which killing the developing human being becomes a crime.

Is it relevant that the embryos Bush seeks to protect are *potentially* beings with the higher mental capacities we have been discussing? He may have been suggesting the relevance of this when he pointed out that some of the frozen embryos that are in excess after successful IVF have been implanted in adoptive mothers and developed into healthy children. But for Bush to argue that the potential of the frozen embryos in fertility clinics makes them precious or entitles them to protection is a difficult undertaking. Such an argument faces two insuperable objections. The first is simply that there is no general argument of the kind "X is a potential Y, therefore X now has the rights of a Y." In the American electoral system, for example, the winners of presidential elections do not have the rights of the president until they have been sworn in. So we cannot assume that a being with the potential to develop higher mental capacities has the rights of a being who has developed those capacities.

This leads to the second objection. Infertile couples wanting to have children value the embryos that might become their longed-for child, but once they have had all the children they desire, most of them no longer value the embryos at all. Some of them are willing to give them up to other infertile couples. Others do not like the idea of their genetic children being brought up by strangers, so they prefer to have their surplus frozen embryos destroyed. If Bush thinks that these embryos are precious and should be protected, what is he proposing to do about them? Does he think that the female partner of such couples should be forced to accept the transfer of the embryo to her uterus? Does he believe that the embryos should be taken away from the couple concerned, and given to a woman who is willing to carry the embryo to term? If there are more embryos frozen in laboratories than there are women willing to volunteer for this duty, should the federal government pay women willing to become adoptive mothers? Could the couple who plans to donate their embryos for research be taken to court and treated as unfit parents who abuse their children? Or should the government simply prohibit IVF, since it leads to the destruction of embryos?

The implanted embryo will, in the normal course of events, and in the absence of deliberate human intervention, become a child. The embryo frozen in the clinic can only become a child if several people strive cooperatively to make that happen—and even then it will probably fail to become a child, because the chance of a given embryo being used in IVF making it through to birth is still well below 50 percent, and in many clinics below 10 percent. In the present legal and medical situation, as Bush himself said, most of these embryos "are going to be destroyed anyway." As long as that remains the situation—and no one is proposing legislation to prevent it—how can Bush argue that frozen embryos are too precious to be used for research?

One might well ask why Bush has not urged federal legislators to pass a law preventing parents and fertility clinics from destroying embryos. Such a law could well be constitutional, for it does not directly interfere with a woman's control of her body, and hence does not violate her right to privacy in the way that the majority of the Supreme Court in *Roe v. Wade* saw laws prohibiting abortion as doing. The real reason seems to be that Bush—and his "pro-life" allies—know that few people really care about early embryos. This applies even to opponents of abortion, like Utah's Senator Orrin G. Hatch. He was speaking for many when, in support of stem-cell research, he said: "I just cannot equate a child living in a womb, with moving toes and fingers and a beating heart, with an embryo in a freezer."

On further reflection, however, we can see that having moving toes and fingers and a beating heart is not really morally decisive either. Ape and monkey fetuses have them, too. Religious grounds aside, it makes sense to see human life as intrinsically precious and in need of protection only when it has developed some other capacities—at a minimum, the capacity to feel something, possibly some degree of self-awareness. The embryos that are used to generate stem cells are still far from the point at which they have even the minimal capacity to feel something. That is why Bush's opposition to the use of embryos to create stem cells can't be adequately defended on secular grounds.

Capital Punishment

Apart from the United States, few countries use the death penalty. Only China and Iran execute more people than the U.S. No member-nation of the European Union uses it. Under the European Convention for the Protection of Human Rights and Fundamental Freedoms, it is regarded as a human rights violation, so no nation can be admitted to the European Union if it still has the death penalty on its books.

When Bush was elected president, the federal government had not used the death penalty for thirty-eight years. Bush reinstated it. When he was governor of Texas, that state had more executions than any other, and Bush signed 152 death warrants—more than any previous governor of Texas, or any other American governor in modern times. Typically, he made his life-and-death decision after a half-hour briefing with his legal counsel. Only once, as governor, did he stop an execution.

Millions of viewers watching the second presidential debate in October 2000 were shocked when Bush described the fate of the three men who murdered James Byrd: "Guess what's going to happen to them? They're going to be put to death. A jury found them guilty and—it's going to be hard to punish them any worse after they get put to death." The words alone do not convey the exultation, almost glee, that appeared on Bush's face when he spoke of the coming execution of the men who had been convicted of murder. (As a questioner from the audience in the third presidential debate put it, Bush seemed to "overly enjoy" the fact that Texas leads the nation in the execution of prisoners. Bush denied that this was the case, but those who saw his expression in the earlier debate must have had difficulty in believing his assurance.) Undoubtedly the crime was dreadful, but such levity about the infliction of the death penalty makes a poor fit with the idea of promoting a culture of life.

To support the death penalty while opposing the killing of embryos or fetuses need not be inconsistent. As Bush said in *A Charge to Keep:* "Some advocates of life will challenge why I oppose abortion yet support the death penalty. To me, it's the difference between innocence and guilt." But to hold the two positions consistently, one would at least need to be very careful about supporting the death penalty. Since humans are fallible, any legal system that puts a large number of people to death will risk executing people innocent of the crimes for which they were charged. Several studies list people who have been condemned to death, and in some cases executed, who were later shown to be innocent. The Death Penalty

Information Center has a list of 102 people wrongly sentenced to death in the United States between 1973 and 2000. An investigation by the *Chicago Tribune* of all 682 executions in the United States between 1976 and 2000 found that at least 120 people were put to death while still proclaiming their innocence, and in four of these cases there was evidence supporting the claim of innocence. When Florida Supreme Court Justice Gerald Kogan retired, he said that there were several cases in which he had "grave doubts" about the guilt of people executed in Florida. If Kogan had doubts, then so should we—he was chief prosecutor of the Homicide and Capital Crimes Division of the Dade County State Attorney's Office before becoming a circuit judge and then Chief Justice. Even a highly critical study of the Death Penalty Information Center list, published on a pro-death-penalty Web site, acknowledges that there were thirty-four people sentenced to death who were released on the basis of serious claims of innocence. After reaching that figure, the study points out that this is less than half of 1 percent of all defendants sentenced to death in that period. But even if 199 out of 200 people sentenced to death are guilty, that does not erase the wrong done to the one who is innocent.

Bush's attitude toward the risk of putting to death the innocent is in contrast to that of another Republican state governor who had once been a supporter of the death penalty. In 1999, Governor George Ryan of Illinois became concerned about the risk of putting innocent people to death when an investigation by students in a journalism class at Northwestern University proved that another man committed a murder for which Anthony Porter, a death-row inmate for sixteen years, was about to be executed. Ryan set up a commission that, over three years, conducted the most thorough study of the death penalty ever carried out in a single state. It concluded that thirteen condemned prisoners were innocent. The commission's findings, Ryan later said, showed that "Our capital system is haunted by the demon of error, error in determining guilt and error in determining who among the guilty deserves to die." The commission proposed changes to the criminal justice system that were repeatedly rejected by the Illinois legislature. Finally, just before he left office, Ryan felt he could no longer live with the risk of executing the innocent: he commuted all death sentences in Illinois to terms of imprisonment.

No matter how careful Bush may have been, it remains possible—the Illinois experience suggests that, given the larger number of executions in Texas, one could say "probable"—that during his tenure as governor of Texas, an innocent person was put to death. To justify taking this risk of executing the innocent, one would need to be very sure of one's grounds for supporting the death penalty. How sure is Bush entitled to be? He has written: "I support the death penalty because I believe, if administered swiftly and justly, capital punishment is a deterrent against future violence and will save other innocent lives." In the third of his debates with Vice President Al Gore, when asked by Jim Lehrer, the moderator, whether he believed that the death penalty "actually deters crime," he committed himself even more firmly, saying, "I do, that's the only reason to be for it. Let me finish that—I don't think you should support the death penalty to seek revenge. I don't think that's right. I think the reason to support the death penalty is because it saves other people's lives."

The problem with this defense of capital punishment is that most of the evidence is against it. Whether the death penalty is a deterrent is a factual question. Since it is not difficult to compare murder rates before and after the abolition or reinstitution of the death penalty, or in different jurisdictions that do and do not have the death penalty, there is relevant data. For example, after the 1976 U.S. Supreme Court ruling that the death penalty is constitutional, a dozen states chose not to enact laws allowing it. These states have not had higher homicide rates than the states that did enact such laws—in fact, ten of them have had homicide rates lower than the national average. South Dakota has it, and North Dakota does not. The homicide rate is higher in South Dakota than in North Dakota. Connecticut has it, and Massachusetts does not. Again, the homicide rate is higher in the state with the death penalty. The states in these pairs are roughly comparable in terms of their economic and ethnic mix. Moreover, homicide rates have risen and fallen in roughly symmetrical patterns in states with and without the death penalty, suggesting that the existence or absence of the death penalty has little effect on the incidence of homicide.

In 1992 California carried out its first execution in twenty-five years. Homicide rates in Los Angeles rose. Something similar happened when Oklahoma restored the death penalty. Keith Harries and Derral Cheatwood took the scrutiny down to the county level, comparing 293 pairs of neighboring counties, differing in their use of the death penalty but otherwise carefully selected to be similar in respect of their location, history, economy, and inhabitants. They found no deterrent effect from capital punishment, executions, or whether a county has a population on death row. They did, however, find higher violent crime rates in death penalty counties. Finally, it is worth noting that a study of the effect of executions in Texas from 1982 until 1997 (and thus including part of Bush's term as governor) concluded that the number of executions was unrelated to murder rates.

Admittedly, there are some studies that suggest that the death penalty does have a deterrent effect. On closer examination, they usually turn out to have serious flaws. In any case, if Bush supports the death penalty only because "it saves other people's lives," he should, before signing 152 death warrants, have taken a hard look at the evidence to see whether it really does save lives. If he had done so he probably would have concluded that the death penalty does *not* save innocent lives. Or at the very least, even if he were to take the most skeptical possible view of the abundant evidence against the deterrent effect of the death penalty, and a more favorable view of the few studies suggesting that it does have such an effect, he would have realized that he cannot possibly have any confidence that the death penalty *does* save other people's lives. Given that, and the risk—slight in any particular case, perhaps, but substantial when the death penalty is used frequently, as it was in Texas when he was governor—that an innocent person will be executed, someone who is concerned about protecting innocent human life should oppose the death penalty.

There is one other respect in which Bush's hard-line support for the death penalty does not fit well with his support for the protection of innocent human life. A person who is seriously mentally retarded is likely to be incapable of understanding right and wrong, and thus to be morally innocent, even if he or she did commit the crime. As a national consensus against executing the mentally retarded began to build, Bush, as governor of Texas, came out against a bill that would have prohibited the use of the death penalty against profoundly retarded criminals, with IQs of less than 65. His explanation for his position was simply: "I like the law the way it is right now." Although Texans strongly support the death penalty, on this issue Bush was more extreme than most of his constituents—a 1998 poll showed that 73 percent of Texans were opposed to executing the retarded. The bill was passed by the Texas Senate, which is dominated by Republicans, but with Bush opposing it, it failed in the House. In May 1997, Bush denied an appeal for clemency on behalf of Terry Washington, a thirty-three-year-old mentally retarded man with the communication skills of a seven-year-old. Washington was executed.

If Bush supports the death penalty because he believes that it saves lives by deterring potential murderers, and if mentally retarded people are morally innocent, then in signing the death warrant for Terry Washington, Bush was deliberately causing the death of a morally innocent human as a means of saving the lives of others. That is, of course, exactly what he refuses to support in the case of human embryos.

In June 2002, the U.S. Supreme Court ruled that, given the growing national consensus, executing retarded persons is "cruel and unusual punishment" and hence a violation of the Eighth Amendment to the U.S. Constitution.

Killing in War

In defending his decision to refuse federal funds for research that involves destroying human embryos, Bush said, as we have seen, "I worry about a culture that devalues life, and believe as your President I have an important obligation to foster and encourage respect for life in America and throughout the world." Yet in Afghanistan and in Iraq he unleashed wars that killed, according to the most conservative estimate, more than 4,000 civilians—at least 1,000 in Afghanistan and more than 3,000 in Iraq. Whether these were justifiable wars is an issue to be discussed in a later section of this book. For the present, I shall assume that both in Afghanistan and in Iraq, there was a just cause for war. Is it consistent for someone who holds Bush's views about the sanctity of human life to be the supreme commander of armed forces that use bombs and missiles in areas where civilians are sure to be killed?

In order to gauge the significance of these wars—and the way they were fought—in terms of the loss of innocent human life, we need to know some details about what happened. Here are some examples from the war that Bush launched in Afghanistan in order to destroy Al Qaeda bases in that country, and to overthrow the Taliban regime that had harbored them. On October 22, 2001, at Chukar Kariz, a small village not far from Kandahar, U.S. bombs killed at least thirty-six civilians. A survivor, Nasir Ahmad, could count twenty dead relatives. There were no combatants in the area. In Kandahar on October 27, a bomb aimed at the Taliban Ministry for the Promotion of Virtue and the Suppression of Vice hit a house across the street, killing three brothers and two passersby. On November 1, American planes bombed Ishaq Suleiman, a group of mud huts, because a Taliban truck had been parked in one of the streets. The truck left before the bomb hit, but twelve local villagers were killed and fourteen injured. On the night of November 10, after American planes came under antiaircraft fire, bombs and cruise missiles destroyed the village of Khakriz, about half a mile from the site of the antiaircraft fire. About seventy people were killed. There were no Taliban or Al Qaeda fighters in the village. At Bekhere on December 20, Musa Khan, a young shepherd, lost four brothers and three sisters when warplanes struck the family home. "We are just poor people," he said. More than forty people were killed in the attack on the village, which the villagers believe was prompted by the headlights of a convoy that had stopped near the village because of snow blocking a road. The convoy itself was attacked because the military believed that it contained Taliban leaders, but survivors said that it consisted of tribal elders en route to the inauguration of the U.S.-backed interim prime minister, Hamid Karzai. There are many more such stories of innocent lives being lost. Hundreds of children were among the victims. Moreover, even though the war is widely regarded as having been brief, hostilities continue in many parts of the country and they also take their toll of civilian lives. In April 2003, for example, an American air strike aimed at a group of rebels instead killed a family of eleven while they were sleeping. In December 2003, a total of fifteen children were killed in two separate incidents when U.S. raids against Taliban suspects missed their targets.

In Iraq, too, most civilian casualties were caused by bombs and missiles. Bush has said that "targets were carefully examined to protect the innocent from harm." We now know that to be a highly misleading statement. There was a procedure in place that required the approval of Defense Secretary Donald Rumsfeld for air attacks that were considered likely to kill more than thirty civilians. More than fifty such attacks were proposed, and Rumsfeld approved all of them—risking the lives of a minimum of 1,500 civilians. That does not sound like the careful examination of targets to protect the innocent from harm.

Here is an example of what may have been one of those raids—or maybe it was one that did not even need Rumsfeld's approval, because it was estimated to be unlikely to kill more than twenty-nine civilians. On the morning of April 5, 2003, a civilian neighborhood in Basra was bombed. British military officials said the bombs were aimed at General Ali Hassan al-Majid, known as "Chemical Ali" because of his use of chemical weapons against Iraqis. Four months later, when al-Majid was captured alive, it became clear that the bombs had missed their intended target. But one of the bombs hit the home of the Hamoodi family, a well-respected, educated family in Basra, none of whose members belonged to Iraq's ruling Baath Party. Of the extended family of fourteen, ten were killed. A *New York Times* reporter covering the tragedy was shown a photo of Zeena Akram, aged twelve, smiling brightly in a pink dress. She was killed. So too were her brothers, Mustafa Akram, thirteen, a keen reader, and Zain El Abideen Akram, eighteen, who wanted to be a doctor like his father. Her sister, Zainab Akram, nineteen, who loved fashion and the latest European music, was another victim. Hassan Iyad, ten, was killed because he had begged his father to let him stay at Grandpa's house. A younger grandchild, Ammar Muhammad, not yet two, died despite his grandfather's attempts to give him mouth-to-mouth resuscitation. A baby, Noor Elhuda Saad, was killed. So too were Wissam Abed, forty, who was to be married in June, and Dr. Ihab Abed, thirty-four, who had come to her father's house because she was frightened of the fighting near her home. The matriarch of the family, Khairiah Mahmoud, mother of ten and grandmother of many more, was the tenth victim.

Mr. Abed Hamoodi, the seventy-two-year-old patriarch of the family, survived to tell *The New York Times*: "I consider what was done to be a crime of war. How would President Bush feel if he had to dig his daughters from out of the rubble?" Mr. Hamoodi's question is well put. Would Bush have thought his decision to attack Iraq, and to use bombers to break Iraqi resistance, was justified if he had had to dig his daughter out of the rubble caused by American bombs? Or if the civilians killed were, though not his immediate family, his fellow Americans?

Ethical discussions about the principles to be observed when there is a danger of causing the death of civilians in war are usually cast in terms of the traditional just-war doctrine. Over the last two decades, a document adopted by the United States Bishops Conference in 1983, entitled *The Challenge of Peace*, has been repeatedly cited as a careful and authoritative statement of just-war theory, the development of which goes back many centuries. It is still widely favored by Christian thinkers, but it has gained acceptance beyond specifically Christian circles. In addition to spelling out when it is just to go to war, the doctrine offers separate principles on how a war may justly be conducted. These principles are generally given as:

> *The Immunity of Noncombatants*
>
> Only those who are combatants are legitimate targets. Civilians are not to be directly attacked, and the greatest possible care must be taken to avoid harming them indirectly, and when that cannot be done, to minimize the harm done.

Proportionality

Gaining an objective should not involve inflicting harms that are disproportional to the value of the objective itself. In particular, causing disproportionate harm to civilians cannot be justified, even when the harm is not directly intended.

Right Intention

The intention with which each act is carried out must be just, so indiscriminate violence is wrong, even in the course of a war.

The first principle relies on a distinction between direct and indirect killing. To aim at killing civilians is always wrong. On the other hand, a government conducting a just war may bomb important military targets, even if it foresees that inevitably some of the bombs will go astray and kill civilians. In that case, however, the second principle—proportionality—must be followed. The harm caused to civilians must be significantly less than the benefit gained in terms of advancing the just cause for which the war is being fought. Even Jean Bethke Elshtain, professor of social and political ethics at the University of Chicago, and author of *Just War Against Terror,* a book supporting Bush's military policy, writes: "According to just war thinking, it is better to risk the lives of one's own combatants than those of enemy noncombatants."

When pressed about the civilian casualties inflicted on Afghans and Iraqis by American missiles and bombs, those speaking on behalf of the Bush administration have stressed that civilians are never directly targeted and that the greatest care is taken to minimize civilian casualties. They express their deep regret that despite this great care, some innocent civilians are killed, but that cannot be avoided. Defense Secretary Rumsfeld said, "War is ugly. It causes misery and suffering and death, and we see that every day. But let's be clear: no nation in human history has done more to avoid civilian casualties than the United States has in this conflict." General Tommy R. Franks, the commander of both wars, said more or less the same thing, but with the emphasis on results rather than intentions. Referring to the war in Afghanistan, he said, "I can't imagine there's been a conflict in history where there has been less collateral damage, less unintended consequences."

Franks's remarks about civilian casualties in Afghanistan are easy to refute: in Kosovo, NATO forces dropped more bombs than the U.S. dropped in Afghanistan, yet the Afghanistan bombing killed twice as many civilians. More innocent people were killed in the two wars Bush initiated than were killed on September 11, 2001. As a proportion of the national population, the U.S. bombing of Afghanistan caused more than three times as many civilian deaths as the terrorist attacks of September 11 caused in the United States, and the war in Iraq caused more than ten times as many. The more important falsehood in the Rumsfeld-Franks justification, however, has nothing to do with mere numbers. It relates to the lengths that the American forces did or did not go to avoid killing innocent Afghans. For example, in responding to the attack on Ishaq Suleiman that killed twelve villagers, a Pentagon spokesman said that even in villages, trucks and equipment belonging to the Taliban were still "authorized military targets." Granted, the civilians were not the direct target of the attack, but what about the principle of proportionality? The U.S. military seems not to have trained its commanders—or even its spokespeople—to ask the crucial question: is the destruction of a truck so important a military target that destroying it justifies risking the lives of innocents? The same Pentagon spokesman said of the destruction of Bekhere, where more than forty were killed, that it was "an active staging and coordinating base for Al Qaeda activities and preparations for escape from Afghanistan." Again, the statement appears to assume that it is right to bomb a village at night if there might happen to be, among the innocent families sleeping there, some Al Qaeda members trying to flee Afghanistan.

The same thing happened in Iraq. The bombing of Basra was an attempt to kill General Ali Hassan al-Majid, the man responsible for deadly poison gas attacks on Kurdish and Iranian villages in 1988. Was his death so important that it was worth killing twenty-three innocent people in an attempt to kill him that was by no means sure of success? The death of a number of civilians—it might be only one or two, or it might be fifty—is always predictable when a civilian neighborhood is bombed. The principle of proportionality seems to have been forgotten here. So, too, has the idea of fostering and encouraging respect for life throughout the world.

Just a day or two after most of the Hamoodi family and many of their neighbors were wiped out, Bush administration officials said that an attempt had been made to kill Saddam Hussein and two of his sons. This was the second such attempt—the first, the opening blow of the war, was an attack on one of Saddam's palaces. The second was directed at a restaurant in a residential neighborhood. Four 2,000-pound bombs were dropped. Not surprisingly, there were civilian casualties—fourteen, according to one report. Whether Saddam and his sons were really there is still not known—certainly they were not killed on that occasion, for subsequently Saddam was captured and his sons killed. Killing Saddam and his sons would have had greater military significance than killing Ali Hassan al-Majid, but by the day of the bombing, April 7, U.S troops were already in central Baghdad, and it was evident to all, with the possible exception of the laughably sanguine Iraqi information minister, Mohammed Saeed al-Sahaf, that the days of Saddam's regime were numbered. Did it really matter so much, at that point, whether he lived or died? Did it matter enough to kill innocent people?

Two months later, U.S. special forces, still in pursuit of Saddam and his sons, attacked a convoy of cars moving across the border into Syria. About eighty people were killed, including civilians living in the area of the attack. The information on which the attack was based turned out to be false. No members of the Hussein family were in the convoy; instead it consisted of smugglers seeking to evade Syrian taxes. But by the time the error was discovered, it was too late. Those attacked were dead. The incident showed, as veteran journalist Seymour Hersh reported, that the special unit assigned to this operation was "not interested in prisoners" and "obviously shoots to kill."

On the ground, too, American troops appear not to have valued the lives of innocent Iraqis in the same way that they would have valued the lives of innocent Americans. After a suicide bomber at a military checkpoint killed four soldiers, American forces put into effect new "rules of engagement." They put up a sign on the road that said in Arabic, "Roadblock ahead. Leave the area or we will fire." Lt. Col. Scott E. Rutter, commander of the Second Battalion, Seventh Infantry, bluntly described the new rules: "Five seconds. They have five seconds to turn around and get out of here. If they're there in five seconds, they're dead." He wasn't exaggerating. On March 31, American soldiers opened fire on a van approaching a military checkpoint, killing seven civilians inside, including five children. The soldiers were understandably edgy, but they were clearly violating the rule of ethical conduct in war that Elshtain described, that it is better to risk the lives of one's own combatants than those of enemy noncombatants. In another instance, observed by Ellen Knickmeyer, an Associated Press reporter, an old man with a cane approached American Marines. He received a warning to stop, but appeared disoriented, and continued forward. He was shot dead. Knickmeyer quoted a Marine as saying: "They shouldn't be out—they got the memo."

To what extent was Bush himself responsible for the loss of civilian life in Afghanistan and Iraq? Beyond the specific decisions made to attack targets where the risk of civilian death and injury was out of proportion to the significance of the military objective, the civilian deaths also reflect back on the ethics of Bush's larger decision to use "bombers coming from all directions" against the Taliban, rather than specifically to go after Al Qaeda, and to use bombing to produce "shock and awe," and thus demoralize Saddam's army, in Iraq. It must have been obvious that using America's supremacy in the air to wage war in this way, rather than largely on the ground, while likely to reduce American casualties, would dramatically increase civilian casualties. In *Bush at War,* Bob Woodward's account of Bush's leadership of the Afghanistan war, we learn that when Bush gave the order for the bombing to begin, pilots had to "abide by the rule of low collateral," meaning that they had discretion to hit targets "as long as they expected it would only cause minimal damage to civilians." That suggests that Bush was concerned about innocent human life. But evidently, the "rule of low collateral" failed to prevent substantial numbers of civilians being killed. So what did Bush do when reports of civilian casualties being caused by American bombing in Afghanistan began coming in? The accounts of Bush's meetings and discussions about the progress of the Afghanistan war in *Bush at War* contain no mention of reports of civilian casualties. The book's index does not include such words as "civilians," "innocents" or "noncombatants." It does list three references to "Afghanistan, collateral damage in." Two of these refer to separate occasions on which U.S. jets bombed Red Cross warehouses. No one was killed, but supplies intended for humanitarian purposes were destroyed. The third reference is to damage done when supplies were being dropped to friendly forces from the air, and half the parachutes did not open. Thus none of the references mentions civilian deaths caused by U.S. attacks. Yet within the first two weeks of U.S. bombing, the Taliban were claiming large numbers of civilian casualties, and Bush administration officials were denying these claims. Major U.S. newspapers published articles discussing the truth of the matter. As reports of the deaths of numerous civilians came in, including the bombing of Chukar Kariz, General Musharraf, the highly supportive president of Pakistan, called for an early end to the bombing. It is inconceivable that Bush was unaware of these reports and of President Musharraf's call. If *Bush at War* is reasonably complete—and its author, one of the nation's leading investigative journalists, had the cooperation of Bush, Powell, and other key figures in compiling his full and detailed account—Bush never pushed Rumsfeld, Franks, or CIA Director George Tenet to give him accurate information on the civilian casualties American bombers were causing. On the only occasion reported in Woodward's book when there was a discussion of the "collateral damage" issue, Bush was more concerned with the public relations aspect of such damage than with probing whether more could be done to avoid it. He is reported as saying, "Well, we also need to highlight the fact that the Taliban are killing people and conducting their own terror operations, so get a little bit more balance here about what the situation is."

In Iraq, too, there is disconcerting evidence that Bush was more concerned with image than with reality. In a lengthy interview with NBC's Tom Brokaw, Bush describes how, just as the war with Iraq was about to begin, Rumsfeld called him and said that they had information from an agent in Baghdad that Saddam Hussein and his sons would be in a particular location, and would like permission to bomb that location. Bush told Brokaw:

> I was hesitant at first, to be frank with you, because I was worried that the first pictures coming out of Iraq would be a wounded grandchild of Saddam Hussein . . . that the first images of the American attack would be death to young children.

The concern Bush expresses here is not about the risk that American bombs might kill or wound children—who would, even if they were Saddam's grandchildren, be innocent of his crimes. It is that images of the dead or wounded children would be "the first pictures coming out of Iraq." Taken in isolation, one might think that Bush was simply speaking carelessly; but the similarity between Woodward's account of his thoughts about the public relations aspects of civilian casualties in Afghanistan, and this remark about children being killed in Iraq, suggests that this focus on the images rather than the actual deaths is an accurate reflection of Bush's thinking.

A Selective Culture of Life

Bush's support for the death penalty, in the face of evidence that it is not an effective deterrent, plus the evidence that the American system of justice allows some innocent people to be executed, is not consistent with his professed ethic of respect for innocent human life. Even more glaringly at odds with this ethic are the American military activities he authorized in Afghanistan and Iraq. Bush's concern for the lives of innocent people on death row, and for innocent men, women, and children in Afghanistan and Iraq falls far short of his concern with protecting embryos that might be used for stem-cell research. On any sensible scale, this is a bizarre set of priorities. The frozen embryos that scientists wish to use will be destroyed anyway, if they are not used. They have no future. But even if that were not the case, none of them have, or have had, any conscious awareness, any hopes or desires of their own. No embryos are mothers or fathers, no embryos will leave sorrowing children behind when they are killed. No one keeps photos of dead embryos and grieves over their loss, as Abed Hamoodi grieved, and will continue to grieve as long as he lives, over the deaths of his children and grandchildren.

Some moralists might argue that one can oppose killing embryos for research, but accept the deaths of civilians in war, because the former are intended, but the latter are not. That view, however, places more weight on the difference between "foreseeable" and "intended" deaths than that distinction can bear. Moralists who support the distinction usually say that whether you intended an outcome of your action can be determined by asking if you would have acted as you did if you believed that the outcome would not have occurred. So, for example, Bush could truthfully say that he would have bombed the restaurant in which Saddam was believed to be even if that would not have killed any civilians. But similarly, the scientists who seeks to derive stem cells from embryos could say that they would have extracted the stem cells even if that procedure did not result in the death of the embryo. In neither case would the deaths be intended, according to this test.

In his speech on the use of embryos to obtain stem cells, Bush said: "Even the most noble ends do not justify any means." So perhaps his view is that the evil we bring about must not be a means to the end we are seeking, but we may allow the same evil to occur as a side effect of achieving a just and sufficiently important end. On this view, Bush might claim that the civilian deaths were a side effect of his attempt to kill Saddam, and not a means to it. But again, the scientists could equally well claim that the death of the embryo is not a means to extracting the cells they require, but a side effect of that extraction.

Michael Walzer, perhaps the most influential contemporary theorist about ethics and war, has argued that for an act of war that harms civilians to be permissible, the military forces must, in addition to not intending to harm civilians, make sacrifices in order to avoid or minimize such harms. As we have seen, Jean Bethke Elshtain endorses this view. As supreme commander, Bush could have ordered the American armed forces to take much greater care to avoid civilian deaths. For example, he could have ordered them not to bomb residential areas, even if Saddam Hussein or other leading members of his regime were believed to be hiding there. He did not issue such orders. Apparently he does not consider that the way in which he commanded the American armed forces in Afghanistan and Iraq is incompatible with the obligation he has acknowledged, "to foster and encourage respect for life in America and throughout the world." But surely it was.

The issue of intentions is also relevant to Bush's attempt to portray the distinction between his own acts and those of terrorists in starkly black-and-white terms. In a speech to the United Nations General Assembly in November 2001, he said: "In this world there are good causes and bad causes, and we may disagree on where the line is drawn. Yet there is no such thing as a good terrorist. No national aspiration, no remembered wrong, can ever justify the deliberate murder of the innocent." The crucial term here is "deliberate," because Bush knew that the attacks he launched on Afghanistan and Iraq would kill the innocent. Those attacks in fact killed more innocent people than the terrorist attacks of September 11, 2001. This of course does not mean that Bush is an evil person in the way that Osama bin Laden is evil. Intentions are relevant to our judgments about people, and it was not Bush's intention to kill the innocent. But it is important to notice that Osama bin Laden has appealed to exactly the same distinction between what we intend, and what we foresee will happen as a result of our actions, in order to deny that the attacks of September 11, 2001, were contrary to Islamic law. In an interview with Al-Jazeera television correspondent Tayseer Alouni in October 2001, he agreed that "the Prophet Mohammed forbade the killing of babies and women." He then went on to say that the men who carried out the attack on September 11 "did not intend to kill babies; they intended to destroy the strongest military power in the world, to attack the Pentagon that houses more than 64,000 employees, a military center that houses the strength and the military intelligence." Alouni then asked about the attack on the twin towers, and bin Laden replied: "The towers are an economic power and not a children's school. Those that were there are men that supported the biggest economic power in the world."

It is, of course, outrageous to claim that all the men in the World Trade Center and the Pentagon on the morning of September 11 were legitimate targets merely because they happened to work in those buildings. But let us focus on bin Laden's assertion that those who carried out the attacks did not violate the prohibition on killing women and children. It was obvious that the attacks would kill hundreds of women and at least a few children. (Eight children under the age of twelve died in the attacks, all passengers on planes that the hijackers deliberately crashed.) Bin Laden must therefore be assuming that the attackers did not violate the Prophet's rule because they did not *intend* to kill babies and women, although they foresaw that babies and women would be killed as a result of their attacks on centers of American military and economic power. In other words, he implicitly attributes significance to the distinction between what someone directly intends, and what someone foresees will happen as a result of his or her actions, but does not directly intend. This distinction makes it possible for him to claim that the attackers were not acting contrary to a rule that should have made it impossible for any devout follower of Mohammed to perpetrate such atrocities. That should give pause to those who wish to use this same distinction to justify the deaths of innocents in the American bombing of Afghanistan and Iraq. If we allow Bush to justify acts that he knew would kill innocents by saying that killing innocents was not his intention, then we should be aware that others, too, can use the same distinction between intention and unwanted consequences to reconcile their deadly deeds with a religious ethic that would otherwise rule them out. According to his own twisted logic, in planning the terrorist attacks of September 11, 2001, Osama bin Laden was not involved in the deliberate murder of the innocent. A distinction that allows bin Laden to reach such a conclusion offers no useful guidance as to which actions are right and which are wrong.

It might be possible to justify the loss of innocent life caused by the American bombs that, it was hoped, would kill Iraqi leaders, by making a utilitarian calculation that killing those leaders would save more lives in the end. That purported justification needs to be scrutinized carefully. We need to ask if it is quite certain that the facts are really as they are claimed to be. Is the goal worth pursuing? Will our actions really help us to achieve it? Is it important enough to justify the loss of civilian lives? Are we not giving more weight to protecting the lives of American combatants than to protecting Iraqi civilians? But such an argument leads not to black-and-white distinctions between evil terrorism and good military bombings of residential districts, but to shades of gray. In any case, Bush cannot consistently use a utilitarian argument to justify the civilian deaths he has brought about in Afghanistan and Iraq, for that is precisely the kind of justification that he refuses to use when it comes to scientific research that leads to the deaths of human embryos. He cannot be an absolutist in one situation and a utilitarian in the other. The conclusion is inescapable: Bush's actions cannot fit within a coherent ethic of respecting human life.

Chapter 4

The Freest Nation in the World

We have a collective responsibility as citizens of the greatest and freest nation in the world.

—*A Charge to Keep*, p. 240

The freest nation?

George W. Bush has often expressed a belief that many Americans share: the United States is "the freest nation" in the world. But as a newcomer to the U.S. who has lived most of his life in other liberal democracies, it isn't at all obvious to me that the United States is a freer nation than Australia, Canada, the United Kingdom, or the Netherlands, to give just a few possible rival candidates. Freedom can mean many things: that there is freedom of speech and thought, that people can associate with whomever they like and come and go as they please, that no one can be imprisoned without a fair trial, that each citizen has an equal voice in who governs them, that the government leaves people alone as long as they do not harm others, that people have the opportunity to realize their potential and prosper in the way they choose. These aspects of freedom are different in kind, and there is no single scale on which we can measure the extent to which one country is more free than another. In any case, our focus is on Bush's understanding of the value of freedom and the protection of individual rights, rather than on whether the United States really is the freest nation in the world. Nevertheless, at least since Bush became president, the two are linked. If Bush is not a true champion of freedom, then it becomes considerably less likely that the country over which he presides can truly claim to be the freest nation in the world.

A philosophy that trusts individuals

When Bush was a candidate for the presidency, his view of the state seemed clear. One of his most constant refrains was that he believes in "the power of each individual" and is opposed to big, remote governments. This, he said, is part of what he means by "compassionate conservatism":

> My philosophy trusts individuals to make the right decisions for their families and communities, and that is far more compassionate than a philosophy that seeks solutions from distant bureaucracies. I am a conservative because I believe government should be limited and efficient, that it should do a few things and do them well . . . I am a conservative because I believe government closest to the people governs best.

This paragraph suggests two distinct elements to Bush's philosophy of government. First, there is a focus on leaving as much as possible to individuals, and second, there is an emphasis on government that is close to the people rather than remote from them. In the context of a federal system of government, the first of these suggests that government at both the state and federal levels should leave as large a sphere as possible in which individuals are free from government interference. The second element suggests that where it is not possible to leave individuals alone, the federal government should seek, whenever it can, to avoid interfering with decisions made by state governments. Bush referred to both these elements in his inaugural address as governor of Texas:

> "Texans can run Texas," I told my fellow Texans. "I will ask the federal government to return to us the power to set our own course. My guiding principle," I said, "will be government if necessary, not necessarily government."

Bush hammered home the same themes again and again, in a variety of different contexts, before he became president. In the presidential debate at Wake Forest University, he said, "I don't believe in command and control out of Washington, D.C." In the next presidential debate, at Washington University in St. Louis, he said that he was opposed to a national health scheme because "I don't want the federal government making decisions for consumers . . . I trust people; I don't trust the federal government. I don't want the federal government making decisions on behalf of everybody." On the *Larry King Show,* in response to a question about a hypothetical state vote on gay marriage, he replied, "The states can do what they want to do. Don't try to trap me in this states' issue." To an inquiry about South Carolina flying the Confederate flag outside the state capitol, he declined to give an opinion, beyond saying, "I trust the people of South Carolina to make the decision for South Carolina." Asked what he thought about the medical use of marijuana by people who were ill and found that it helped them, Bush replied, "I believe each state can choose that decision as they so choose." (A spokesperson for the Marijuana Policy Project, a lobby group for medical marijuana, praised Bush's position as "courageous" and "consistent on states' rights.") Finally, in promoting his plan for a big tax cut and criticizing Gore's more limited proposal, Bush accused Gore of supporting "big, exploding federal government that wants to think on your behalf."

Hostility to government in the name of promoting freedom is a distinctively American philosophy, particularly when it is part of a conservative, rather than left-anarchist, outlook. In the nations of the European Union, or in Canada, Australia, and New Zealand, conservatives often favor a paternalistic government that ensures that people do what is right (in the opinion of the conservatives) in their private lives. *On Liberty,* the finest defense of individual liberty against government interference in the English language, was written by the liberal utilitarian John Stuart Mill. In opposition to conservatives who wanted to use the power of the state to stamp out prostitution, sodomy, and suicide, Mill urged that the state should restrain individual liberty only to prevent harm to others. It was, in his view, wrong for the state to interfere with an individual "for the good of the individual," whether physical or moral. For a century after the publication of *On Liberty,* conservatives in both Britain and the United States resisted Mill's view, defending laws that restricted individual liberty in circumstances that could not be shown to cause harm to others—for instance, laws that intruded into the bedrooms of consenting homosexuals, that made prostitution criminal, or that restricted the access of adults to sexually explicit films, books, and magazines.

Since Bush has been so plain in his identification of conservatism with limited government and with fostering individual responsibility, we might assume that these battles between liberals and conservatives are now over. The Bush administration, one imagines, would seek to limit the power of the federal government and promote maximum freedom for adults to make their own decisions in matters that do not harm others. But soon after Bush took office, his belief that "government closest to the people governs best" was severely tested—as was his commitment to trusting individuals.

Choosing how to die

In 1994 a majority of voters in the state of Oregon approved a proposal to allow physicians to prescribe, but not to administer, a lethal dose of drugs to patients who are terminally ill. Two doctors must confirm that the patient is likely to die within six months; the patient must be informed and mentally competent; and he or she must make three requests, two oral and one written, for assistance in dying. The requests must be made at least fifteen days apart.

Opponents of the new law took the state of Oregon to court, delaying the law's implementation. Three years later, they succeeded in getting the issue placed on the ballot again. But despite a well-funded campaign against the law by pro-life organizations, mostly drawing their support from Roman Catholics and other conservative Christians, Oregon voters reaffirmed their support for physician-assisted suicide by a considerably larger majority than in 1994. Further attempts to stop the law through the courts failed when the Ninth U.S. Circuit Court of Appeals held that the law was constitutional and the U.S. Supreme Court refused to hear an appeal. The law went into effect, and has allowed those who make use of it to end their lives in a manner they consider dignified. There is no evidence of abuse or a "slippery slope" to less justified uses of physician-assisted suicide. The number of people making use of the law has remained small. Between 1997, when the law took effect, and 2002, 198 lethal prescriptions were issued, according to state records, and 129 patients used their prescriptions to end their lives. The overwhelming majority of them had cancer, and their median age was sixty-nine.

After losing twice at the polls and failing in the courts, the opponents of the Oregon law turned to that "distant bureaucracy," the federal government. The use of prescription drugs, including drugs prescribed by physicians to patients seeking to end their lives, is controlled by federal regulations. President Clinton's attorney general, Janet Reno, was asked to rule that it was illegal for a physician to prescribe federally controlled substances for the purpose of allowing patients to end their lives. She said that she could find nothing in the federal laws governing prescription drugs that forbade their use for this purpose, and did not make the requested ruling. Oregon's law therefore remained in operation.

Few decisions can be more closely tied to people's individual values than when and how their lives shall end if they should be terminally ill. Some will seek to prolong life by all possible means, others will reach a point at which they decline further medical treatment, and a third group, burdened by illness and with no reasonable prospect of recovery, will want to take death into their own hands. This would seem exactly the kind of situation in which a philosophy that trusts individuals to make the right decisions really is "far more compassionate than a philosophy that seeks solutions from distant bureaucracies." Someone who opposes a national health scheme because he doesn't want the federal government making decisions for consumers should also support the right of health-care consumers to make the crucial decision as to when they want to end their lives. Similarly, a state governor who thinks that Texans can run Texas should presumably also believe that Oregonians can run Oregon, and deplore attempts by the federal government to take from Oregon powers that it still has. For all these reasons, and whatever his personal views about the rights and wrongs of physician-assisted suicide might be, one would expect Bush's administration to follow the path set by Clinton's, thus keeping the distant federal bureaucracy from hindering procedures that the voters of Oregon had already twice supported, and at the same time keeping the federal bureaucracy out of the lives of individual Oregonians.

Contrary to that very reasonable expectation, on November 9, 2001—a time when he surely had issues of greater urgency to contemplate—Bush's attorney general, John Ashcroft, reversed Reno's decision and asserted that federally controlled substances could not be used in physician-assisted suicide. Ashcroft's decision was not based on any change of law since Reno's decision. Instead it rested on a dubious legal opinion from the Justice Department, which in turn had relied on the decision of the Supreme Court in *United States v. Moore,* the case of a doctor who was, in effect, acting as a drug dealer, prescribing addictive drugs on request without medical grounds, and charging his patients on the basis of the number of drugs prescribed. The doctor's right to prescribe drugs, the court said, holds only "within accepted limits" and when the drugs are prescribed "in the course of professional practice or research." But the Oregon doctors who prescribe drugs for terminal patients who want to die are doing so as part of their professional practice, and they are doing it within limits that are accepted by the majority of Oregon voters. Ashcroft's opinion mounts a case against the Oregon law only by insisting that the idea of "accepted limits" must mean accepted at the national level rather than at the state level—precisely the kind of idea that a proponent of states' rights should vigorously resist.

Another part of Ashcroft's opinion appeals to a 1984 amendment to the Controlled Substances Act, the law regulating controlled drugs, that allows the attorney general to revoke a doctor's federal license for acts inconsistent with the "public interest." This amendment was also concerned with the abuse of the drug laws, and had nothing to do with physician-assisted suicide. Moreover, there is ample legal precedent for the view that the determination of the public interest, in regard to health care, is properly the province of the states. The Justice Department assumes that decisions about what is or is not in the "public interest" cannot be left to the states, but must be decided in Washington, and is better decided by a single unelected official—the attorney general—than by the voters or by the legislature. This is in direct opposition to the view of the U.S. Supreme Court, which specifically upheld the states' role in the area of physician-assisted suicide in its 1997 decision, *Washington v. Glucksberg*. Ashcroft was, as an amicus brief filed by a number of bioethicists and lawyers against the attorney general put it, "hijacking an unrelated statute in order to capture new powers for the federal government."

How did the champion of trusting individuals, a staunch opponent of distant bureaucracies, and a champion of states' rights view his attorney general's decision? Ari Fleischer, the president's press secretary, said, "The president believes that we must value life and promote a culture that respects the sanctity of life at all its stages," adding that Bush "opposes physician-assisted suicide" and "believes it is the proper role of the federal government to regulate controlled substances such as narcotics or other dangerous drugs." The reference to "narcotics or other dangerous drugs" obscures the issue, for while the drugs patients use to end their lives may be narcotics, the same drugs are already used to relieve pain. When prescribed under the circumstances specified in the Oregon legislation, these drugs are not going to cause addiction, are not likely to fall into the wrong hands, and pose no danger to anyone other than the person who chooses to take them, fully understanding their effects. It is difficult to see why a president with a philosophy of trusting individuals to make the right decisions would not allow terminally ill, mentally competent individuals to decide when they have had enough and wish to die.

In any case, Fleischer's comment fails to address the issue of federal-state relations. The point is not whether Bush supports or opposes what Oregon decided to do. The point is whether the issue should be decided by the voters of Oregon, or by a Washington-based federal official. A president can hardly claim to be a supporter of the rights of states to run their own affairs if he only allows them to pass laws that he personally supports. Just as genuine supporters of free speech must defend the rights of people to express views they consider obnoxious, so Bush's support for states' rights should lead him to defend states that pass laws with which he disagrees.

I happen to think that terminally ill people should have lawful access to the help of a physician to end their lives, if that is their considered wish. Nelson Lund, a professor of law at George Mason University's school of law, does not. But as a supporter of James Madison's idea of federalism, he also thinks that Ashcroft is wrong to attempt to thwart the Oregon legislation. Writing in *Commentary,* he pointed out that, no matter how bad the effects of legalizing physician-assisted suicide may be, "they will be visited almost entirely on Oregonians, and will not threaten the citizens of other states." Oregon's policy will only spread to other states if the people of those states are persuaded that the Oregon experiment is a success. This in itself is a reason for federal restraint. In fact, Lund says, as far as the case against federal intervention is concerned, "physician-assisted suicide is a pretty easy case."

The Oregon governor, John Kitzhaber, called Ashcroft's ruling a "slap in the face to Oregonians" and "an unprecedented federal intrusion on Oregon's ability to regulate the practice of medicine." Subsequently, Ashcroft got his own face slapped when U.S. District Judge Robert Jones of Portland, Oregon, ruled that the Justice Department "overstepped its authority" in attempting to nullify Oregon's physician-assisted suicide law. In granting Oregon state officials a permanent injunction against Ashcroft's ruling, Jones wrote that the federal government is not authorized to "act as a national medical board" and regulate how doctors treat patients. Justice Department officials have appealed the decision.

Choosing what drugs to take, and whom to marry

During the 1999 election campaign, as we have seen, Bush said that he would allow the states to decide on the medical use of marijuana, and he also handled a question on gay marriage by saying, "Don't try to trap me in this states' issue." The medical use of marijuana issue was the first to put his words to the test. By 2000, eight states—California, Alaska, Arizona, Colorado, Hawaii, Maine, Oregon, and Washington—had decided in favor of allowing people who were ill to take marijuana, under some circumstances. California's voters, for example, had approved a ballot initiative permitting the cultivation and use of small amounts of marijuana for medical purposes. Once in office, however, Bush appointed Asa Hutchinson to head the Drug Enforcement Agency, and Hutchinson soon acted in ways very different from Bush's words. Granted, in contrast to Ashcroft's attack on Oregon's physician-assisted suicide law, Hutchinson acted in accordance with federal law, which prohibits the use of marijuana. The United States Supreme Court had held that the medical use of marijuana was not exempt from this law. So Hutchinson, and Bush, could say that they were merely enforcing the law. Nevertheless, if Bush had been true to his frequent statements of support for individual liberty—and to his explicit preelection statement on the issue—he could have shown leadership and asked Congress to amend the law, as he has asked it to enact or change many other laws, with a high rate of success. He could also, given his focus on improving homeland security and fighting terrorism, very reasonably have decided that the weeks following September 11, 2001, was not the time to worry about sick people taking marijuana.

Instead, under the Bush administration there have been raids involving dozens of federal government agents on cooperatives that distribute marijuana to people who are ill. In classic "distant government" style, the raids were carried out by armed federal agents who did not inform state law enforcement officials of their plans. After a cooperative in Santa Cruz that had been scrupulous in following California law was raided and two of its organizers arrested, California attorney general Bill Lockyer commented, "A medical marijuana provider such as the Santa Cruz collective represents little danger to the public and is certainly not a concern [that] would warrant diverting scarce federal resources." It seems hard to disagree with that statement.

The issue of gay marriage arose after Canada had opened the way to same-sex marriages and Vermont had recognized a ceremony, separate from marriage, for gay unions. In response to a question at a press conference about his attitude toward homosexuality, Bush said that he believed "marriage is between a man and a woman" and added that he thought "we ought to codify that one way or the other" and he had lawyers looking at the best way to do that. The statement was widely understood to express support for a constitutional amendment to rule out same-sex marriages, and Bush did nothing to rebut that understanding. His close ally, the Republican Senate Leader Bill Frist, already supports such an amendment. But marriage has always been an issue handled by the states—as Bush himself said when he was campaigning for the presidency. No genuine advocate of small government would seek to take from the states the right to decide whether people of the same sex can marry.

The Environment

One area in which Bush has lived up to the pledge to cut back the role of the federal government is the environment. Under Bush, the administration has proposed rules removing federal controls over up to 20 percent of the country's wetlands, which means that many developers will no longer require a federal permit before filling these wetlands in. Although officials said that their action was a response to a Supreme Court decision limiting the scope of the Clean Water Act, the administration's response seemed to go well beyond what was required by the Supreme Court's decision. Similarly, the administration supports more local control over the 436 million acres of public land under the authority of the Department of the Interior. Gale Norton, Bush's appointee as secretary of that department, has spoken in support of the governors of Western states who want more mining and drilling on federal lands in their region, and she has explicitly rejected new rules introduced under the Clinton administration—after three years of public hearings—that gave the federal government a veto over any mine that threatened "irreparable damage" to the environment. She also declared that she would end reviews of Western landholdings to ascertain if they have wilderness values—thus at a stroke releasing more than two hundred million acres of federal land for potential development, at the discretion of the states. Another result of listening more to local interests is allowing more off-road vehicles onto fragile landscapes. The Bush administration has rescinded rules developed during Clinton's presidency to phase out snowmobiles from Yellowstone National Park, and it plans to reopen sensitive federal lands in southeastern California to dune buggies. After a *New York Times* editorial criticized these decisions, pointing out that public lands are owned by all of us, not just the locals, Norton responded by reiterating her support for local involvement: "We are at a time when we must move beyond command-and-control and punitive approaches," she said in an article published in the *New York Times* for Earth Day 2002.

Under the Bush administration, the federal government has played a reduced role in enforcing environmental protection. In his first budget submission to Congress, Bush proposed cutting the Environmental Protection Agency's enforcement staff by 225 positions. Congress rejected that move, but during the first two years Bush was in office, the EPA nevertheless lost one hundred positions by attrition and non-replacement. The average fine levied by the EPA dropped from $1.3 million under Clinton to $600,000 under Bush, and the monthly average total of fines levied, excluding the Superfund toxic waste program, fell from $10.6 million under Clinton to $3.8 million.

Eric Schaeffer, who had directed the EPA's Office of Regulatory Enforcement since 1997, was so dismayed by the way in which the Bush administration undermined his office's efforts to enforce the Clean Air Act and other national environmental legislation that, after a little more than a year of attempting to work under the Bush administration, he quit. Among the ways in which Bush's appointees have thwarted proper enforcement, he says, is their attitude that "what little environmental enforcement is necessary should be left to states." This approach, according to Schaeffer, is not the way to get environmental legislation enforced properly.

First, many states, especially in the South and West, are hostile to the very idea of enforcing many environmental laws. States are consistently more lenient to big corporations than the federal EPA. Even if they do want to enforce the laws, with the exception of the largest states like New York and California, they don't have the resources needed for proper enforcement. (Ironically, as Schaeffer points out, when Christine Whitman, Bush's first head of the EPA, was governor of New Jersey, she eliminated the state environmental prosecutor and made deep cuts in the state budget for environmental enforcement.) In any case, even for those states that can afford to enforce the laws, it is wasteful to have similar efforts duplicated in several state offices. Since enforcement problems tend to be national rather than specific to particular states—for example, there are similar problems across the country, or at least in many different states, in enforcing controls on diesel engine emissions, emissions from old coal-fired power plants, and pollution from large animal feedlots—it is more cost-effective to use a federal office to put in the thousands of skilled staff-hours that are often needed to bring a successful lawsuit. Then the results of one court victory can, with relative ease, be made to flow through the industry. The main area in which Bush has lived up to his pledge to reduce the power of the federal government is one in which, for anyone who thinks that laws to protect the environment really ought to be enforced, handing power to the states makes little sense.

The Rights of American Citizens

One aspect of the relationship between government actions and individual liberty is the extent to which governments protect or interfere with a realm of individual freedom for all their citizens. Thus, if the government succeeds in forbidding physician-assisted suicide and the medical use of marijuana, all Americans have lost some freedom—whether they would ever wish to exercise these particular freedoms or not. But there are other ways in which governments can act that have an impact on a mere handful of people, but nevertheless weaken the basic constitutional guarantees that secure the liberties of every citizen.

Tom Paine, the supporter of American independence and author of *The Rights of Man*, wrote:

> He that would make his own liberty secure must guard even his enemy from oppression; for if he violates this duty he establishes a precedent that will reach himself.

Since the terrorist attacks of September 11, 2001, Bush's commitment to freedom has been subject to what we might call "Tom Paine's Test." Just as the true test of our support for freedom of speech comes when we are asked to defend the rights of some whose views we abhor, so, as Paine points out, the true test of our support for the rights of the individual comes when the person whose rights have been violated is one we consider an enemy.

Bush and Ashcroft consider Jose Padilla to be an enemy of the United States. Padilla was arrested in May 2002 on a "material witness" warrant claiming that he was a witness to the crimes committed by Al Qaeda terrorists on September 11, 2001. In accordance with the law relating to material-witness warrants, he was assigned a lawyer. The lawyer challenged his detention, and a court hearing on the challenge was set for June 11. On June 9, Bush issued a presidential order designating Padilla an "enemy combatant." Ashcroft announced on national television that Padilla was an Al Qaeda agent and part of a conspiracy to build and explode a so-called "dirty bomb"—not a nuclear weapon, but a conventional bomb that would disperse radioactive material. His arrest, according to Ashcroft, had disrupted an "ongoing terrorist plot." Padilla was transferred to military custody and denied the right to see his lawyer on the grounds that civilian courts no longer had jurisdiction over him. When civil liberties organizations challenged this, the Bush administration contended that it was legally and constitutionally entitled to hold indefinitely anyone it designated as an enemy combatant in military facilities, without access to counsel and without meaningful judicial review, until the threat from Al Qaeda was over.

The American Civil Liberties Union (ACLU) filed suit to challenge the government's decision to hold Padilla without filing charges. In its brief, the ACLU argued that Padilla's detention violates the right to due process of law guaranteed in the Fifth Amendment to the Constitution. That amendment declares that "no person shall be . . . deprived of life, liberty, or property, without due process of law." The ACLU urged that there is ample authority, going back to an 1866 decision of the Supreme Court in a Civil War case known as *Milligan,* that the Constitution of the United States applies "equally in war and in peace, and covers with the shield of its protection all classes of men, at all times and under all circumstances." The brief also argued that there is no legislative authority for the executive to detain American citizens, and that, on the contrary, Congress had specifically prohibited such detention. Moreover, in the USA Patriot Act, passed after 9/11, Congress only authorized the detention of aliens—not U.S. citizens—suspected of terrorism for seven days, after which the alien must be charged with an offense. The idea that Congress had, in authorizing the president to use military force against Al Qaeda, intended to allow him to detain U.S. citizens indefinitely would only make sense on the implausible assumption that Congress intended that the rights of aliens should be better protected than those of U.S. citizens.

In December 2002 Judge Michael Mukasey upheld the government's right to hold enemy combatants, whether U.S. citizens or not, and whether arrested on U.S. soil or not, during the period of hostilities without bringing charges. But the judge ordered the government to produce "some evidence" to support the president's conclusion that Padilla was engaged in a mission against the United States "on behalf of an enemy with whom the United States is at war." The judge also ordered that Padilla be allowed to see a lawyer for the purpose of contesting the evidence that the government offered. A spokesperson for the ACLU said that the ruling was "a crucial rejection of the Bush administration's claim of almost unbridled power to unilaterally detain an American citizen and hold him indefinitely and incommunicado." Laurence Tribe, a professor of constitutional law at Harvard University, said that the decision "sends a signal to the executive that should discourage the sort of careless or profligate use of the detention power."

Like Padilla, Yasser Esam Hamdi is an American citizen. Hamdi was born in Louisiana to a Saudi Arabian father working for Exxon, but returned to Saudi Arabia with his parents when he was only three years old. Unlike Padilla, he was captured in Afghanistan, with a Taliban unit, rather than on American soil, so his designation as "enemy combatant" is less contentious. Nevertheless, the fact that he has been held captive for more than two years at the time of this writing, along with the government's claim that he has no right to see a lawyer or receive any form of judicial review, again raises questions about the limits of executive powers. Federal Judge Robert Doumar, who heard an application on Hamdi's behalf to have his detention declared unlawful, said that he had tried and failed to find a case of any kind, in any court, where a lawyer couldn't meet with a client. In that regard, the judge said, "This case sets the most interesting precedent . . . in Anglo-American jurisprudence since the days of the Star Chamber." (The Star Chamber was a court set up by Henry VIII to try his enemies in secret. It was abolished in 1641.) Doumar, a Reagan appointee who was a delegate to three Republican national conventions, granted Hamdi a lawyer, but the Department of Justice appealed and, in January 2003, the U.S. Federal Court of Appeals overturned Doumar's decision, ruling that a "wartime" president can indefinitely detain a United States citizen captured as an enemy combatant on the battlefield and deny that person access to a lawyer. In December 2003, the Pentagon suddenly agreed to allow Hamdi to meet a lawyer. Yet the Justice Department continued to argue, in a brief to the Supreme Court, that the president has the power to hold a U.S. citizen in custody indefinitely, without access to a lawyer.

For our understanding of Bush's political philosophy, the truth or lack of truth in the government's contentions that Padilla has plotted with Al Qaeda to carry out terrorist acts, and that Hamdi is a trained terrorist, are irrelevant. The significance of the cases lies in the Bush administration's attempt to deprive American citizens of their liberty, indefinitely and without legislative authority or any possibility of judicial review. The right to liberty is one of the most basic human rights. For anyone who believes that individual rights and the rule of law are essential elements in a free society, to deprive a citizen of his or her liberty by executive fiat should be anathema. The fact that Bush was prepared to do it, and not only to do it once, hastily, but to allow his administration to go into court, in two separate cases, and argue that it is right to do it, is inconsistent with an ethic that is committed to respecting human rights.

In addition to the "enemy combatant" cases, the Bush administration has held people for several months under a relatively obscure federal law that permits the detention of "material witnesses" to a federal crime to be held in order to ensure that testimony is available, before a grand jury or elsewhere. These "material witnesses" do have court-appointed lawyers. Nevertheless, under Bush the Department of Justice has used this provision more aggressively than under any previous government. Of forty-four people found by *The Washington Post* to have been held as material witnesses, twenty never testified before a grand jury. Some were held for long periods of time. For as long as it could, the Justice Department shrouded the "material witness" cases in secrecy, refusing to say how many people it had detained, to name the detainees, or to indicate for how long they had been held. When a federal judge ordered it to issue this information, the department appealed. Eventually, in response to concerns from Congress, it issued a report stating that the number of material witnesses held in terrorism investigations as of January was "fewer than 50." Of these, about half had been held for thirty days or less, but 10 percent had been held for more than ninety days.

The Rights of Noncitizens

Bush has said that America's "greatest export is freedom, and we have a moral obligation to champion it throughout the world." But what kind of freedom has Bush been championing since 9/11? Two months after 9/11, Bush announced that military tribunals would be used, at his discretion, to try noncitizens that he declared to be suspected terrorists. As originally planned, these tribunals could be secret. They were to be conducted under special rules laid down by the secretary of defense. The ordinary rules of evidence would not apply, and the offense did not have to be proved beyond a reasonable doubt. A two-thirds majority would suffice to declare a defendant guilty, and the death penalty could be applied. The only appeal was to the secretary of defense or to the president. Even long-standing permanent residents of the United States could be tried in this way. This announcement provoked an outcry. Conservative columnist William Safire said that Bush's military order set up "kangaroo courts for people he designates before 'trial' to be terrorists" and "turns back the clock on all advances in military justice, through three wars, in the past half-century." A prominent Spanish judge pointed out that the European Convention on Human Rights would prohibit European nations from extraditing any suspects to be tried before such tribunals.

Initially, Bush defended his tribunals by saying that "non-U.S. citizens who plan and/or commit mass murder are more than criminal suspects. They are unlawful combatants who seek to destroy our country and our way of life." But the whole question is whether those who the president suspects of planning or committing mass murder really have planned or committed such crimes. If we could take the say-so of the executive branch as reliable proof of guilt, we wouldn't need to have an independent judiciary at all. Bush, in this statement, appeared to have forgotten that one of the foundations of basic liberties is the presumption that a person is innocent until proven guilty.

In the end, as a result of widespread disapproval from conservatives as well as liberals, the tribunal plan was modified, and at the time of this writing, no one has been tried before them. That Bush could make such an announcement, however, is indicative of either a lack of understanding about what basic human rights require, or a lack of commitment to protecting the human rights of noncitizens. As Ronald Dworkin, an American who has held the chair of jurisprudence at the University of Oxford, commented, "If any American were tried by a foreign government in that way, even for a minor offense, let alone a capital crime, we would denounce that government as itself criminal."

Although the military tribunals appear to be in abeyance, the United States is, at the time of this writing, still holding more than six hundred noncitizen enemy combatants captured in Afghanistan. Since January 2002, they have been imprisoned at Guantánamo Bay, a U.S. military base held on long-term lease from the government of Cuba. The Bush administration asserts that as enemy combatants they have no right to a lawyer, nor to communicate with their families, and the decision to incarcerate them outside the United States has been effective in keeping them beyond the reach of U.S. courts. They have not been charged with any offense, and have had no access to any kind of impartial tribunal. Both the United Nations Human Rights Commissioner at the time, Mary Robinson, and the International Committee of the Red Cross have said that these captives should be declared prisoners of war, and are entitled to the rights of such prisoners under the Geneva Convention. The Bush administration denies that they are prisoners of war. But the Geneva Convention also provides that where the legal status of prisoners is in doubt, it should be determined by a competent tribunal. This, too, the United States has refused to do.

The detainees are thus, as the British Court of Appeal has put it, in a "legal black hole." That expression was used by Lord Phillips of Worth Matravers in a case brought by the mother of Feroz Abassi, a British subject detained in Guantánamo Bay, seeking a court order that the British foreign secretary should intervene with the U.S. government. The three senior British judges who heard the case agreed that the detention was "in apparent contravention of fundamental principles recognized by both English and American jurisdictions and by international law." It was objectionable, the court said, that Abassi should be subject to indefinite detention in territory over which the United States had exclusive control with no opportunity to challenge the legitimacy of his detention before any court or tribunal. Although the court concluded that it had no power to order the foreign secretary to intervene, it left no doubt that it considered the conduct of the Bush administration incompatible with the rule of law.

Bush's solicitor general, Theodore B. Olson, asserted that there was nothing for U.S. courts to discuss about the detainees. In effect, the administration was trying to erect a legal fence around the detainees that would keep the courts out, as well as the detainees in, for as long as it pleased. But that strategy was dealt a significant blow in November 2003, when the Supreme Court decided that there was a case to be heard in respect of the Guantánamo Bay detainees, and agreed to consider an appeal from some of the prisoners there. As of this writing, the Court has yet to deliver its verdict.

In addition to those held at Guantánamo Bay, the Bush administration has also mistreated hundreds of illegal immigrants. In June 2003, the Justice Department's Inspector General Glenn Fine reported on 762 cases involving illegal immigrants held after September 11, 2001. He found that few of them had clear ties to terrorism, and by the date of his report, fewer than twenty-four suspects were still being held, but many had been released only after being held for months in harsh conditions, often without access to lawyers. Most were detained at traffic checks or as a result of anonymous tips. The ground for suspicion, it appears, might be no more than Middle Eastern origin and the fact that they registered a motor vehicle at the same department office as one of the hijackers. Some of those detained were subjected to physical and verbal abuse. Although the Justice Department said it would alter some procedures in the wake of Fine's report, Ashcroft and his aides also said that they "make no apologies" for doing what they could to deter another attack on America.

The Question of Torture

Though imprisoning people for months or years when they have not been charged with any offense is a clear violation of human rights, the treatment of captured alleged Al Qaeda members held for interrogation by the CIA in Afghanistan and on Diego Garcia, a U.S. base on an island in the Indian Ocean, is even more disturbing. Neither reporters, nor military lawyers, nor the Red Cross have access to these prisoners. According to a *Washington Post* report based on interviews with U.S. national security officials, these prisoners are subjected to "stress and duress" techniques, which include an initial beating to "soften up" the captives, followed by sleep deprivation through bright lights and loud noises, being kept standing or kneeling for hours in spray-painted goggles or black hoods, being bound in painful positions, and, if they were wounded before capture, having painkillers selectively withheld. In some cases, the CIA has handed over prisoners to the intelligence services of nations that have a reputation for violating the human rights of their opponents. *The Washington Post* quotes an anonymous U.S. national security officer who is involved in such transfers as saying, "We don't kick the [expletive] out of them. We send them to other countries so *they* can kick the [expletive] out of them." Officially, little has been said about interrogation methods, but at a joint hearing of the House and Senate intelligence committees the head of the CIA Counterterrorist Center said, "There was a before nine-eleven, and there was an after nine-eleven. After nine-eleven the gloves come off."

The U.S. State Department, in its annual human rights report, denounces other countries for depriving prisoners of access to lawyers, and for "Torture and other Cruel, Inhuman, or Degrading Treatment or Punishment." Under that heading, it lists sleep deprivation, beatings, and tying up in contorted positions as torture techniques. For example, in the 2002 report, released by Secretary of State Colin Powell in March 2003, Jordan is cited for human rights violations in the following terms:

> Police and security forces sometimes abused detainees physically and verbally during detention and interrogation, and allegedly also used torture. Allegations of torture were difficult to verify because the police and security officials frequently denied detainees timely access to lawyers, despite legal provisions requiring such access. The most frequently alleged methods of torture included sleep deprivation, beatings on the soles of the feet, prolonged suspension with ropes in contorted positions, and extended solitary confinement.

About Azerbaijan, the report states:

> There were widespread and credible reports that the authorities have withheld medical treatment from selected inmates, especially political prisoners. . . . Authorities severely limited opportunities for exercise and visits by lawyers and family members of prisoners in maximum security prisons. Some prisoners were kept in "separation cells" often located in basements, in which prisoners reportedly were denied food and sleep in order to elicit confessions from them with no physical evidence of abuse.

It appears that the Bush administration is now doing exactly what its own State Department denounces others for doing. Under the Bush administration, prisoners are denied access to lawyers—indeed in this respect current U.S. practice is actually worse than Azerbaijan's practices, because access to lawyers and family members of the prisoners held at Guantánamo Bay is not "severely limited"—it is nil. Like Jordan and Azerbaijan, the Bush administration uses solitary confinement. It seems that, like Jordan, its officials tie prisoners up in painful, contorted positions, and like Azerbaijan, they deny a form of medical treatment—pain relief—to prisoners from whom they are seeking information.

In one case, the Bush administration transferred an Al Qaeda suspect to Syria, which has been, according to the U.S.'s own listings, one of the worst violators of human rights. The suspect held dual German and Syrian citizenship, and the German government strongly, but unavailingly, protested his transfer to Syria. Officials said the CIA does not know of any of these suspects being tortured by the intelligence services of the countries to which they are handed, but as one official commented, "If we're not there in the room, who is to say?" Although during the Clinton administration, the U.S. cut off contacts and funding with the Egyptian general intelligence services because of their torture of prisoners, a Bush administration official said, "You can be sure that we are not spending a lot of time on that now."

After *The Washington Post* published its report, the New York–based Human Rights Watch called on Bush to make it clear that U.S. policy does not condone torture, to investigate the "stress and duress" techniques allegedly used by the CIA on some of its captives, to take immediate steps to stop any use of such techniques, and to prosecute anyone involved in their use. The organization also insisted that the U.S. must not be complicit in torture by handing suspects over to other governments that use such methods. A U.S. government spokesperson responded that combatants are held "humanely, in a manner consistent with the third Geneva Convention." But Bush has not ordered any investigation, and the U.S. continues to deny outside observers or lawyers access to virtually all of those it detains.

Failing Tom Paine's Test

The most blatant announcement of an intention to ignore fundamental principles of the rule of law was made by Bush himself in his 2003 State of the Union address. On that solemn occasion he told Congress and the world that his administration had "arrested or otherwise dealt with many key commanders of Al Qaeda." Then Bush said:

> All told, more than 3,000 suspected terrorists have been arrested in many countries. Many others have met a different fate. Let's put it this way—they are no longer a problem to the United States and our friends and allies.

The president of the United States was referring to the fact that agents of his administration were killing people without any judicial process at all. He appeared to be proud of that fact. President Gerald Ford had banned secret assassinations by the CIA in 1976, after reports of botched attempts had come to light. Now, as the media had reported a month earlier, Bush has opened the way for the CIA to resume extrajudicial killing. In an example of its actions, six Al Qaeda suspects traveling in a car in Yemen were killed by a missile fired from a pilotless aircraft. One of them was a U.S. citizen.

The deprivations of liberty and of rights of due process that Bush has authorized and defended place national security ahead of rights so basic that they are usually taken for granted in a society governed by the rule of law. The most plausible defense of these deprivations is in straightforward utilitarian terms. A utilitarian might claim that the costs to a few innocent people who may be killed or imprisoned because of poor intelligence information are outweighed by the costs to many more innocent people if, because of an overzealous insistence on civil liberties, a terrorist is set free and manages to explode a "dirty bomb" in Manhattan, or to spread the smallpox virus across America. In the case of people detained without trial, Ronald Dworkin has argued that if violations of the right to liberty are to be defended in this manner, we should acknowledge that some of those detained may be being treated unfairly, and do everything we can to minimize their discomfort and suffering. We should also insist that the unfair deprivation of liberty is inflicted on as few as possible—and for this, we would still need some form of due process, so that we can be sure that government does not become arbitrary, careless, or arrogant in its use of power. As Dworkin put it, "When we treat individual people unfairly for our own safety, we owe them as much individual consideration and accommodation as is consistent with that safety."

If we compare Dworkin's statement about what we owe to those we deprive of liberty without proof of their guilt with conditions in the U.S. detention camp at Guantánamo Bay, the contrast is striking. For the first few months the prisoners—many of whom were, after being held for more than a year, acknowledged to be innocent and released—were kept in small, wire-mesh cells roughly six by eight feet in size. The cells had a wooden roof, but the sides were open to the hot afternoon sun, as well as to wind and rain. In that tiny space, the prisoners slept on the ground, with just two blankets and a prayer mat. They also went to the toilet in their cells. They were able to leave the cells only once a week, for a one-minute shower. Then, after months of complaints and a hunger strike, prisoners were allowed to extend the shower to five minutes, and exercise once a week for ten minutes, although the exercise was still within another cage that is only about thirty feet long. At the time of this writing (December 2003) most prisoners are still allowed out of their cells for only two fifteen-minute periods each week, to shower and exercise. (The cells have been improved, and supplied with beds and running water.) Some prisoners found themselves confined with other prisoners from different ethnic groups with whom they had no common language, and thus for months they were unable to talk to anyone at all. The uncertainty about when, if ever, they would be released was hard to bear. In the first eighteen months of the detention camp, there were twenty-eight suicide attempts.

Dworkin is surely right to say that if we violate people's rights to liberty, we must do so in a way that minimizes the harm we do to them. The Bush administration has failed to do that in regard to those it is detaining at Guantánamo Bay. But Dworkin's principle cannot be applied to torture and assassination—there is no way to minimize the harm they do to the person tortured or killed (who has not been convicted in any court, and could be innocent). Utilitarians might, in extreme circumstances, be prepared to defend torture and assassination in the same way that they might defend a violation of due process rights in the hope of preventing a tragedy that could kill and maim millions. But given the propensity of human beings to abuse others in their power, utilitarians could also argue that torture and assassination should be ruled out on the grounds that the slim chance of preventing a major tragedy by the use of these methods is outweighed by the much greater probability of their misuse. Interrogators may come to enjoy the exercise of brutal power over a hated enemy (who, of course, in the case of those held by U.S. forces after 9/11, have not, at the time of this writing, been proved guilty of any crime). Officials empowered to order secret assassinations wield a frightening power of life and death, unchecked by the extensive judicial safeguards that are required in extradition procedures and criminal trials. They may become callous in the way they use this power, or, with the best of intentions, they may be misled by agents playing a double game (as was the case in Afghanistan, where feuding warlords apparently managed to call in U.S. air strikes against their rivals by telling the U.S. that they were Taliban). So even utilitarians are generally strong supporters of the rule of law, since the long-term consequences of supporting it are almost always better than the consequences of breaching it.

Freedom and the Bush Philosophy

Whatever Bush may have said as governor of Texas, or as a candidate for the presidency, his record as president suggests that neither the promotion of individual rights and freedoms, nor the curtailment of the powers of the federal government, is a high priority for him. When individuals make decisions that he thinks are wrong—whether it is terminally ill patients who wish to end their own lives, or people who find smoking marijuana helps them deal with illness—he will try to prevent them from acting on their decisions. When states pass laws that allow their citizens freedoms that Bush thinks they ought not to have, he will try to use the power of the federal government to overturn or thwart those laws. The chief area in which he has been ready to support states' rights and local decision-making is the environment—that is, where he is more sympathetic to the views of state governments and local interests than he is to the policies that federal agencies have pursued.

The only coherent philosophy consistent with these decisions is one that ranks the specific values that Bush is seeking to protect above the values of individual freedom and states' rights. Thwarting physician-assisted suicide must be more important to Bush than the combined value of trusting individuals to make their own choices and the value of allowing Oregonians to make decisions for Oregon. Something similar must also be true of the value Bush places on stopping the medical use of marijuana.

Despite Bush's boast that the United States is the "freest nation in the world," I can't say that I feel any freer as a resident of the United States than I did when I lived in Australia. To the extent that Bush is successful in forcing Americans to do what he thinks to be right, America will fall behind other nations in terms of freedom. Residents of the Netherlands and Belgium, for example, have more freedom than Americans to choose how they die. In those countries, patients who are terminally or incurably ill, and suffering in ways that cannot be relieved, may ask a doctor to assist them in committing suicide, or to give them a lethal injection. About 2 percent of all deaths in the Netherlands occur as a result of such a request. A rather larger number obtain the assurance of their doctor that if their suffering becomes unbearable, the doctor will end their lives, but, having received this assurance, they do not find it necessary to make use of it. So this is a freedom that is used by a significant number of Dutch people. (And, despite much propaganda from pro-life groups suggesting that more people in the Netherlands are put to death by doctors without their consent, there is no evidence to indicate that this happens more frequently in the Netherlands than in other countries in which voluntary euthanasia has not been legalized.) The Dutch are also freer than Americans with regard to the use of marijuana. In the Netherlands the possession and sale of small quantities of marijuana is tolerated to such an extent that some cafés have a sign in their window indicating that they sell joints. Admittedly, there are some respects in which Dutch residents are less free than most Americans—it is, for example, not so easy to buy a gun in the Netherlands. To balance the respects in which the Dutch are more or less free than Americans would take us beyond the scope of this book, and in any case would require argument about which freedoms are more important. By my values, though, the Netherlands comes out as a freer nation than the United States.

It used to be possible to say that the rights and liberties of Americans are more secure than those of the citizens of other countries because they are protected by a written constitution that is upheld by an independent judiciary. Under Bush, it is no longer possible to say this. Basic rights to liberty and due process have been denied, and the Bush administration has resorted to secret assassinations of those it suspects of terrorism.

In the previous chapter, when examining the killing of civilians in Afghanistan and Iraq, we saw that Bush's support for the right to life is less absolute than his statements about abortion and the rights of embryos would lead one to expect. In this chapter we have found that his support for other basic human rights is highly variable. In allowing government officials to use interrogation methods that the State Department describes as forms of torture or as violations of human rights when used by other nations; in abrogating basic rights to liberty and due process; and in resorting to secret assassinations, Bush has shown that he does not regard human rights as inviolable. He is prepared to take risks with the lives and liberties of innocent people in order to protect America from terrorism. He is, it seems, an advocate of absolute rights on some occasions, and of utilitarian arguments—of dubious quality—for overriding such rights on others. His views and actions on freedom and the limits to government lack any clear and consistent philosophical underpinning.

Chapter 5

The Power of Faith

A charge to keep I have,
A God to glorify,
A never dying soul to save,
And fit it for the sky.
To serve the present age,
My calling to fulfil,
O may it all my powers engage
To do my Master's will!

—From the hymn by Charles Wesley, as quoted by George W. Bush, *A Charge to Keep*, p. 44.

I recognize that government has no business endorsing a religious creed, or directly funding religious worship or religious teaching. That is not the business of the government.

—George W. Bush, speaking to a White House Conference on Faith-based and Community Initiatives, Philadelphia, December 12, 2002

Religion in America

George W. Bush is a Christian. His heart, he has told us, is committed to Jesus. As war with Iraq loomed, he read the Bible every day. He also prays daily. He believes in "a divine plan that supersedes all human plans." He carries his faith into his public life. He says that liberty is "the plan of Heaven for humanity." He thinks that a president should speak for "the power of faith." In the Bush White House, as his former speechwriter David Frum put it, "attendance at Bible study was, if not compulsory, not quite uncompulsory." He opens cabinet meetings with a prayer. When he ordered General Franks to attack Iraq, he asked God to bless him and the troops. He speaks on the radio—on the day before Easter—about relying on "the Creator who made us," and placing "our sorrows and cares before him." When the space shuttle *Columbia* was lost, he drew on words of the prophet Isaiah, saying "The same Creator who names the stars also knows the names of the seven souls we mourn today." Obviously, such an important part of Bush's life and beliefs, and one so closely intertwined with his ethical views, is relevant to any inquiry into Bush's ethics. We also need to ask to what extent it is appropriate for the elected leaders of pluralist societies to invoke their religious faith on official occasions, in speeches, and radio broadcasts, and to use it as a basis for policy on issues that affect others in the community who do not share such beliefs.

Religion and politics in America make a curious mix. On the one hand, the First Amendment prohibition on Congress making any law "respecting an establishment of religion, or prohibiting the free exercise thereof" has led to church and state being much more strictly separated than in many other liberal democracies. In Britain, for example, there is an established church, and the Queen is both the head of state and the head of the Church. Some Anglican schools (but not schools adhering to any other religion) are fully state-funded. In Australia, although there is no established church, private schools, including those that are religious, are eligible for state financial assistance. In secular Australian state schools, there is often a Christmas concert at which children sing Christmas carols they have been taught in class. These practices rarely cause much controversy—Australian organizations defending civil liberties reserve their energies for more serious battles. Similar things could be said about most European countries. But that is not because the Britons, Australians, or French are highly religious people, pleased to see the state supporting religion. On the contrary, poll after poll shows that Americans are much more religious than the citizens of any other developed country. In Europe, fewer than 20 percent of the population go to church once a week or more. In North America, if we can believe what people tell pollsters, it is 47 percent. More than eight out of ten North Americans say that God is important in their lives; fewer than half of all Europeans say that. About 94 percent of Americans believe in God, 89 percent in heaven, and 72 percent in hell and the devil. These differences are also reflected in politics. It is the role of religion that has kept the issue of abortion at the center of American politics, when it has long ceased to be a key issue in other developed nations, with the exception of Ireland.

How then can we understand the greater scrutiny paid to the separation of church and state in the U.S. as compared with other developed countries? One explanation might be that it is precisely where religion is most fervently held that the need to limit its scope is strongest. To most Australians, Christmas carols are traditional songs, some quite beautiful, that small children, whether or not they believe in Jesus, enjoy singing. Political leaders are generally careful to keep their religious beliefs—if they have any—separate from their public life. They rarely, if ever, mention God or their religious faith, and if they were to finish a political speech by saying "God bless Australia," people would wonder why they feel it necessary to make public reference to their private beliefs. Indeed, surprising as it may seem to many Americans, other liberal democracies often elect leaders who are open about not being religious and not attending church or any other form of worship. When taking the oath of office, the German chancellor Gerhard Schröder refused to say the customary words "so help me God." This did not prevent him from being reelected. This is scarcely imaginable in America, where polls have shown that although there is now near-universal willingness to vote for a Catholic or Jewish candidate, only a minority is prepared to vote for an atheist. It seems that the line separating church and state does not need to be so strictly policed in other liberal democracies, not because the environment is more favorable to religion, but because it is less favorable. In the U.S. religion has a more serious prospect of changing the nature of society than it has in any other developed country.

Funding Faith-Based Charities

In the American media, the big issue about religion and politics that Bush's presidency has raised is whether state funding of faith-based charities, a key part of Bush's Compassionate Conservatism social agenda, breaches the constitutional barrier against establishing a religion. Soon after taking office, Bush began pushing for legislation to enable religious organizations to get government funds, arguing that past treatment of religious organizations by the federal government was unfair. He gave examples: an Iowa organization was told to return grant money to the government because the board of directors was not secular enough; a South Dakota shelter for the homeless was denied a grant because voluntary prayers were offered before meals; and a New York Council on Jewish Poverty was discouraged from applying for federal funds because it had the word "Jewish" in its name. The House of Representatives passed a version of the legislation he sought, but the Senate rejected it. So in December 2002 he signed an executive order informing federal agencies that religious organizations are eligible for public funding. "If a charity is helping the needy," the president told a White House Conference on Faith-based and Community Initiatives just before signing the order, "it should not matter if there is a rabbi on the board, or a cross or a crescent on the wall, or a religious commitment in the charter. The days of discriminating against religious groups just because they are religious are coming to an end."

Bush said that under his executive order, "no funds will be used to directly support inherently religious activities," but he then promised that "no organization that qualifies for funds will ever be forced to change its identity." To make both of those statements hold will require some exceedingly difficult line-drawing. The Interfaith Housing Coalition in Dallas, for example, is an organization about which Melvin Olasky, Bush's guru on compassionate conservatism, is enthusiastic. It helps homeless people find housing and employment—after they begin the day with a "motivational Bible lesson." Will the staff be funded from private sources when they conduct the Bible lesson, but funded from government sources when they advise people on finding employment? That will require a lot of careful accounting—and checking up on it would need just the sort of bureaucratic red tape that Bush deplores. The situation is made even worse by a plan to allow federal funds to be used for buildings where religious worship is held, as long as a part of the building is used for social services. How will the cost of building a church be separated from the cost of building rooms within the overall structure in which nonreligious forms of counseling are offered?

No doubt the courts will eventually decide what is or is not constitutional in this area. From an ethical perspective, there is nothing inherently wrong with using the resources of the state to support faith-based charities that assist the poor and homeless, or those on drugs, as long as the charities are supported strictly on the basis of their ability to help those in need, and the help that the faith-based charities provide is also available to those who do not wish to take part in religious activities. Again, this appears to be Bush's view. He told the White House Conference on Faith-based and Community Initiatives, "When decisions are made on public funding, we should not focus on the religion you practice; we should focus on the results you deliver." Assessing results isn't easy. We can measure the number of people helped by different organizations who become self-supporting, drug free, and stay out of prison, but some programs are selective about who they help, and drop people if they don't follow strict rules. Comparing success rates between organizations is meaningful only when the organizations have similar pools of people they are helping, and count those who they reject as well as those they "graduate" from their program. Despite some hopeful claims for faith-based charities, Anna Greenberg of the

John F. Kennedy School of Government at Harvard University concluded a survey of the field by observing that there "is little hard evidence that faith-based communities do a better job than government at solving our society's social and economic problems."

A more difficult issue raised by Bush's measure is that it allows faith-based organizations that receive federal aid to take the religion of job applicants into account when hiring. So a Christian organization could receive federal funds and then use them to advertise a position for which only Christians with a set of religious beliefs similar to those of the organization itself would be eligible. This has led to claims that the government is "funding religious discrimination." But an organization working on the assumption that religious faith helps overcome poverty can hardly do anything else. A secular person could not convey the faith that, the organization believes, the poor need to help them get out of poverty. The organization is, therefore, appointing those it views as best for the task it wishes to undertake, and these people will necessarily share the organization's religious faith.

Whether this really will work—whether faith can be used as a means of helping large numbers of people out of poverty, hunger, drugs, and homelessness—remains to be seen. Whether it is a good thing if it does work, is a question of values. There is a cost to be paid for inculcating religious faith. It could diminish the inquiring spirit that is the basis of scientific investigation and technological progress. It leads to forms of belief that are potentially divisive and dangerous, because they are beyond argument and outside public reason. Nevertheless, those dangers are speculative and many people will think that, even if religious faith is a delusion, a delusion that reduces poverty, hunger, drug use, and homelessness is worth having.

To an observer from a more secular liberal democracy, it is a mistake for defenders of the separation of church and state to focus all their attention on Bush's proposal to fund faith-based charities, as if this were the only, or even the main, issue raised by his presidency about religion and its role in political life. When political leaders are religious, we should ask whether they use their official positions to push their own religious views onto the community as a whole, and to what extent decisions they make on behalf of the state are influenced by religious teachings and ways of thinking. On that basis, there may well be more to be concerned about than the funding of faith-based charities. But first, I want to ask a question about something that few Americans would ever contemplate challenging: the ethics of Bush's faith.

The Ethics of Belief

The nineteenth-century English mathematician and philosopher William Clifford wrote an essay on the ethics of belief that began with a story about a shipowner about to send off to sea a ship full of emigrants. He knew that the ship was old and needed repairs, so he had doubts about whether it was seaworthy, and wondered if he should go to the expense of having it thoroughly overhauled and refitted. But he decided instead to put his trust in Providence, which could hardly fail to protect all those families leaving their homeland to seek a better life abroad. So he convinced himself that all would be well, and watched the ship sail without any qualms. When the ship sank with great loss of life, his losses were covered by the insurance company.

Clifford's point is that the sincerity of the shipowner's belief does not absolve him of guilt for the lives lost, because on the evidence he had before him, he had no right to believe that the ship was fit to make the voyage. As Clifford says, "He had acquired his belief not by honestly earning it in patient investigation, but by stifling his doubts." Even if the ship had proved to be sound and had made the journey safely, that would not mean that the owner was justified in believing it seaworthy. He would still have been wrong to allow the lives of the passengers to hang on his faith, rather than on sound evidence that the ship was seaworthy.

In the light of this example, consider Bush's own account, in *A Charge to Keep*, of his decision to "recommit my heart to Jesus Christ." He traces this to his walk along the beach in Maine with the Christian evangelist Billy Graham. Conversing with Graham, Bush was, he says, "humbled to learn that God had sent His Son to die for a sinner like me." After his decision to recommit himself to Jesus, Bush tells us, he began to read the Bible regularly, and joined a Bible study group. Later, when Bush describes a visit to Israel that he and his wife Laura made in 1998, we get a further insight into his view of the gospels as history. George and Laura went, he tells us, to the Sea of Galilee and "stood atop the hill where Jesus delivered the Sermon on the Mount." It was, he adds, "an overwhelming feeling to stand in the spot where the most famous speech in the history of the world was delivered, the spot where Jesus outlined the character and conduct of a believer and gave his disciples and the world the beatitudes, the Golden Rule, and the Lord's Prayer." Bush concludes his account of his visit to Israel by saying he knows that faith changes lives, because "faith changed mine." This faith is something that enables him to build his life on "a foundation that will not shift."

Bush here presents a picture of a man who accepts what he is told without asking himself any critical questions about it. The question of how people come to have religious faith is too large a topic to discuss here, but there is still something about such unquestioning acceptance that should make us uneasy. Reflective people who are used to questioning what they are told will struggle over the decision to embrace the Christian idea that the world is made according to a divine plan. They will notice that the single chief determinant of belief in the Christian religion is being brought up as a Christian, and that few people brought up in Islamic, Hindu, Jewish, and Buddhist homes believe that Jesus is the son of God. Bush seems to believe that only Christians have a place in heaven. Most Muslims believe, just as fervently, that only Muslims do. They cannot both be right (although they can both be wrong). Is the Christian claim to know the truth any better founded than the Islamic, Jewish, Hindu, or Buddhist claim? We should be skeptical of claims to know something when belief in that thing is so immune to any objective evidence or argument that it depends largely on what one's family believes, and on the customs and beliefs of the society in which one was raised.

None of this seems to trouble Bush in the least. He "learns" that God sent his only son to die for sinners, as if it were just like learning that George Washington was the first president of the United States. When he goes to Israel, he is so confident that he is standing on the hill where Jesus delivered the Sermon on the Mount that the reader might assume he had come across an inscription recording the event carved by the disciples who were present. It never crosses his mind that since the gospel according to Luke tells us that the sermon was given "in the plain," the gospels might not be entirely reliable. Most New Testament scholars believe that whoever wrote the Gospel According to Matthew himself composed the Sermon on the Mount, basing it on various sayings of Jesus that had been written down earlier. If that is right, we needn't bother about the problem of identifying the hill (or plain) from which Jesus preached the Sermon, since he never preached it at all.

Many Americans will not see a problem here. They share Bush's faith, and are all the more ready to vote for him because of it. But we are considering the ethics of his beliefs, not whether they are widespread, or politically convenient. Even if many Americans share Bush's naive beliefs, the rest of us need to ask what we are to think, ethically, of someone who bases his or her life on unquestioning faith. In other words, what are we to think of someone who, although he talks and writes a lot about his religious belief, shows no signs of having struggled with the question at all—someone for whom religious belief is an unquestioned "foundation that will not shift." As the philosopher Karl Popper aptly said, the difference between science and dogma is that a scientific theory must always be open to falsification, on the basis of evidence. Bush seems almost to boast that his view of the truth is not open to falsification on the basis of evidence.

It will also be said that our religious beliefs are a private matter, and therefore not a proper subject of ethical evaluation. But Bush has made his religion a matter of public interest by referring to it frequently and asserting that it influences his public decisions. It matters to us all because Bush's faith, like that of Clifford's shipowner, may make him more certain that he is right than he should be. In 1999, as he prepared to run for president, he assembled leading pastors in the Texas governor's mansion and told them that he had been "called" to seek a higher office. After September 11, 2001, he told Karl Rove, his political adviser, "I'm here for a reason." In the month before he launched a war against Iraq, Bush attended the convention of National Religious Broadcasters, and listened without demur while he was described as "God's chosen man for this hour in our nation." Howard Fineman, writing on Bush in *Newsweek,* says that faith "helps Bush pick a course and not look back." We don't have to look far to see where such an attitude toward belief can lead. Those who planned and brought about the deaths of 3,000 innocent Americans on September 11, 2001, were people of deep religious faith who prayed frequently and, before they died, commended their souls to God's care. One of the ironies of American life is that these attacks by religious fanatics brought about even more public displays of religious belief than is usual in American public life, including the televised singing of "God Bless America" by members of Congress on the night of the attacks. Experts on Islam, hastily summoned before television cameras, said that the problem was not Islam, let alone religious faith itself. The terrorists had misinterpreted their own religion. But if everything depends on faith, then why should terrorists not have faith that their particular version of Islam is right? Why should they not "learn" from an eminent religious teacher that God wants them to destroy the greatest power standing against an Islamic way of life?

Of course, there is a crucial moral difference between those whose faith tells them to murder innocent people, and those whose faith tells them to respect life. But the difference is not something we can get from faith. The Islamic militant who believes he is doing the will of God when he flies a plane full of passengers into the World Trade Center is just as much a person of faith as the Christian who believes she is doing the will of God when she spends her days picketing a clinic that offers abortions. Faith cannot tell us who is right and who is wrong, because each will simply assert that his or her faith is the true one. In the absence of a willingness to offer reasons, evidence, or arguments for why it is better to do one thing rather than another, there is no progress to be made. If we try to dissuade people from becoming radical Islamic terrorists, not by persuading them to be more thoughtful and reflective about their religious beliefs, but by encouraging them to switch from one unquestioned religious faith to another, we are fighting with our hands tied behind our backs. Much better, therefore, to insist that there is an ethical obligation to base one's views about life on evidence and sound reasoning. Bush, unfortunately, is in no position to insist on such an ethical obligation, for his own religious beliefs are no more based on critically examined evidence than are the religious beliefs of Osama bin Laden.

One further comment by Clifford about the effect of credulity takes on new significance in the light of the recent controversy about the administration's claims that Iraq had weapons of mass destruction and links with Al Qaeda:

> The harm which is done by credulity in a man is not confined to the fostering of a credulous character in others, and consequent support of false beliefs. Habitual want of care about what I believe leads to habitual want of care in others about the truth of what is told to me. Men speak the truth to one another when each reveres the truth in his own mind and in the other's mind; but how shall my friend revere the truth in my mind when I myself am careless about it, when I believe things because I want to believe them, and when they are comforting and pleasant? . . . The credulous man is father to the liar and the cheat. . . .

When, more than a century after Clifford wrote those words, doubts were raised about the Bush administration's use of questionable information to build its case that Iraq possessed weapons of mass destruction, Greg Thielmann, a proliferation expert who worked for the State Department's Bureau of Intelligence and Research, explained what had happened in terms that Clifford would have seen as confirming his view. Thielmann said: "This administration has had a faith-based intelligence attitude: 'We know the answers, give us the intelligence to support those answers.' When you sense this kind of attitude, you quash the spirit of intellectual inquiry and integrity." Former vice president Al Gore said something similar when he pointed out that Americans have always believed that democracy depends on open debate and "a shared respect for the rule of reason as the best way to establish the truth"—and then added that the Bush administration does not respect that process because they "feel as if they already know the truth" and are "true believers in each other's agendas."

Religion in Public Life

In his inaugural address, Bush uttered the following three consecutive sentences:

> And this is my solemn pledge: I will work to build a single nation of justice and opportunity.
>
> I know this is in our reach because we are guided by a power larger than ourselves who creates us equal in His image.
>
> And we are confident in principles that unite and lead us onward.

The first and the third sentences refer to the desirability of unity among Americans, but they are separated by a sentence that introduces a divisive note. Even if a large majority of Americans share their president's belief that we are guided by a power larger than ourselves who created us equal in his image, there remain millions who do not.

One of the virtues of a democratic system of government is that it offers a peaceful way of resolving disagreements between people with fundamentally different views. But within a broadly democratic system, there are varying models of how such a resolution should occur. One way is to regard democratic politics merely as a method of deciding who shall exercise power. On this model, those who win elections gain power and use it to impose their will on society as a whole. If religious fundamentalists gain power, they may send homosexuals to jail, or prohibit the sale of contraceptives and prevent stores and cinemas from opening on the sabbath. In defense of such laws, in this view of democracy, they need give no better reason than that they believe it to be God's will, and that they were elected by a majority who shares this belief. With this model there is no incompatibility between democracy and theocracy, as long as the theocrats allow free and fair elections, and the supporters of theocracy continue to win at the ballot box.

A succession of elected theocracies, however, is not the model of democracy that the American founders envisaged. They wanted limits on the power of the majority. They enacted a constitution protecting freedom of expression and opinion, so that people can say what they want, and have the opportunity to persuade others to change their minds. Judging that better decisions emerge from open discussion, they created public arenas, like town meetings and the two chambers of Congress, so that political debates could help to build an educated and informed citizenry, and an effective democracy. They did not want adherents of one religion, no matter how large a majority they might be, to impose their religious beliefs on the remainder.

Bush has said, as the quotation at the start of this chapter indicates, that "endorsing a religious creed" or "directly funding religious teaching" is "not the business of the government." It is against this background that we should look at Bush's frequent references, while speaking as president, to his religious beliefs. For if the head of state and chief executive of the nation is constantly referring to God, or his faith, in his speeches on official occasions, is that not a government endorsing a religious creed? Simply by referring to God in the singular, he leaves out many—polytheists who believe in more than one god; Buddhists, who are generally considered to be religious, but do not believe in a God or gods; agnostics, who are doubtful about the existence of God; and atheists, who are convinced that there is no God. Even when he makes no specific reference to Christianity, what Bush professes in his public statements as president is a religious creed, and the most senior employee of the U.S. government is endorsing and teaching it. (I am not the only one to think this. The quotation just referred to comes from a speech so religious in tone and content that while Bush was delivering it, one audience member called out "Preach on, brother!" and the audience, consisting largely of members of faith-based organizations, applauded.)

Philosophers and political theorists holding a wide variety of philosophical views use the terms "public reason" and "public justification" to describe a broad framework for a discussion in which everyone in a community can take part. Supporters of the idea of public justification see democratic politics not so much as a battle for power, settled by elections, but rather as a kind of public conversation about issues of common concern, with a decision-procedure for reaching temporary closure on these issues when the time for action has come. When we take part in this conversation, we seek to justify our views to others, and in so doing we should acknowledge the fact of political and religious pluralism. We should show that we recognize that we live in a community with a diversity of political and religious views. Hence we should offer reasons that can appeal to all, not only to other members of our own community of belief. Otherwise there can be no public conversation that embraces the entire society; we are implicitly dividing society into separate communities that do not seek to persuade each other. That is a recipe for increasing antagonism and mutual hostility between separate groups, divided along lines of belief. From Northern Ireland to Sudan, in Nigeria and in India, we have many examples of such societies, and the destructive conflicts to which they give rise, from past history and from our own times. Debates within a broad framework of public reason are one way to cross the divisions that separate these communities of belief.

Consider some examples of public policy discussions on controversial issues in ethics. We have already looked at the issue of killing human embryos for research. Obviously the argument *for* doing such research—improving the chances of finding cures for diseases that affect 128 million Americans—is something everyone can appreciate, so it is a justification that falls within the arena of public reason. Against that argument, someone might say:

> We all agree that it is wrong to kill a normal human being. But human development from conception to maturity is so gradual that there is no place at which we can sensibly draw a line and say, "Here, and not before, the developing human being gains a right to life." Hence we should accept that the developing human has a right to life from the moment of conception.

This argument also offers a public justification, and of course it is open to responses within the same framework of public reason, perhaps suggesting places where a line can be drawn to indicate when the developing human gains a right to life. We may end up disagreeing, but our disagreements are within a shared framework of reason and argument. We can each understand what moves the other, and accept that it is a reason, of some kind, even if we are not fully convinced by it.

Now take another issue. Suppose someone says, "We should clone human beings because aliens have told us to do so." We would, if we were to take this ridiculous claim seriously, ask for evidence that these aliens really exist, that they have told us to clone humans, and that there is some reason why we should do what they tell us to do. Suppose that the response to our questions is, "I have encountered these aliens in moments of deep despair, and they have entered into my head and my heart, and I love them and know I can trust them. Open your hearts to them, and you too will come to love them and see that they are right." If we are told that no evidence for the existence of the aliens will be offered, and we should take these claims on faith, we would, rightly, refuse to pay them any further attention. So suppose, then, that someone tells us that human embryos should not be destroyed because "human life is a sacred gift from our Creator." He also refuses to offer evidence, and when asked how he knows this, says it is a matter of faith, and we should open our heart to the Lord, and to Jesus, his only son, and we too will see things as he does. That answer may be more widely held than the justification that the bizarre Raelian sect has given for setting out to produce a human clone, but as a justification for public policy within the sphere of public reason, it fares no better.

The same point applies to other areas of public policy. Most prominent are those relating to the sanctity of human life from the moment of conception, like Bush's immediate reinstatement of Reagan's "global gag rule" that denies U.S. assistance to any foreign nongovernmental organizations that provide information to women on the option of legal abortion and where they can get safe abortion services, even if the organizations fund such activities separately. (Bush's apparent belief that it is not possible to separate the provision of information about planned parenthood from the provision of abortion services makes an odd contrast with his belief that when funding faith-based organizations it is possible to separate the provision of social services from religious activities.) Or there is Bush's statement, in signing the Partial Birth Abortion Ban Act, that the right to life "cannot be granted or denied by government because it does not come from government, it comes from the creator of life." But there are also other policy decisions on issues where principles like equality and individual freedom run counter to traditional Christian principles.

In one of the debates he held with Vice President Gore, Bush was asked what he thought about gay marriage. His answer was, "I think marriage is a sacred institution between a man and a woman." The term "sacred" suggests a religious basis for his opposition to some civil recognition of unions between people of the same sex, and Bush apparently saw no need to provide any other arguments that would appeal to those who did not share his religious views. In office, he has not favored giving gays and lesbians the legal protection that would provide health and tax benefits to their domestic partners. He also expressed his confidence in a leading Republican senator, Rick Santorum, who compared sodomy to incest, and stated his support for laws making sodomy a crime—a position that the Supreme Court shortly afterward decisively rejected.

The Bush administration's attitude toward providing information about contraception and the use of condoms to prevent both teenage pregnancy and sexually transmitted diseases is very difficult to explain on any grounds other than that it is driven by religious faith. The government's Centers for Disease Control had evaluated a number of sex education programs for teenagers to see which were most effective in reducing teenage pregnancies. In 2002, under an initiative called "Programs That Work," it identified on its Web site five effective programs. None were promoting only abstinence, without the use of contraception. Subsequently, without any scientific justification, the Centers for Disease Control ended its "Programs That Work" initiative and put on its Web site a message saying: "The CDC has discontinued PTW and is considering a new process that is more responsive to changing needs and concerns of state and local education and health agencies and community organizations." In a similar manner, Bush adminstration officials pulled from government Web sites science-based information about the effectiveness of condoms in preventing transmission of HIV and replaced it with much vaguer and less positive language. The Department of Health and Human Services appointed an inspector general to investigate AIDS programs to see if their content is too sexually explicit or promotes sexual activity.

Similar attitudes have been put forward at an international level, although with less success. At the Fifth Asian and Pacific Population Conference, held in December 2002, the U.S. delegation sought to prevent reaffirmation of a 1994 agreement, at the International Conference on Population and Development, which committed the governments of the world to take specific action for women's health and rights. Although the U.S. had been a willing party to the agreement when it was first reached, Bush's adminstration objected to the terms "reproductive health services" and "reproductive rights," and tried to remove language that supported the use of condoms to prevent the spread of HIV, the virus that causes AIDS. The U.S. delegation also stated that "the United States supports the sanctity of life from conception to natural death." (One member of the U.S. delegation was John Klink, who served as the Vatican's representative to the United Nations from 1994–2000, and therefore had plenty of experience in advocating such positions.) The Bush administration's proposal was defeated by a vote of 32–1.

On the other hand, to his great credit, when Bush in 2003 finally became convinced of the need for a major U.S. initiative to tackle HIV/AIDS at a global level, he did not insist on avoiding talk of condoms altogether. Although the president used biblical language to urge funding for his HIV/AIDS initiative ("When we see the wounded traveler on the road to Jericho, we will not—America will not—pass to the other side of the road") in the face of a crisis that threatens tens of millions of lives, he was prepared to put compassion ahead of religious fears that condoms condone promiscuity. The bill he signed stipulated only that one-third of the funds going to prevention should be set aside for programs that exclusively promote sexual abstinence until marriage; the remainder was available for use in programs promoting condom use.

At this point those seeking to extend the influence of religion into politics will object that to define public reason in a manner that excludes appeals to religious faith is to do what the theocrats do, but in reverse: to impose a secular framework on public life, thereby unfairly excluding religious perspectives. This sounds like a strong argument, until we realize that it is not religious beliefs, as such, that are excluded from the realm of public reason, but methods of reaching those beliefs that are not accessible to public justification of a kind that we accept in every other area of decision-making. There is no reason or principle why claims about the existence of God, and what he or she wishes us to do, should not be part of public political debate. The problem arises only when religious belief is put into a realm that protects it from the usual rules of scrutiny. If someone tells us that embryo research should be prohibited because human life is a sacred gift from our Creator, then it is reasonable to ask how we know this. If the answer is that it is written in scripture, we need to know why those particular writings are to be believed. If this depends on historical claims about the origins of these scriptures, then experts on the texts may be called in to consider whether these claims are sound . . . and so on. If all these questions can be given answers that are open to the usual rules of critical scrutiny, public justification is satisfied. But if, at some point, further inquiry is cut off with an appeal to faith, then the position is not one that other reasonable people have any grounds to accept, and the original recommendation for the prohibition of embryo research has not been defended within the framework of public reason. It is not the content of the belief—whether it is about God, or gods, or evil spirits, or curses—that determines whether it is a matter of public reason, but the way in which the belief is held and defended. The great medieval Christian philosophers, like Anselm and Aquinas, thought that the existence of God could be proved by rational argument. Whatever we think of their arguments, at least they were concerned to justify their beliefs in terms of what we now call public reason. It is only those who scorn reason who exclude themselves from the field of reasonable public debate.

Appeals to people's religious sensitivities are also not excluded from the sphere of public reason. In debating the proposal to allow federal funds to be used for research that destroys embryos, it is reasonable to assert that millions of Americans believe that only God has the right to take innocent human life, and they will be deeply disturbed if their taxes are used to kill embryos. That is a claim about a matter of fact that can be investigated, and weighed in the balance against competing claims, like the potential of stem cells to cure diseases. From the standpoint of public reason, the fact of offense is the issue, not how well grounded the offense might be. (Although John Stuart Mill and other defenders of freedom have argued that mere offense should not, in the absence of more specific harm, be a ground for infringing individual liberty, once we grant that a risk of offense to some justifies restricting the liberty of others, we have introduced a sweeping argument for prohibiting any kind of behavior, public or private. What offends people is not fixed. People can learn to be more tolerant, and that is a better solution than restricting the liberty of others.)

The suggestion that public policy be debated within the framework of public justification does not seek to restrict freedom of expression or religion. People should, of course, be free to express their religious beliefs, to worship as they choose, and to seek, without coercion, to convert others. The issue is not one of who may say what, but of what reasons should be given weight when we decide issues of public policy, and make laws that affect all members of society. If someone wants to base a policy recommendation on religious beliefs that they hold on faith, they are free to do so, but the rest of us are also free to ignore them—and whether we ourselves are religious or not, we should ignore them, or encourage them to attempt to restate their views in ways that appeal to those who do not share their religious faith. In doing so, we are acting on a sound understanding of what makes for a well-functioning democratic society.

Some will think that public reason is a quaint relic of Enlightenment ideas about reason and progress, properly rejected in the postmodern world in which we now live. They will say it is naive to believe that anyone decides anything on the basis of reason, and will deny that there is any basis for privileging reason and argument above religious faith, or belief in witch doctors, or oracles, or any other way in which people might reach decisions about what to do. But those who say this do not fully think out the alternatives. There are methods of reaching decisions that we use every day, and would not want to do without. We do not want the police to go before the courts saying that they need no evidence that the accused committed the crimes of which he is accused, because they have faith that he did, and faith needs no evidence to support it. We want physicians who have studied what does or does not help sick people—and if we consult alternative healers, we look for evidence that their therapies really work. If we abandon the assumption that reason, evidence, and argument can lead to better decisions, more innocent people will be jailed and more sick people will die. So those who want public justification to fit within the same broad framework are not imposing some narrow, sectional set of standards on the debate. They are seeking standards of argument that everyone uses all the time.

Others will argue that even if we can agree on standards of reasoning for much of everyday life, we cannot prove the truth of any ethical principle. Therefore, since ethics is beyond reasoning and public justification, it is no less acceptable to get one's ethics from religion than it is to get it from one's culture, or one's subjective beliefs. In fact, many Americans believe that the only alternatives to deriving moral judgments from religion are moral nihilism or moral relativism. (Interestingly, this is not an assumption that I have come across outside the United States, presumably because in more secular countries, it is obvious that there are many people who are not religious but still hold that morality is important, and not just a matter of subjective or cultural preferences.) But morality does not have to be religious in order to be real and important. Each of us is concerned about our own well-being, or the satisfaction of our wants and desires. When we think ethically, we should do so from an impartial perspective, from which we recognize that our own wants and desires are no more significant than the wants and desires of anyone else. To base judgments about the rights and wrongs of an action on the impact it will have on the welfare of those affected by it is to base ethics on something that is real and tangible. Because it is based on something that we all want for ourselves, coupled with an argument for a form of impartiality in our reasoning, it meets the standards of public justification. That is why I agree with Bush that it is appropriate to make moral judgments, and that it is possible to educate—not indoctrinate—children to do so. We would be educating them in putting themselves in the place of others. When they are trying to decide what to do, we would encourage them to imagine what it would be like to be those who are harmed by their actions. This is, of course, a form of the Golden Rule, a principle that has been taught by all the major religions, and by secular ethicists, both ancient and modern, as well. Naturally, there is much more to be said on this topic, and there are alternative views of ethics that are defensible. While secular philosophers may disagree about what is the right thing to do, the same is true of religious thinkers, even among those who are Christians.

Bush is aware of the need to broaden his appeal beyond those who share his religious beliefs, and for this reason we may feel that his frequent references to God are innocuous, and it is petty to read too much into them. When he lays out reasons for his policies, he does not rely exclusively on religious grounds. In his speech on the use of embryos for research he states his belief that life is a sacred gift from the Creator, but he also tells us of his concerns about "a culture that devalues life." That phrase suggests a link between permitting federal funds to be used for destroying embryos, and a more general loss of respect for life that we would all oppose, so it is an argument within the framework of public reason.

Not all leading members of Bush's party are so careful. Tom DeLay, the House majority leader, and thus the most powerful Republican after Bush, has said that "Only Christianity offers a way to live in response to the realities that we find in this world—only Christianity." Part of what DeLay means by this can be gleaned from the suggestion he made that the tragic shootings at Columbine High School occurred "because our school systems teach our children that they are nothing but glorified apes who have evolutionized out of some primordial mud." DeLay apparently believes that God is using him to promote "a biblical worldview" in American politics. Though Bush is not responsible for DeLay's views, he does have control over his secretary of education, Rod Paige. Paige has been quoted as saying that he would prefer to have a child in a Christian school, partly because there were too many different values in the public schools to easily arrive at a value consensus. Apart from the fact that Paige was running down the schools it is his responsibility to improve, the remark implies that diversity and debate in ethics are not good, and that it would be preferable for all children to be brought up with just one—Christian—worldview.

Despite his close proximity to people like DeLay and Paige, Bush has said that "We ought not to worry about faith in our society. We ought to welcome it into our programs. We ought to welcome it in the welfare system. We ought to recognize the healing power of faith in our society." This has caused concern even for some religious organizations, at least the more broad-minded of them. The Baptist Joint Committee, for example, decided that the president needed to be reminded that he had been elected "the political leader of the whole nation, not one segment of the religious community." There are real grounds for fearing that using the presidential platform to make religious statements will lead to the promotion of religious faith in general and, more specifically, to the promotion of the religion favored by the president and other leading members of his party. Then the separation of church and state will have broken down, and we will have a society in which non-Christians can no longer feel they are equal participants.

PART II:

AMERICA AND THE WORLD

Chapter 6

Sharing the World

The first question is, what's in the best interests of the United States? What's in the best interests of our people? When it comes to foreign policy, that'll be my guiding question. Is it in our nation's interests?

—George W. Bush, Second Presidential Debate,
Wake Forest University, October 11, 2000

Ethics, the National Interest, and the Leader's Role

Bush's frank statement of his commitment to the national interest came in response to a question that Jim Lehrer, moderator of the 2000 presidential debates, put to both candidates, asking them about their guiding principles for exercising the enormous power that one of them would shortly be wielding as leader of the most powerful nation in the world. Vice President Gore said that "America's real power comes, I think, from our values" and urged that America must stand up for human rights at home, in order to set an example to the rest of the world. His answer, although a little equivocal, gestured toward universal values like human rights that look beyond the borders of his own country. Bush's characteristically more direct appeal to national self-interest put the two candidates on opposite sides of a deep ethical divide. When a nation's interests are in conflict with the interests of the people of the world as a whole, to what extent should national leaders make decisions on the basis of what is in the interests of the nations over which they rule, and to what extent should they take into account the interests of the rest of the world? How much of an obligation does a leader have to ensure that his nation acts as a good global citizen, rather than as a country concerned only with protecting its own interests?

When we consider individuals, rather than nations, there is no doubt about what is right for each individual to do. Consider a situation that resembles the global problem of greenhouse-gas emissions, but at the level of individuals. Our cars used to run on fuel containing lead, which was hazardous for everyone's health, especially for children. It is now illegal to sell leaded fuel in the United States. Suppose that someone we will call John supports this policy, because he is concerned about the health of his own young children. But he also likes the better performance his car gives when it runs on leaded fuel. His car is the biggest in town, and he drives a lot, using more fuel than anyone else in town. John lives near the border of a country that still sells leaded fuel. Every week, he drives across the border and fills his tank. There is nothing illegal about this, but John is pleased that very few others in the town where he lives do the same. (Those who do are mostly much poorer than John, and buy their fuel across the border only because they can't afford the higher gas prices in their own town. They drive cars with very small engines that put much less lead into the atmosphere than John's car does.) As John drives around his town, enjoying the increased responsiveness of his large engine, he knows that his car is putting lead into the air, but he also knows that, since so few others in town use leaded fuel, the lead that his own car emits is not going to create dangerous levels of lead in the area in which he and his children live.

Is John acting ethically? He has no special reason for needing a better-performing car, he just likes the feel of driving one. Others in the community also regret the loss of performance that unleaded fuel has brought, and they too could fill their tanks with leaded fuel on the other side of the border, but they think about the interests of the community as a whole, and they run their cars on unleaded gas. In these circumstances, John's choice is selfish and unfair.

If John is selfish, unfair, and doing the wrong thing, does that also mean that a country that acts like John, obtaining advantages for itself and its own citizens while gaining the benefit of the restraint of others, is being selfish, unfair, and doing the wrong thing? And does it mean that the leader of that country is also acting wrongly? So-called "realists" in international relations answer these questions in the negative. Realists believe that morality works only within a community that has some common values, a source of authority, and a means of enforcing laws. Between nations, as the English philosopher Thomas Hobbes pointed out in the seventeenth century, the "state of nature" still prevails: there is no community, no authority, and no enforceable law. Hence neither nations nor their leaders can be judged by the standards we apply to individuals.

Bush's choice of Condoleezza Rice as his foreign policy adviser during the campaign and as his national security adviser after the election made many people assume that he was a realist. Rice attacked the Clinton administration for confusing foreign policy and morality, and promised, as a realist would, to "refocus the United States on the national interest and the pursuit of key priorities." Bush's answer to Jim Lehrer about what he would do if elected president reinforced this assumption, for it certainly sounded like a realist's answer. At least since September 11, 2001, however, it has become obvious that Bush is not a realist. He has consistently painted the international scene in moral terms. His "axis of evil" speech is merely the best-known of many examples. Not only in his speeches on Iraq and Saddam Hussein, but also when speaking about foreign aid, free trade, and the Kyoto Protocol, Bush puts his views in moral language. His moralism is the polar opposite of the realist approach.

If we are working within a moral, rather than a realist, framework, we have to come back to the question posed above: if something would be wrong when done by an individual, is it also wrong when done by a national leader? One way of answering that question in the negative is to say that the role of a national leader carries specific duties. Just as parents are expected to provide for their own children, rather than for the children of strangers, so too in accepting the office of president of the United States, George W. Bush has taken on a specific role that makes it his duty to protect and further the interests of Americans. Other countries have their leaders, with similar roles relating to the interests of their fellow citizens. For example, the Australian foreign minister, Alexander Downer, has defended his government's determination to advance Australia's national interests by arguing "if we don't, no one else will." In the absence of a global community, we must have nation-states, and the leaders of those nation-states must give preference to the interests of their citizens.

There is some merit to this argument. If you are sick and in the hospital, the philosopher Robert Goodin argues, it is best to have a particular doctor made responsible for your care, rather than leaving it up to all the hospital doctors in general; so too, he says, it is best to have one state that is clearly responsible for protecting and promoting the interests of every individual within its territory. An American government that devoted more resources to building schools in Mexico than it did to building schools in America might be accused of neglecting its responsibilities to its own citizens. Specific duties assigned by roles may be justified on the grounds that a system of roles with corresponding duties provides a better framework for achieving the results we want, whether it is a safe and nurturing environment in which children can grow up, or good government that protects the well-being of citizens. A father who takes his children to the local playground is not, however, entitled to push his children ahead of others who have been waiting to use the swing. The chief executive of a corporation has a duty to make profits for shareholders, but that does not mean that he is entitled to engage in dishonest business practices in order to do so. Something similar holds for national leaders. The duties of a role do not trump the obligation to consider the interests of others, and to deal fairly with them. Today, especially, it is important for nations to be good global citizens, and governments must balance that obligation with concern for the interests of the nation they govern. How does

Bush's ethics hold up by this standard when it comes to a range of issues that reach beyond America's borders, issues like foreign aid, free trade, the International Criminal Court, and global warming?

Aiding Others

If doing what is in the interests of the United States and its citizens is Bush's declared guiding principle in foreign policy, there is one field in which he appears to have violated that principle by acting in a manner that is more compassionate and more ethical than a commitment to national self-interest would suggest. That field is foreign aid, or the extent to which wealthy nations like America should assist the world's poorest people to feed themselves and their families, to educate their children, to have at least a minimum of health care, and generally to be able to improve their way of life.

The first significant Bush initiative on foreign aid came in March 2002, during the buildup to a United Nations Financing for Development conference in Monterrey, Mexico. Bush spoke movingly about the need to do something about the fact that nearly half the world's people live on less than $2 a day. He talked about Malawi, where life expectancy has fallen to only thirty-eight years, about Sierra Leone, where nearly one-third of babies die before the age of five, and about Sudan, where only half the children attend school. Though he linked poverty and the despair that it causes to terrorism, thus suggesting that it was in America's interests to help people rise out of poverty, he also said that the growing divide between the wealthy and the poor is "a challenge to our compassion," and that working for prosperity and opportunity is "the right thing to do."

Most importantly—and in contrast to his similar language about creating a land of justice and opportunity within the United States—Bush was prepared to put additional resources behind these words, above those that had been allocated to foreign aid in recent years. He announced that the United States would increase its development assistance by $5 billion over three years, leading to, at the end of that period, a substantial 50 percent annual increase over current levels. In order to make this additional money as effective as possible in overcoming poverty, it is to go into a new "Millennium Challenge Account," reserved for projects in countries with governments that satisfy certain eligibility requirements—they must, in Bush's words, "govern justly, invest in their people and encourage economic freedom." This means rooting out corruption, respecting human rights, and adhering to the rule of law, as well as allowing markets to operate freely. The idea behind the Millennium Challenge Account is to forge a "Compact for Development" with those countries that are developing sound policies. "When aid is linked to good policy," Bush said, "four times as many people are lifted out of poverty compared to old aid practices." The United States will show that it stands ready to help, if the governments of the developing nations will do their part to remove internal obstacles that keep their people in poverty. Once established, the compact would serve as an example to other nations, showing them that the path of reform will bring rewards.

Separately from the Millennium Challenge Account, Bush has also made a substantial commitment to the global struggle against AIDS. It took some time for him to become involved with this struggle. At an AIDS conference in Nigeria in April 2001, UN secretary-general Kofi Annan outlined the size and urgency of the AIDS catastrophe that is overwhelming Africa and other parts of the world. By that date, seventeen million people had already died from the disease in sub-Saharan Africa alone, and worldwide, thirty-six million were infected with the virus that leads to the disease. Annan called for a multimillion-dollar global fund to fight AIDS, saying that $7 billion to $10 billion was needed every year to reverse the spread of the disease. Microsoft founder Bill Gates, whose foundation has pledged $126 million to the International AIDS Vaccine Initiative, challenged world leaders, starting with Bush, to make "new and unprecedented financial commitments" to the fight against AIDS. Nine months later, however, the Bush administration had made only a very modest commitment to the global AIDS fund—$200 million for 2002, and the same amount for the following year. The fund was languishing, and its advocates were blaming America for setting such a poor example. Leading conservative Republican senators Bill Frist and Jesse Helms announced that they were planning legislation that would authorize an increase of $500 million in U.S. funds, aimed especially at preventing transmission of the AIDS virus from mothers to their children. Frist, a surgeon who had been to Africa to care for AIDS patients, also put forward a bipartisan bill with Democratic senator John Kerry urging the allocation of $4 billion over two years for the fight against AIDS, but the Senate rejected this proposal. In June 2002 Bush announced his own $500 million initiative, but advocates for AIDS victims pointed out that this sum, to be spent over two years, was still far less than what was needed, and also fell short of what other developed nations were putting into the global fund, relative to the size of their economies.

Bush's thinking on what he ought to do about AIDS may have begun to change in December 2002, when Frist became Senate majority leader. Now, as one of the two most powerful members of Congress, he was in a position to do something about the victims of AIDS. A month later Bush surprised even well-informed AIDS activists when, during his 2003 State of the Union address, he turned from terrorism and the threat posed by Iraq to the plight of the thirty million Africans, including three million children under fifteen, infected by the AIDS virus. Bush pointed out that AIDS can be prevented, and that the cost of the drugs needed to extend life for many years had dropped from $12,000 a year to under $300 a year. (This was a remarkable statement in itself, since the reduction in price was the result of the use of cheap generic drugs that Bush's administration had, in response to lobbying from pharmaceutical corporations, tried to restrict.) The lower cost of the antiretroviral drugs, Bush said, "places a tremendous possibility within our grasp . . . seldom has history offered a greater opportunity to do so much for so many." He then asked Congress to commit $15 billion over the next five years, including nearly $10 billion in new money, to "turn the tide against AIDS in the most afflicted nations of Africa and the Caribbean." Congress rapidly did as requested and four months later Bush signed into law what he said was "the largest single up-front commitment in history for an international public health initiative involving a single disease."

How significant are Bush's initiatives to increase U.S. aid, both for development and to fight AIDS? To answer that question, we need to begin by clarifying Bush's confusingly phrased statement about the additional amount he was proposing for the Millennium Challenge Account. Although he spoke of $5 billion over three years, this figure did not match his reference to a 50 percent increase in U.S. development assistance. When officials later clarified the proposal, they confirmed the higher figure—a 50 percent increase, meaning that the amount of aid given will increase progressively over the next three fiscal years, until at the end of that period—for the fiscal year 2006—it will be $15 billion, or roughly 50 percent, higher than the level prevailing at the time of Bush's speech. Since some additional money will be available in the fiscal years 2004 and 2005, the total extra amount of money over the three years in question will be significantly more than $5 billion. When, in February 2003, Bush submitted budget proposals to Congress extending as far ahead as 2008, they included a total of $20 billion over five years for the Millennium Challenge Account. Including the additional money for AIDS, Bush is proposing increasing annual U.S. development and humanitarian assistance from $10 billion in 2002 to $18 billion in 2008.

This is, then, a big increase over present aid levels. Nevertheless, even if all goes according to plan, the U.S. will, in 2008, still be giving an ungenerously low level of aid. In 2001, the latest year for which figures are available, Denmark gave a little over 1 percent of its gross national income in foreign aid. The United Nations has set a target of 0.7 percent. Apart from Denmark, four other nations—Norway, the Netherlands, Luxembourg, and Sweden—have exceeded that target. Major European nations, like the United Kingdom, France, and Germany, gave approximately 0.3 percent. Japan, the nation with the world's second largest economy, gave 0.23 percent. The United States gave only 0.11 percent, or just 11 cents in every hundred dollars the nation produced—the lowest proportion of all the developed nations. (These figures are for government aid. Private donations from the U.S. are higher than from other nations, but including them moves the U.S. proportion of gross national income given as aid up only to 0.145 percent, still among the lowest of the developed nations.) If the United States had given $18 billion in 2001, it would still have ranked below all of the nations I have mentioned. To be on the same footing as Sweden, Norway, the Netherlands, and Luxembourg in the amount of aid it gives relative to the size of its economy, the U.S. would have to increase its annual foreign aid not to $18 billion, but to approximately $80 billion. Moreover, even that figure underestimates the shift toward genuine development and humanitarian aid that would be required. The top five recipients of U.S. development aid in 2001 were, in diminishing order of magnitude, Egypt, Pakistan, Colombia, Jordan, and the former Republic of Yugoslavia. Compare this with the leading recipients of Danish aid—Tanzania, Uganda, Vietnam, Mozambique, and Ghana—and it is easy to see that Denmark's aid is going to the countries with far greater needs. What the United States terms "development aid" goes largely to countries of strategic or other special interest to the United States (for example, ensuring that Egypt is a partner in the Middle East peace process, or attempting to stop Colombian drug exports).

We can also compare Bush's proposal with the aid that was given by the United States in recent decades. In 2006, with the Millennium Challenge Account fully phased in and the commitment to the special fund for AIDS met, U.S. foreign aid would be well below the average of 0.2 percent of national income that the U.S. gave during the 1980s. It would still be below the level currently being given by virtually every other industrialized nation, and only about a quarter of the UN recommended target.

Most illuminating of all is a comparison between Bush's additional foreign aid spending and defense budget increases in the same period. In his budget proposal for 2003, released just a month before he announced his Millennium Challenge Fund initiative, the Department of Defense received an increase of $48 billion over the previous year. A year later, shortly after he had asked Congress to approve spending $15 billion dollars over five years to fight AIDS, he proposed adding another $15 billion to the defense budget for 2004, bringing the Department of Defense budget to a total of $380 billion. Since this increase was for a single year, it was five times the spending he was proposing for the fight against AIDS.

Then in March 2003, as the attack against Iraq was launched, Bush went back to Congress asking for an additional $75 billion for the "war on terrorism," of which $63 billion was specifically for military operations in Iraq. In September 2003, Bush again went to Congress, this time seeking an extra $87 billion for the occupation and reconstruction of Iraq. Months after Bush had declared major combat operations in Iraq "over," the occupation of Iraq was still costing the Pentagon, every month, 30 percent more than Bush had promised to spend on AIDS in a full year.

Taking the Millennium Challenge Fund and the AIDS funding together, Bush has sought an eventual increase in foreign humanitarian and development assistance of $8 billion annually. Of that sum, $5 billion annually is to help more than two billion people living in poverty, and $3 billion annually is to assist more than thirty million people infected with the AIDS virus, who will die if they cannot get access to drugs costing $300 a year, as well as untold millions more who will be infected if efforts to reduce the spread of the virus are inadequate. Bush knows these numbers—they are taken from his 2003 State of the Union address. He also knows what happens to people with AIDS in Africa. Here are his words:

> Because the AIDS diagnosis is considered a death sentence, many do not seek treatment. Almost all who do are turned away. A doctor in rural South Africa describes his frustration. He says, "We have no medicines. Many hospitals tell people, you've got AIDS, we can't help you. Go home and die." In an age of miraculous medicines, no person should have to hear those words.

It doesn't take much arithmetic to calculate that $3 billion is not enough to ensure that no person will hear those words. The other developed nations are doing their part as well, but even if the total is $9 billion, since much of this will have to go toward educating people about preventing further infections, it will fall well short of providing every victim of AIDS with the drugs they need. The contrast between the sums that Bush sought for fighting poverty and AIDS and those he sought for the defense budget and for the war with Iraq is an indication of his priorities. So too is the lengthy delay that has occurred since his State of the Union address without anything really happening on the ground. In the words of Jeffrey Sachs, professor of economics and director of the Earth Institute at Columbia University, "Despite a lot of talk and one famous speech, and one plan that isn't in operation, they've essentially accomplished nothing." Since more than seven million Africans have died of AIDS since Bush was elected to office, history would, Sachs thought, judge him "severely" for this "utterly inexcusable" delay.

There are other concerns about Bush's humanitarian initiatives. Critics of globalization see the criteria that developing nations must satisfy to obtain assistance from the Millennium Challenge Account as a ruse to force them to open up their economies to global trade. That, the critics suggest, will actually disadvantage their poorest citizens, who will find their markets lost to more efficient and often subsidized goods produced by the industrialized nations. Nor will those who are at the bottom of the least developed nations of the world be able to take advantage of the opportunities that global trade offers, for they lack the skills and infrastructure needed to make goods that the rest of the world is willing to buy. Critics of Bush's AIDS program point out that at least one-third of the AIDS-prevention funds must be used to promote abstinence. Some believe that promoting abstinence is not effective, and others point out that this provision will restrict the flow of funds to groups that work with prostitutes, whose cooperation is important in preventing the spread of AIDS, but who are hardly likely to respond to efforts to promote abstinence. But even if promoting abstinence is not the most effective way to fight AIDS, it can do some good under some circumstances, and there is still a considerable (if inadequate) sum available for other ways of preventing AIDS, as well as for preventing mother-child transmission of the virus, and for providing lifesaving drugs to people who have AIDS. Another serious concern is that the legislation Bush signed does not mandate the spending of the $3 billion a year for five years; the money still has to be allocated each year by Congress, and the White House asked for an allocation of only $2 billion for 2004. Nevertheless, and even if Bush was slow in appreciating the scale of what was needed, his AIDS initiative was a major step forward. Until then, it seemed possible that the developed world would do little or nothing to prevent a humanitarian catastrophe on a scale that dwarfs the Nazi Holocaust, the killing fields of Cambodia, and the massacre of Tutsis in Rwanda. Now it seems that, with other developed nations joining in, something significant will be done.

Credit should be given where it is due. While Bush has certainly not done—by his own standards—nearly enough to fight poverty or AIDS, during the Clinton era, U.S. aid declined both in proportion to the size of the economy, and in proportion to government spending. In reversing this alarmingly selfish and shortsighted trend, Bush has, as USAID administrator Andrew Natsios has put it, "taken development off the back burner and placed it squarely at the forefront of our foreign policy." Though the outcome is still uncertain, it is possible that by insisting that the additional aid included in the Millennium Challenge Account go only to nations that govern justly, invest in their people, and allow economic freedom, Bush's initiative will help to set these nations on a better path. In any case, in giving both more money and more prominence to development aid and the fight against AIDS, Bush has taken steps that have the potential to improve and prolong the lives of millions of people.

Trade

From the time when he was a candidate for the presidency, Bush has been a forthright advocate of international free trade, on ethical as well as economic grounds. In *A Charge to Keep* he said that support for free markets and free trade was part of what made him a conservative. Honoring Ronald Reagan in 1999, he said that the case for trade "is not just monetary, but moral. Economic freedom creates habits of liberty." At the Summit of the Americas in Quebec City in April 2001, he affirmed his intention to "vigorously pursue a free trade agenda" unaffected by anti-globalization protests. A month later, he said: "Open trade is not just an economic opportunity, it is a moral imperative." Signing the Trade Act of 2002, he described free trade as "a proven strategy for building global prosperity" and said that it has helped lift "millions of people, and whole nations, and entire regions, out of poverty and put them on the path to prosperity." In May 2003 he told Coast Guard cadets, "America's national ambition is the spread of free markets, free trade, and free societies."

Despite all the rhetoric from Bush and the leaders of other industrialized nations about breaking down barriers against trade and assisting the world's poor, when developing countries export to rich countries, they have to overcome tariff barriers that are four times higher than those encountered by rich countries for their products. These trade barriers deprive the developing countries of annual earnings of about $100 billion, or roughly twice what they now receive in aid from the rich nations. That is one reason why some protest against economic globalization. They say that the industrialized nations, including America under Bush, have skewed the terms of trade to their own advantage, forcing developing countries to open their doors to goods and services produced in the industrialized world, but refusing to allow the free market to determine the fate of their own industries.

Oxfam, the international aid agency, has compiled a "Double Standards Index" to measure the gap between a nation's rhetoric about free trade, and the reality of what it actually does to allow developing countries access to its markets. Of the four major industrialized trading nations or blocs, the European Union comes out as the worst offender, but the United States is in second place with a record rated worse than those of Japan and Canada. Among the major blots on the U.S. record are huge subsidies on agricultural products; a tariff in excess of 120 percent on groundnuts, a staple product of some African nations; the failure to remove more than a quarter of the restrictions on the import of textiles and clothing that the U.S. committed itself to remove under the World Trade Organization Agreement on Textiles and Clothing; higher tariffs on processed food than on unprocessed food, thus deterring developing countries from creating jobs by adding value to their exports; and a sharp rise in the number of "anti-dumping" actions taken against low-cost producers in developing countries. ("Dumping" involves the sale of goods abroad below their cost of production, or more cheaply than they are sold at home. While countries are entitled to protect themselves from such unfair trade practices, claims of "dumping" are often a cover for protection against legitimate competition.)

Bush's own record is mixed. He has supported one important initiative for some of the world's poorest nations, the African Growth and Opportunity Act (AGOA). This legislation, enacted under Clinton's presidency but enhanced in August 2002, allows free-market access for selected products from thirty-eight African nations. In remarks videotaped for broadcast at the 2003 summit of nations participating in AGOA, Bush said that "AGOA shows the power of trade to lift people out of poverty." Exports from AGOA nations to the United States were "rising dramatically," he said, and the legislation was "helping to reform old economies, creating new incentives for good governance, and offering new hope for millions of Africans." It is true that during 2002 exports from AGOA nations to the U.S. increased by 10 percent, but more than three-quarters of these imports were petroleum products, which do less to generate employment than more labor-intensive products like textiles, and are unlikely to do much to "reform old economies." Excluding petroleum products, all the thirty-eight AGOA nations together exported only a modest $2.2 billion worth of goods to the U.S. (For comparison, Australia, with a population of nineteen million, or about one-twentieth of the combined total of the AGOA nations, had exports to the U.S. of more than $6 billion.) The "dramatic" rise is therefore from a very small base, and the growth in imports from AGOA nations was not enough to offset a more substantial decline in imports from other sub-Saharan African nations, which meant that overall U.S. imports from sub-Saharan Africa actually fell by more than 15 percent in 2002. The African Growth and Opportunity Act is a step in the right direction, and Bush's support for it is commendable, but even for the nations that come within its scope, it falls well short of eliminating all barriers to trade.

In other respects, Bush's commitment to free trade does not live up to the principles he espouses. In announcing his candidacy for the presidency, he said: "I'll work to end tariffs and break down barriers everywhere, entirely, so the whole world trades in freedom.

The fearful build walls. The confident demolish them." Yet as president, Bush imposed tariffs of nearly 30 percent on most types of steel imported from Europe, Asia, and South America. That was scarcely a move that showed confidence in American industry. The tariff increase offered the Chinese trade minister Shi Guangsheng an irresistible opportunity to complain that "advanced economies [that] once preached free trade are now undermining free trade." For once, conservatives agreed with the Chinese leadership. *The Weekly Standard* described the tariff as "perhaps the worst piece of trade legislation in half a century." Columnist George Will said the tariff was a case of "compassionate conservatism for government-addicted corporations" and added the ultimate conservative condemnation: on this issue, Bush had proven himself "less principled than Bill Clinton." Predictably, foreign nations affected by the tariffs, led by the European Union, took their case to the World Trade Organization. No one was surprised when the WTO ruled the steel tariffs illegal. Even then, it wasn't until the European Union threatened to put punitive tariffs on imports from electorally sensitive U.S. states like Florida that Bush finally withdrew them.

In the election year of 2002, Bush's free-market principles melted away again, apparently unable to take the political heat he would have received for opposing a farm bill that gave away huge amounts of tax revenues to farmers—and mostly, to wealthy corporate farmers. *The Wall Street Journal* called the legislation "a 10-year, $173.5 billion bucket of slop" that "would embarrass even the French." The Farm Security and Rural Investment Act of 2002 increased subsidies to producers of crops like corn and wheat by $50 billion over ten years, a 70 percent increase over previous levels, and a complete reversal of the attempt made in the previous comprehensive farm bill (passed in 1996, in the Clinton era) to wean American farmers off subsidies. Instead of refusing to sign so blatant a violation of free-market principles, Bush expressed his pleasure that the law "provides a generous and reliable safety net for our nation's farmers and ranchers" and signed it.

If Bush really considers free trade a moral imperative, he ought to have vetoed the Farm Security and Rural Investment Act of 2002.

Less than six months earlier, at a meeting of the World Trade Organization in Doha, Qatar, the United States and other members of the World Trade Organization had agreed to remove barriers to farm trade. The so-called "Doha Round," initiated at that meeting, was made much more difficult by the jump in U.S. subsidies to farmers. The subsidies may threaten trade agreements that limit the amount the U.S. can spend on what are known as "trade-distorting" subsidies. It also makes it much harder for the U.S. to credibly complain to the European Union about its farm subsidies—for as European Union trade commissioner Pascal Lamy caustically noted, the U.S. now pays three times more per farm than does the EU.

James Wolfensohn, president of the World Bank, has pointed out that farm subsidies in the rich nations amount to six times what those countries provide in foreign aid to the entire developing world. Moreover, whereas the aid is distributed among the almost five billion people living in developing nations, the subsidies go mainly to a relatively small number of agribusinesses and large corporations. The Farm Security and Rural Investment Act of 2002 has infuriated Brazilians, who claim that the subsidies deprive their soybean and cotton farmers of $1.5 billion a year in exports. The Act also doubled subsidies on cotton, to nearly $4 billion annually. These subsidies threaten the livelihood of some of the world's poorest people, including those that the African Growth and Opportunity Act is supposed to help. West African cotton growers say that despite their lower costs, they cannot compete with U.S. cotton, exported for a price that is 57 percent below the cost of its production. The American subsidies are paid to only 25,000 cotton growers, with an average net worth of $800,000. In the African nation of Burkina Faso, where cotton is the principal export crop, the average annual income is $200. According to Oxfam, U.S. cotton subsidies have caused a 12 percent drop in Burkina Faso's export earnings, with smaller but still significant drops in the earnings of several other poor African nations. The Bush administration spends more on subsidizing its 25,000 cotton growers than it provides in aid, through the U.S. Agency for International Development, for all of Africa. African cotton producers in Benin, Burkina

Faso, Chad, and Mali joined with Brazil in an official complaint to the WTO against cotton subsidies paid in the United States and Europe. In September 2003, the round of talks begun in Doha came to an abrupt halt when negotiations broke down at the WTO meeting in Cancun, Mexico. The refusal of the United States to reconsider its cotton subsidies was one factor in that setback to further progress in liberalizing trade. The long-term effects of the farm bill on efforts to create a global free-trade environment are clearly negative.

As an ethical goal, global free trade is controversial, but defensible. It is consistent with Bush's other professed values, including the value of free markets in general. But it is not ethical to preach the value of free trade to the world and then bow to political pressure to protect American industries that cannot compete in their own marketplace. Nor is it ethical to subsidize wealthy domestic producers so that, with the assistance of American taxpayers, they can take markets from producers in developing countries. That, however, is what Bush has done.

The International Criminal Court

In July 2002, more than one hundred countries celebrated the birth of the International Criminal Court, or ICC. The ICC is the successor to a line of tribunals that goes back to the Nuremburg Tribunal, set up by the victorious Allies to try the Nazi leaders for the crime of waging a war of aggression and also for genocide and crimes against humanity. Other tribunals followed, to deal with crimes against humanity in Bosnia after the breakup of Yugoslavia, in Rwanda during the Hutu massacre of Tutsis, and by Indonesian-supported militias in East Timor. In setting up the ICC, the participant nations have attempted to move beyond the justice of the victors over the defeated, and instead give international criminal justice a more impartial and permanent basis. The court will have a prosecutor who can bring charges of genocide, crimes against humanity, and war crimes against individuals as long as they are a national of a state that has ratified the treaty, or the crime was committed on the territory of such a state, or a specific case is referred to the court by the United Nations Security Council. The aim is to ensure that there is no legal refuge anywhere in the world for those who commit such crimes. That objective, one might have thought, is one that fits well with American values, with support for universal human rights, and for the principle that power should be restrained by the rule of law.

In the final days of his presidency, Clinton signed the treaty setting up the ICC. Since then, an additional important reason has emerged for the U.S. to support the ICC. If, in the wake of the terrorist attacks of September 11, 2001, other nations doubt the impartiality of American justice and are reluctant to hand over one of their citizens suspected of terrorism to a U.S. court, they might instead accept the jurisdiction of an international court. But although 139 nations had signed and ninety-two had ratified the treaty as of December 2003—well above the sixty required to bring the court into existence—the United States was not one of those ratifying the treaty. Bush has said he would not submit the treaty to the Senate for ratification and denied that any legal obligations arise from his predecessor's signature. In taking the second of these steps, he was not only opposing the ICC, he was also acting contrary to the authority of the Vienna Convention on the Law of Treaties, which requires states to refrain from undermining treaties they sign, whether or not they later ratify them.

Bush and his aides have said that participating in the court would mean ceding U.S. sovereignty to an international prosecutor, and that the court could initiate capricious prosecutions of American officials and military personnel. Had the U.S. supported the court, it could have played a role in developing safeguards to prevent such misuse. Instead the Bush administration's preoccupation regarding the court has been to negotiate—under threat of a withdrawal of U.S. aid—agreements with individual nations guaranteeing that U.S. citizens in their jurisdiction will not be extradited to the ICC. It has also persuaded the UN Security Council to pass resolutions extending immunity to U.S. citizens. In June 2003, the Security Council agreed to another year of immunity for U.S. citizens, but the fact that the U.S. was once again seeking special treatment for its own citizens raised an important question in the minds of the international community: is the United States willing to play its part, as one citizen among others, in creating an international system of law and order, or will it stand apart and require special treatment, different from that which other nations are willing to accept?

In July 2003, the Bush administration announced that it was suspending military aid for thirty-five nations that had refused to pledge to give American citizens immunity before the International Criminal Court. Some of these countries, like Colombia and Ecuador, were considered vital for efforts to bring stability to the Western Hemisphere, while others, like Croatia, were being assisted in efforts to join NATO. Richard Dicker, a director of Human Rights Watch in New York, pointed out that the administration had created a dilemma for itself, because now it had to choose between supporting democratic nations and its ideological campaign against the ICC. Dicker then added pointedly, "I've never seen a sanctions regime aimed at countries that believe in the rule of law rather than ones that commit human rights abuses." No wonder that other nations see Bush's insistence on special treatment for Americans as a stumbling block to international cooperation. At a European Union summit held in Greece in June 2003, the member nations issued a pointed rebuke to the Bush administration, saying, "The European Union strongly supports the ICC as an important step forward in the implementation of international law and human rights. We will continue to work actively for the universality of the court and contribute to its effective functioning."

Ironically, while Bush had been insisting that U.S. citizens are not to be brought before the ICC, despite all its safeguards ensuring proper political process, his administration was continuing to hold, at Guantánamo Bay, hundreds of citizens of other countries, not charged with any offenses, unable to see lawyers or have any of the rights that the ICC would allow to those accused of crimes under its statute. It was during negotiations between the U.S. and Australia—to ensure that Americans in Australia would be immune from prosecution by the ICC—that the Bush administration announced that it would try David Hicks, an Australian citizen captured in Afghanistan, before a military tribunal. The tribunal rules do not respect the normal procedural right of the accused to confidential communication with his or her lawyer, reject the usual courtroom standards of admissible evidence, and allow a two-thirds majority of the "judges" (of whom only one need be legally qualifed) to decide on the guilt of the accused. From this tribunal the only avenue of appeal is to a panel of three military officers that meets behind closed doors.

Many non-Americans regard Bush's concern about protecting U.S. citizens from the ICC, while himself detaining people for years without trial and even (as we saw in Chapter 4) ordering the assassination of the citizens of other nations, as sheer hypocrisy. That impression is reinforced by the fact that Bush's attitude to the ICC runs parallel to his approach to another, arguably more momentous, global issue that also requires international cooperation between sovereign nations: global warming.

Climate Change, or Being Evenhanded

The idea that Americans come first has enormous importance for dealing with the paradigmatically global problem of climate change. Our planet's atmosphere is a common resource. No individual, and no nation, owns it, or any part of it. We all need it—not only to breathe, but also to absorb the waste gases we produce, of which carbon dioxide is the most significant. The more fossil fuels we use, the more carbon dioxide we put into the atmosphere. We now have strong—many atmospheric scientists would say overwhelming—evidence that the carbon dioxide produced by human use of fossil fuels is changing our planet's climate. The predicted change in climate is already happening, with nine of the hottest ten years ever recorded occurring since 1990.

If every nation in the world goes ahead with "business as usual," doing nothing to reduce the amount of greenhouse-gases it is putting into the atmosphere, the results will be bad for the people of the world as a whole, for most nonhuman animals, and for the preservation of many endangered species of animals and plants. A relatively small number of people and animals, living in areas like Siberia and northern Canada, are likely to be better off, but their gains will be outweighed by the losses to others who will suffer from more severe droughts and floods, increased frequencies of tropical storms (extending beyond their present climatic zones), and also spreading tropical diseases. The Asian monsoon, on which hundreds of millions of peasant farmers in India and several other Asian nations rely to grow their food, will become less reliable. As polar ice melts, sea levels will rise by between four and thirty-five inches. Even the lowest estimate will pose a threat to tens of millions of people farming the fertile but low-lying delta regions of Bangladesh and Egypt. These lands are already prone to flooding from the sea when storms and high tides coincide. If the higher estimate turns out to be nearer the truth, they will lose their land, and small island nations in the Pacific will disappear beneath the waves. Species unable to adapt to climate change, or move to a cooler environment, will become extinct. Australia, for example, has unique alpine ecosystems that depend on winter snowfall. But since Australia's mountains barely reach 7,000 feet, if the climate warms, these mountains will cease to receive snow. Animals and plants found nowhere else will be trapped on their isolated peaks like animals on high ground about to be drowned by rising floodwaters.

When, shortly after taking office as president, George W. Bush was asked what he would do about global warming, his answer was, "We will not do anything that harms our economy, because first things first are the people who live in America." Asked whether the president would call on drivers to sharply reduce their fuel consumption, the White House press secretary, Ari Fleischer, replied, "That's a big no. The President believes that it's an American way of life, and that it should be the goal of policymakers to protect the American way of life. The American way of life is a blessed one." Under Bush's leadership, the U.S. has refused to accept the Kyoto Protocol, which requires its member nations to reduce greenhouse gases to, on average, 5 percent below 1990 levels. (By 1999, the U.S. was already 11.7 percent above its 1990 emissions level, and this figure has been growing with every passing year.)

"First things first are the people who live in America" endorses the same kind of national selfishness that is evident in the answer Bush gave to Jim Lehrer's question in the second presidential debate. It is an implication of this view that the rights of Americans to drive large, gas-guzzling cars outweigh the rights of people in other countries to live on their land, undisturbed by changing rainfall patterns and rising sea levels. But it is not surprising that people in other nations should consider that this way of thinking fails to deal fairly with those who are not Americans. Romano Prodi, at the time president of the Commission of the European Union, and a former prime minister of Italy, responded to Bush's statement by saying that "If one wants to be a world leader, one must know how to look after the entire earth and not only American industry."

At times Bush has acknowledged, and apparently accepted, the view of the National Academy of Sciences that global warming is "due in large part to human activity." At other times he has backed away from that admission. In 2002, when his own State Department submitted to the United Nations a report by the Environmental Protection Agency that emphasized the seriousness of the problem of global warming, Bush dismissed it as a "report put out by the bureaucracy." The following year, when the EPA prepared a comprehensive report on the state of the environment, the White House forced the deletion of a section stating that emissions from factories and cars contribute to global warming. Bush's aides wanted to drop references to a 2001 report by the National Research Council, which Bush himself had commissioned, and to a 1999 study showing a record rise in global temperatures over the previous decade. In place of the original wording, they proposed a few paragraphs drawing on a report commissioned by the American Petroleum Institute that came to no specific conclusion about global warming. In an internal memo leaked to *The New York Times*, an EPA official stated that the White House version "no longer accurately represents scientific consensus on climate change." Christine Todd Whitman, Bush's appointee as administrator of the EPA, thought it would be better to have no discussion of global warming in the EPA report than the wording that the White House proposed. She resigned her position about this time.

Admittedly, there are gaps in what we know about global

warming—for example, how much of the rise in temperatures is due to natural causes, how fast our planet is likely to warm, and what impact some of our actions could have. Officials in the Bush administration have suggested that given these uncertainties, costly measures to reduce climate change, such as those required to comply with the Kyoto Protocol, are unjustified. Even if we agree that there are these uncertainties, however, the risks of not taking immediate action are so great that they outweigh the much more limited costs of taking action. Carbon dioxide remains in the atmosphere for one hundred years. The carbon in the exhaust of Henry Ford's original Model T is still trapping heat. By the time the gaps in our scientific knowledge are closed, it may be too late to undo the consequences of our past actions. The "better safe than sorry" approach—sometimes more formally referred to as "the precautionary principle"—suggests that even in the absence of complete information, we should be prepared to incur reasonable costs to avoid a significant chance of a disastrous outcome. The evidence on climate change is that the risk is quite considerable. As University of Chicago law professor Cass Sunstein has pointed out, Bush's attitude toward the risk of Iraq having weapons of mass destruction was that it is better to act preemptively, even in the absence of complete information, to ensure that the disaster of such weapons being used is averted. This precautionary stance is exactly what Bush's critics are urging him to take regarding climate change. The cost of restricting greenhouse-gas emissions, however, is far less than the many thousands of deaths and injuries caused by the war in Iraq.

From a collective standpoint that takes everyone's interests into account, it would be best if all countries with high levels of emissions made significant reductions in the amount of greenhouse gases they produce. But from the standpoint of an individual nation, this is not necessarily the best possible outcome, for the national costs associated with reducing greenhouse-gas emissions could outweigh the national benefits. To cut emissions substantially, instead of using the cheapest fuel available to generate electricity or drive our cars, we would have to take into account the amount of carbon dioxide we are producing. We may have to switch to natural gas, which produces less carbon dioxide than coal, but in some regions is more expensive. We may need to use more expensive, but more fuel-efficient, cars. Or we may simply have to consume less energy, which may mean that our houses are a little warmer in summer, and cooler in winter, than we would otherwise wish them to be.

When Jim Lehrer asked Bush why he would refuse to sign the Kyoto Protocol, Bush said:

> I'll tell you one thing I'm not going to do is I'm not going to let the United States carry the burden for cleaning up the world's air, like the Kyoto treaty would have done. China and India were exempted from that treaty. I think we need to be more evenhanded. . . .

Regrettably, neither Lehrer nor Gore asked Bush what he meant by being "more evenhanded." Thus a chance to learn more about Bush's ethical thinking was missed and we can only speculate about why he thinks that the fact that the treaty did not require any reductions in emissions from developing nations means that it is not "evenhanded."

Since Bush believes that people should be held responsible for their actions, he should be sympathetic to the principle that the person who breaks something is the one who ought to fix it. How does that idea apply to the atmosphere? Well, there is a problem right now about climate change, because over the past century or more, industries in the developed nations pumped a lot of carbon dioxide into the atmosphere. Most of that carbon dioxide is still there. Although the developed nations have only about one-fifth the population of the developing nations, at present rates of emissions the contribution that the developing nations, including China and India, have made to the problem will not begin to match the contributions of the developed nations until 2038. (That calculation includes gases released by clearing forests, the one area in which the developing countries are now worse than the developed countries.) In other words, if the developed nations had had, over the past century, per-capita emissions at the level of the developing nations, there simply wouldn't be a problem at present, and there would be plenty of time to prevent any problem coming about. As far as the atmosphere is concerned, the developed nations broke it. If those most responsible for breaking something should do the most to fix it, then the developed nations owe it to the rest of the world to fix the problem. Instead, they are making it worse—and the United States is the chief culprit. Despite having less than 5 percent of the world's population, it is the largest producer of greenhouse gases, responsible for 25 percent of all emissions. China, with more than four times the population of the United States, emits only 60 percent as much carbon dioxide.

Some say that because the United States has planted so many trees in recent decades, it has actually soaked up more carbon dioxide than it has emitted. But this is an arbitrary way of calculating emissions, for the United States has only been able to reforest because it had previously cut down much of its great forests, thus releasing the carbon into the atmosphere. The balance sheet depends on the time at which the accounting is done. If the period includes the era of cutting down the forests, then the United States comes out very badly. If it starts from the time at which the forest had been cut, but no reforestation had taken place, it comes out much better. In any case, forest regrowth offers only a temporary solution to the greenhouse problem. It locks up carbon only while the trees are growing. Once the forest is mature, it ceases to soak up carbon from the atmosphere. U.S. reforestation, therefore, while a good thing for many reasons, does not enable the country to avoid its responsibility for causing a large part of the global warming problem.

Suppose, though, that Bush were to reject the "you broke it, you fix it" ethic. Perhaps he could argue that at the time the developing countries put most of the greenhouse gases into the atmosphere, there wasn't the scientific knowledge we have today. So although the U.S. and other developed nations did cause the problem, they didn't know what they were doing, and shouldn't be held responsible for it.

That would be a dubious argument for a tough-on-crime death-penalty supporter to use, especially one who thinks that even mentally retarded criminals may be held responsible for their actions and executed. And even if we think that today's Americans cannot be held morally responsible for what earlier generations of

Americans did, Americans today are enjoying a higher standard of living because of the actions of their polluting predecessors. By accepting the benefits generated by these earlier emissions, the present generation of Americans could be said to have incurred an obligation to pay for the costs that the acts of earlier generations of Americans imposed on others by using more than their fair share of a common resource.

But suppose we forget about everything that has happened up to now. Is there some other principle of fairness that would not require the developed nations to do more than the developing nations? In other words, let's bend over backwards to avoid any possibility of being unfair to Bush in his attempt to protect the interests of the United States, and put aside the strong argument that the United States—because it did more than any other nation to bring about global warming, and has benefited from doing so—has an obligation to take the lead in remedying it. Starting afresh, we begin with the fact that the atmosphere is a common resource. No one owns it. How should we divide it up? The simplest and most obvious answer is: equally. Not, of course, equally between nations. It would be absurd to give a small nation like Costa Rica the same share of the atmosphere as a large nation like the United States. And not equally in proportion to the area of a nation's landmass, either, because having an extra million square miles of uninhabited desert or frozen tundra doesn't generate any extra emissions. But having an extra million people does. Hence the simplest answer is to divide equally, between every inhabitant of the planet, the atmosphere's capacity to absorb our emissions. Unless someone can show that he or she is entitled to more of the atmosphere than others, equal shares would seem to be a good starting point.

Unfortunately for Bush, this principle would also require the United States to make drastic cuts to its greenhouse-gas emissions, while allowing China and India to avoid any cuts, at least at present. The United States produces more than five tons of carbon per person per year. Japan and Western Europe average below three tons. China emits 0.76 tons per capita and India 0.29. This means that given an "evenhanded" per-capita annual emission limit of one ton of carbon per person (which is not very far off what the Kyoto Protocol aims to achieve) India would be able to increase its carbon emissions to more than three times what they now are. China would be allowed a more modest increase. The United States, on the other hand, would have to reduce its emissions to no more than one-fifth of what they are now. Compared with the mauling that such a reduction would inflict on the U.S. economy, the cut that the U.S. would have had to take if it had signed on to the Kyoto agreement would barely be noticeable.

Are there any other principles of fairness or "evenhandedness" that would give the industrialized nations a better deal? In his speeches on this topic, Bush has referred to the fact that the United States is not only the world's biggest producer of greenhouse gases, but also the world's biggest producer of goods and services. This suggests that he may have in mind a principle of distribution, such as, "To each according to how much they produce." How evenhanded is this? One argument for it might be that if the United States were forced to slow down its economy and produce less, in order to meet an emissions target based on something other than the value of goods and services it produces, then other nations would step into the gap to produce the goods and services now produced in the United States. But they might do so less efficiently. The outcome would be fewer goods from the same level of emissions.

Even if this were true, as a principle of fairness, "To each according to how much they produce" suffers from a major ethical flaw. It's not as if the United States produced all these goods in order to benefit everyone equally. The vast majority of the goods and services that the United States produces are consumed in the United States. The relatively small fraction of goods produced in the United States that are sold abroad also benefit U.S. residents, who gain employment and income from the production and sale of these goods. These benefits are gained in part by the appropriation, without consent or compensation, of a collective resource. Admittedly, it is a resource that everyone freely appropriated up until now, but it is also one that, as every nation (including the United States) agreed at the 1992 Rio Earth Summit, should no longer be seen as available on a "take as much as you want" basis.

In any case, the claim that the United States produces more efficiently, in terms of greenhouse-gas emissions, than other nations has been refuted by figures published by the U.S. Central Intelligence Agency. The United States is well above average in the amount of emissions it produces in proportion to its GDP. The CIA figures show that developing countries like India and China, as well as some European nations like Spain, France, and Switzerland, are the best at producing a high value of goods for a given level of emissions.

Although it is true that the Kyoto Protocol does not initially bind the developing nations, it is generally understood that the developing countries will be brought into the binding section of the agreement after the industrialized nations have begun to move toward their targets. That was the procedure with the successful Montreal Protocol concerning gases that damage the ozone layer, and there is no reason to believe that it will not also happen with the Kyoto Protocol. China, by far the largest greenhouse-gas emitter of the developing nations and the only one with the potential to rival the total—not per-capita—emissions of the United States in the foreseeable future, has already, even in the absence of any binding targets, made significant progress in reducing fossil-fuel emissions, thanks to improved efficiency in coal use. Hence the claim that the Kyoto Protocol does not require the developing nations to do their share is misleading, because they have not yet reached the point at which they are using more than their quota of the planet's capacity to absorb greenhouse gases. When they do, it is reasonable to presume that they will also have obligations under the next international climate agreement to reduce their emissions. The Bush administration's position amounts to saying that the poor nations of the world should commit themselves, in perpetuity, to much lower levels of greenhouse-gas production per head of population than the rich nations have. There is no way in which that principle can be defended as ethical.

Chapter 7

War: Afghanistan

The president wanted to kill somebody.

—Secretary of State Colin Powell, as quoted by Bob Woodward in *Bush at War*

A Defining Moment

On September 11, 2001, watching the television footage of the collapsing World Trade Center and seeing the grief of the families of the victims, it was easy to agree with Bush when he said, "Today, our nation saw evil." In his brief speech to the nation that evening, he used the word "evil" four times, setting the tone for the months and years to come. That the president of the United States would become the leader of a global struggle against terrorism was inevitable, given the target of the attack. A different president might not, however, have jumped to the conclusion that America was attacked because it is "the brightest beacon for freedom and opportunity in the world." That statement ignored America's role in global politics, and especially in the Middle East. It therefore struck many people in other countries as a painful example of just how self-satisfied America is.

Another president might also have made different moral choices about how best to prevent future terrorist attacks. Here the decisions that Bush has made will define his presidency and have an impact on the peace and security of the world for a long time to come. About these decisions, there are many questions to ask. We have already seen that Bush's actions are inconsistent with his professed belief that all innocent human life is precious and must be protected. Other equally significant questions about Bush's decisions include whether they are based solely on the principle of doing what is in the best interests of Americans, or can be justified in terms of the interests of everyone affected by them. Do they prove that America is a nation that "loves peace," as Bush has claimed? Are they applied consistently in different situations? Are they likely to lead to a world in which peace and justice, for Americans and others, are more secure, or less secure?

The Bush Doctrine and the Decision to Attack Afghanistan

The first important policy decision was taken very quickly. On the evening of September 11, when Bush spoke to the nation for just seven minutes, he said that the United States would, in responding to the attack, "make no distinction between the terrorists who committed these acts and those who harbor them." The decision to say this was made by Bush, in discussion with Condoleezza Rice, his national security adviser. No one else—not Vice President Dick Cheney, Secretary of State Colin Powell, Secretary of Defense Donald Rumsfeld—was consulted beforehand. Nine days later, Bush repeated what soon became known as the "Bush Doctrine" to a special joint session of Congress: "From this day forward, any nation that continues to harbor or support terrorism will be regarded by the United States as a hostile regime."

This Bush Doctrine—perhaps better described as the "first Bush Doctrine," since his later assertion of America's right to make preemptive strikes has also been referred to as the Bush Doctrine—significantly changed previous understandings of national sovereignty and support for terrorism. Before September 11, the U.S. government would surely have resisted the application of such a doctrine by another nation. Take Cuba, for example. America harbors Cuban exiles who have used Miami as a base from which to carry out terrorist attacks in Cuba. In 1998 a former senior federal prosecutor told the *Miami Herald* that there was a policy of avoiding prosecution of those plotting terrorist acts against Cuba. So, when a boat loaded with explosives and registered in the name of Tony Bryant, an anti-Castro militant, turned up near Havana, the FBI simply told Bryant not to do it again. The *Herald* article provided that as one of many examples showing what it described as "the weakness of U.S. laws that bar violent acts against foreign governments."

The most notorious example of a country going to war against another nation for harboring and supporting terrorism is still Austria-Hungary's attack on Serbia in 1914, which triggered a world war that cost nine million lives. Austria-Hungary's case for going to war rested on Serbian involvement in the assassination of the Austro-Hungarian crown prince and his wife in Sarajevo. The conspirators admitted that they had been trained, armed, supported, and given safe passage across the border by Serbian government officials. Austria-Hungary handed the Serbian government an ultimatum, demanding that it bring the conspirators to justice and allow Austro-Hungarian officials to supervise the prosecution to ensure that the trail of guilt was pursued to the end. This ultimatum was widely seen as a violation of the principle of national sovereignty. The British foreign minister, Sir Edward Grey, called it "The most formidable document I have ever seen addressed by one State to another that was independent." The American Legion's official history of the Great War denounced it as a "vicious document of unproven accusation and tyrannical demand." Many historians studying the origins of the First World War have condemned the ultimatum as failing to respect Serbia's sovereignty. They are especially critical of the fact that after the Serbian government accepted many, but not all, of the demands in the ultimatum, Austria-Hungary refused to enter into negotiations, instead declaring war.

Although the U.S. administration—unlike the Austro-Hungarian government in respect of Serbia—had no evidence of the involvement of Afghan government officials in the events of September 11, Bush's ultimatum to Afghanistan was no less threatening to that country's sovereignty than Austria-Hungary's was to Serbia. He demanded the closure of all terrorist training camps, and access for U.S. officials to ensure that they were no longer operating. In one important respect, he went further than Austria-Hungary, which was content for Serbia to put those who had aided the terrorists on trial. Bush insisted that Al Qaeda leaders in Afghanistan be handed over to the U.S.—where one might suspect that it would be difficult for them to get a fair trial. (The subsequent history of American procedures for dealing with those captured in Afghanistan has shown this suspicion to be reasonable.)

When, on October 7, 2001, the United States began bombing Afghanistan, there was very little opposition within the U.S. or in the international community to the war against the Taliban. On behalf of the United States Conference of Catholic Bishops, Bishop Joseph Fiorenza wrote to Bush that the use of force against Afghanistan was "regrettable but necessary" and Cardinal Francis George of Chicago said flatly, "This is a just war." At Princeton University I organized a forum on whether a war on Afghanistan would be a just response to terrorism. I invited four distinguished speakers, covering the range of opinion from left to right: Richard Falk, Michael Walzer, James Johnson, and Gideon Rose. I was surprised—and from the perspective of an organizer seeking vigorous debate, disappointed—to find that all four thought that an attack on Afghanistan would be a just war in the light of the events of September 11. For Falk, who had opposed the Vietnam War and the 1991 Gulf War, and subsequently opposed the 2003 war with Iraq, it was the first time that he had supported America going to war.

It is possible that the near-unanimity of support for an attack on Afghanistan was a sign of nothing more than that people were calmly and impartially considering whether such an attack was the right thing to do, and deciding that it was, because the facts were such that no rational person could come to a different conclusion.

But it is also possible that the horrendous nature of the attacks of September 11, still fresh in everyone's memory, swayed people's judgment and prevented the kind of calm reasoning that is desirable before making a momentous decision that puts at risk the lives of many people, including innocents.

The just-war theory to which Bishop Joseph Fiorenza appealed in his letter to Bush has wide acceptance beyond religious circles and provides a convenient framework for assessing whether America's war on the Taliban government of Afghanistan was ethically defensible. As set out in *The Challenge of Peace,* the much-praised statement on when it is just to go to war adopted by the United States Conference of Catholic Bishops, lethal force may only be used when all of the following seven conditions are fulfilled:

The Cause is Just.

The most obvious "just cause" is defense against aggression; another would be to stop grave violations of the basic rights of whole populations.

Competent Authority.

War can only be waged by a legitimate government, with responsibility for keeping order.

Comparative Justice.

The values at stake must be sufficiently critical to override the presumption against killing, and when right is not all on one side, the injustice suffered by one party must significantly outweigh that suffered by the other.

Right Intention.

Force may only be used for just reasons, such as to achieve peace and reconciliation.

Probability of Success.

No matter how just the cause may be, if resorting to arms will be futile, it is wrong to go to war.

Proportionality.

The expected costs of going to war, in terms of loss of life and destruction, must be outweighed by the good expected to be achieved.

Last Resort.

Force may be used only after all peaceful alternatives have been tried and exhausted.

In the case of the U.S. attack on Afghanistan, the first four criteria seem to pose little difficulty. If the cause was to bring those behind the outrage of September 11, 2001, to justice, and to prevent further terrorism, then it was undoubtedly just. The war was undertaken by the American government, the proper authority for the use of force to defend American civilians. The values at stake—protecting people from further acts of terrorism like those carried out on September 11—were of critical importance. The government's intentions were, we can assume, primarily to stop such acts, and secondarily to bring a less oppressive, more democratic government to Afghanistan. The U.S. government was not intending to annex Afghan territory.

On the fifth criterion, the probability of success, much depends on how the objectives of the war are seen. If they were to destroy Al Qaeda's training camps and disrupt its operations, the war was successful. Bringing those behind the 9/11 attacks to justice has proved more difficult. Only a few Al Qaeda leaders have been captured or confirmed killed, and at the time of writing, Osama bin Laden is not among them. Nevertheless, there might have been reasonable expectations that this could be achieved.

Destroying the training camps, bringing its leaders to justice, and temporarily interfering with Al Qaeda's operations, however, were merely the means to the only justifiable goal of the "war on terrorism": to stop, or sharply reduce, terrorist attacks. Was a war on Afghanistan likely to achieve that? The camps were primarily training fighters to support the Taliban in consolidating its hold over Afghanistan, rather than training terrorists to operate against America or other Western nations. Destroying them could not be expected to stop such terrorism. Al Qaeda already had cells in Western nations, and it was from these that further terrorist attacks were likely to come. Indeed, as one study has said, "the 11 September terrorist cells were less dependent functionally on Al Qaeda bases in Afghanistan than on flight schools in Florida." A senior FBI counterterrorism official has estimated that the war on Afghanistan reduced Al Qaeda's capacity to commit "horrific acts" by 30 percent. Even the capture of bin Laden, he said, would cause only a "stuttering" in Al Qaeda operations. The bombings in Bali and the Philippines in October 2002, in Riyadh and Casablanca in May 2003, in Jakarta and Baghdad in August 2003, and in Riyadh, Nasiriya, and Istanbul in November 2003 showed only too vividly that the war in Afghanistan did not succeed in preventing major terrorist attacks. Since we can't rerun history without that war, we really don't know whether it reduced the number of such attacks by 30 percent, by 70 percent, or by any other figure. It may have been reasonable to expect that overthrowing the government that had harbored the terrorists would be a warning to other governments that might consider supporting terrorists or allowing them to use their territory as a base. But as the IRA showed for many years, terrorist organizations do not need the support of a state to carry out their atrocities. It also needs to be asked whether going to war with the government of an Islamic nation would not give rise to more hatred of America among Muslims than a more narrowly focused attack on Al Qaeda. If that is so, in the long run the war may turn out to have contributed to increasing terrorism, rather than reducing it.

Given a proper reading of the objectives of the war on terrorism, then, it is not clear that the requirement of having a reasonable probability of success was fulfilled. Of course, this judgment must be made against a background of other possible actions, and the probability that they would be as successful or more successful in reducing terrorism.

The sixth criterion is proportionality: was the end or goal of the war proportional to the means used or the costs incurred? Even if the cause of a war is inherently just, the costs of achieving justice may be so high that it would be wrong to go to war. In the conflict between the people of Hungary and the Soviet Union in 1956, for example, justice clearly lay on the side of the Hungarians. But if the only way to defend the Hungarians was to start a global nuclear war, then the cost of achieving a just outcome was simply out of proportion to the goal of freedom for Hungary. In the case of the war on Afghanistan, there was no real risk of bringing about a catastrophe on that scale, but there was a serious risk of killing a substantial number of civilians—and this did happen. Since the proportionality principle involves a weighing of costs and benefits, much depends on the uncertain nature of the benefits. If a successful war prevented Al Qaeda from mounting more operations on the scale of 9/11, or from killing even larger numbers with nuclear or biological weapons, then the proportionality criterion was satisfied even if a significant number of civilians were killed.

Finally, there is the criterion of last resort, and it is here that the Bush administration's actions are most difficult to defend. This criterion requires that a nation go to war only when it has tried and exhausted all peaceful alternatives. Bush, however, showed little interest in exploring any option short of war. Already on September 13, according to Bob Woodward's account in *Bush at War,* Powell noticed that "Bush was tired of rhetoric. The president wanted to kill somebody." From then on, although there is occasional talk of the need for patience, Bush frequently pushes for quick action, saying things like, "Time is of the essence," "It's very important to move fast," and "We've got to start showing results."

On September 17, Bush told Powell to issue an ultimatum to the Taliban, ordering them to turn over bin Laden and Al Qaeda, and adding that if they did not comply, "We'll attack them with missiles, bombers and boots on the ground." Then, as Woodward recounts, Bush added, "Let's hit them hard. We want to signal this is a change from the past. We want to cause other countries like Syria and Iran to change their views. We want to hit as soon as possible." Powell was "slightly taken aback" that Bush wanted to give the Taliban an immediate ultimatum. In the end, Bush issued the ultimatum himself, in his speech to Congress—and to eighty million Americans watching on television—on September 20. Shortly before he gave that speech, he had privately told British prime minister Tony Blair that his plan was to use the "full force of the U.S. military" with "bombers coming from all directions."

Remarkably, as far as we can tell from Woodward's account, after giving the Taliban the ultimatum, Bush never discussed, with Rice, with Powell, with the National Security Council, or with any other advisers, the Taliban's response. The reader of *Bush at War* might assume that the Taliban never responded at all. But in reality Mullah Omar, the Taliban leader, asked the U.S. government to provide evidence of Osama bin Laden's involvement in the events of 9/11, and indicated that if this was done, he would be willing to hand bin Laden over to an Islamic court in another Muslim country. (This proposal was later softened to a requirement that the court have at least one Muslim judge.) There was also a suggestion that the Organization of the Islamic Conference, a group of more than fifty Muslim countries, should be consulted. Finally, there was an offer to meet with U.S. officials. The request for evidence of bin Laden's involvement—no such evidence had been made public at the time—was surely a reasonable one, in accord with normal requests for extradition. The U.S. would itself insist on evidence before handing someone within its borders over to another nation wishing to put him on trial for a capital offense. Yet the request, and the proposal for a meeting, appear to have been totally ignored, just as Austria-Hungary ignored Serbia's counteroffer in 1914. In both cases, such treatment of a response to an ultimatum indicates that the intention behind the ultimatum was not to find a satisfactory solution to the problem, but to provide an excuse for going to war. War was not the last resort.

The problem for the impatient president was what kind of action he could take. The original plan was to send in American ground troops simultaneously with the commencement of bombing, but the military did not have the necessary infrastructure in place for getting troops into Afghanistan quickly. Even when it had been decided to bomb first and get troops in later, Bush was impatient with the delay required to prepare the bombing campaign. On September 27, when Rice told Bush that the military was not ready to begin bombing, the president replied, "That's unacceptable!" Bush himself told Woodward that he was "ready to go," "growing a little impatient," "fiery." And he also said, "I rely on my instincts. I just knew that at some point in time, the American people were going to say, Where is he? What are you doing? Where's your leadership? Where is the United States? You're all-powerful, do something."

Since getting American ground troops into Afghanistan was going to take more time than he was prepared to accept, bombs and missiles were the obvious alternative. They could be ordered up more quickly, but Al Qaeda was an elusive target. The Bush war cabinet knew that the training camps were already empty, and Bush was determined to avoid "pounding sand"—a derisive term that he and Rumsfeld used to refer to what they saw as Clinton's tactic of responding to bin Laden's earlier attacks on American embassies by sending a million-dollar cruise missile into an empty tent. The Taliban government, on the other hand, offered more substantial targets. So the goal slid from attacking Al Qaeda to toppling the Taliban regime. In Woodward's account, by September 29, just nine days after the ultimatum had been issued, ousting the Taliban was already the assumed goal of the military operation.

If Woodward's account is accurate—and it is based on extensive interviews with those who were present, including Bush himself, and on notes made at the time by those who were there—the war on Afghanistan fails to meet the criteria for being a just war because it was not a war of last resort. Moreover, because the form that the war actually took—a war to overthrow the Taliban government—arguably went beyond what was necessary to achieve the goal of bringing those behind the outrage of September 11, 2001, to justice, and preventing further terrorism, it is not even clear that the war was fought for a just cause. It was the most aggressive choice among a range of options that had not been adequately explored. It was an option chosen by a leader who was in a hurry to act, to show the American public that he was a leader, and to make an example of Afghanistan, in order to send a signal to other nations. But impatience is not an ethical justification for going to war, and the signal could have been sent in other ways, less costly in human life.

The tone of the discussions that Woodward reports gives little sense that Bush was pondering the deaths that the war was bound to bring to many, including children and other innocent civilians. Rumsfeld has acknowledged, as we have seen, that war makes "misery and suffering and death" commonplace. The inevitability of a major loss of innocent human life in the war Bush was contemplating makes it an ethical imperative to search very hard for an alternative to war. If, on the other hand, a major loss of innocent life was *not* inevitable, then there is all the more reason to blame Bush for the more than a thousand civilian deaths that did occur as a result of the means by which the war was fought. The ethics of inflicting civilian casualties, even unintentionally, feeds back into the ethics of the decision to go to war. A peace-loving president would have been more convincing in trying all other options. That would have been emotionally and politically difficult in the days immediately following September 11, but it was what Bush ought to have done. Then, if those options had failed, when America went to war, it would have been beyond doubt the last resort.

Chapter 8

War: Iraq

Fourteen forty-one, the Security Council resolution passed unanimously last fall, said clearly that Saddam Hussein has one last chance to disarm. He hasn't disarmed.

—George W. Bush, Press Conference, March 6, 2003

Liberty for the Iraqi people is a great moral cause and a great strategic goal. The people of Iraq deserve it.

—George W. Bush, speaking at the United Nations, September 2002

Two Arguments

The slow buildup to the U.S. attack on Iraq in March 2003 gave George W. Bush many opportunities to set out the ethical ideas underlying his actions. He offered two separate arguments for going to war with Iraq. They could be put like this:

Argument 1
The cease-fire that ended the first Gulf War in April 1991 required Iraq to give up weapons of mass destruction and to accept UN inspectors who would inspect and monitor the de-

struction and removal of chemical, biological, and nuclear weapons. The Iraq government led by Saddam Hussein accepted these terms, but Saddam deceived the world, continuing to develop weapons of mass destruction. Hence he was in breach of the cease-fire, and the coalition that had fought Iraq in 1991 was free to resume hostilities.

Argument 2
A change of regime in Iraq would liberate that country from a tyrant who had, during the long years of his rule, been responsible for the deaths of hundreds of thousands of his own people and allowed others to remain in grim poverty while he poured the country's oil revenues into military projects and extravagant palaces for his own luxury.

Weapons of Mass Destruction and the United Nations Resolutions

Bush's primary case for war with Iraq rested on the claim that the Security Council had required Saddam Hussein to get rid of weapons of mass destruction, but he had not done so. It now seems very probable that Saddam Hussein had largely, and perhaps entirely, rid himself of weapons of mass destruction. That simple fact undermines the main reason Bush offered for the war. It also raises important questions about why Bush falsely claimed to know—even insisted that there was "no doubt"—that Saddam possessed weapons of mass destruction. But let us assume, as a purely hypothetical exercise, that Bush's statement was correct and Saddam had not disarmed. We need to make this assumption if we want to scrutinize the ethical basis on which Bush claimed to be acting. The most important question to ask here is: if the facts were as Bush said they were, would the U.S.-led attack on Iraq have been justified by the Iraqi dictator's failure to comply with Resolution 1441?

As Bush said, Resolution 1441, adopted by the UN Security Council in November 2002, gave Iraq "a final opportunity to comply with its disarmament obligations under relevant resolutions of the Council." To that end, it called on Iraq to accept an enhanced system of inspections. Once Iraq accepted the weapons inspectors, the key issue became one of determining whether or not Iraq had destroyed its weapons of mass destruction, as it claimed. But Resolution 1441 was not as clear-cut as Bush's two-sentence summary suggests. The resolution directs the executive chairman of the United Nations Monitoring, Verification and Inspection Commission (UNMOVIC) to report if Iraq is not cooperating with the inspectors or has not fulfilled its obligations to disarm, and reminds Iraq that it has been repeatedly warned that it will face "serious consequences" if it continues to violate its obligations. But the last words of the resolution state that the council "decides to remain seized of the matter." This peculiar wording is used by bodies like the Security Council to indicate that they are maintaining an interest in a particular matter, and have not finished dealing with it. The same wording was used in the earlier Resolution 687, which declared the cease-fire in 1991. The Security Council said at that time that it "decides to remain seized of the matter and to take such further steps as may be required for the implementation of the present resolution and to secure peace and security in the region." In that respect the language of both Resolution 687 and Resolution 1441 is in sharp contrast with the language of the earlier Resolution 678, adopted in August 1990 after the Iraqi army had invaded Kuwait. That resolution authorized member nations to "use all necessary means" to evict Iraqi forces from Kuwait. Thus the Gulf War of 1991 was fought under the auspices of the United Nations. But the formula used in Resolution 687 and Resolution 1441 indicates that the council is keeping the matter under active consideration, rather than handing it over to any nation, or group of nations, to decide whether Iraq was or was not complying with its obligations.

That Resolution 1441 did not authorize any nations to take action was also made clear by France, Russia, and China, who all pointed out at the time the resolution was passed that it did not contain any "automaticity" about the use of force. Each of these nations could have vetoed the resolution, and would probably have done so if it had contained an automatic authorization of force.

Other non-veto members of the Security Council who voted for Resolution 1441, including Mexico, Ireland, Syria, Bulgaria, Norway, Cameroon, and Guinea, made similar points. Many of them stressed that the resolution strengthened the role of the Security Council in deciding issues of international peace and security. The Mexican representative, for instance, was reported as saying, in the United Nations official summary, that the passage of Resolution 1441 "strengthened the Council, the United Nations, multilateralism and an international system of norms and principles." He added that it provided for the use of force to be valid only "as a last resort, with prior, explicit authorization of the Council."

Both the United States and the United Kingdom representatives accepted that Resolution 1441 contained no "hidden triggers" or "automaticity" regarding the use of force, although the U.S. representative, John Negroponte, asserted that it also "did not constrain any Member State from acting to defend itself against the threat posed by that country, or to enforce relevant United Nations resolutions and protect world peace and security." Negroponte's remark about a country defending itself against the "threat" posed by Iraq suggests a justification for war outside the framework of the UN resolutions, and thus is a different argument from the kind we are here examining. The second part of Negroponte's remarks presupposes that there is a relevant UN resolution to be enforced, but does not indicate what resolution that might be, nor why it should be open to the United States, or any other member of the UN, to take it upon itself to enforce a resolution that the Security Council had not asked it to enforce. The UK representative explicitly agreed that "If there was a further Iraqi breach of its disarmament obligations, the matter would return to the Council for discussion."

All this makes it clear that in regard to Resolution 1441, the council was expecting to be informed by its weapons inspectors, and was prepared to take further decisions depending on what they reported. That is, of course, what happened over the next four months. The inspectors reported back to the Security Council on several occasions. Iraq denied having any weapons of mass destruction. Although it did not provide complete documentation of what had happened to some chemical and biological agents it had once possessed, the inspectors failed to find proof that the Iraqis were lying. The inspectors' reports indicate that, after a slow start, Iraq was, by February, showing a significant amount of cooperation. When the inspectors established (using information supplied by Iraq) that one of Iraq's missiles had, in test firings, slightly exceeded the 150 km range set by the cease-fire terms, Iraq agreed to destroy the missiles, and had already destroyed sixty-five, or more than half of them, by the date of the American attack.

Bush asserted flatly that Saddam "hasn't disarmed." In other speeches Bush said, over and over again, that Saddam "has weapons of mass destruction." In the speech in which he issued his forty-eight-hour ultimatum, he said, "Intelligence gathered by this and other governments leaves no doubt that the Iraq regime continues to possess and conceal some of the most lethal weapons ever devised." Even at the time he made these statements, there were good reasons for doubting the evidence that the Bush administration offered in support of its claims. In his 2003 State of the Union address, Bush said, "The British government has learned that Saddam Hussein recently sought significant quantities of uranium from Africa" and went on to say that Saddam has attempted to purchase high-strength aluminum tubes suitable for nuclear weapons production. In support of the claim that Saddam had tried to import uranium from Africa, Colin Powell presented to the United Nations documents purporting to show that Iraq had attempted to buy 500 tons of uranium from Niger. These documents were soon—before the war began—shown to be, as Powell and the White House later admitted, clumsy forgeries. One of the documents, dated October 2000, bore the signature of a man who by that date had not held the post of foreign minister of Niger for several years. Other evidence that Bush and Powell presented was inconclusive. For example, as chief weapons inspectors Hans Blix and Mohamed Elbaradei later said, no evidence was ever produced to show that the aluminum tubes to which Bush referred were intended for anything other than the production of conventional missiles.

The intelligence information to which Bush referred was unreliable, and could be seen to be unreliable before the war began. In these circumstances it was entirely reasonable for France, China, and other members of the Security Council to take the view that inspections should be allowed to continue in order to establish whether Saddam had or had not disarmed. Despite American outrage at the French threat to veto a resolution authorizing an attack on Iraq—an outrage that went to such absurd lengths as U.S. citizens boycotting French goods and renaming "French fries" as "freedom fries"—French president Jacques Chirac had good grounds for resisting Bush's rush to war. He considered that Bush and Powell had not succeeded in showing, in a way that would justify war, that Iraq was in violation of its obligations under Resolution 1441. Subsequent events suggest that he was right, and that Bush and Powell were wrong.

Whatever view one takes of the evidence, however, whether Iraq was or was not in compliance with its obligations was not a decision for the U.S., or any other country, to make. (Similarly, the decision as to whether Israel is or is not in compliance with UN resolutions relating to the occupied territories is not a decision for, say, Russia to make.) Under Resolution 1441, the Security Council had retained the right to make that decision for itself, and to decide also on the nature of the consequences that would follow if Iraq was found to be in violation of its obligations. That is why the Bush administration tried so hard to obtain a second resolution declaring that Iraq had not disarmed and authorizing the use of force against Iraq. When it became apparent that France, and perhaps Russia and China, too, would use their veto to prevent the passage of such a resolution, the administration began to suggest that if a majority voted for the resolution, that would provide some sort of moral authority for action in accordance with it, even if a veto prevented its formal acceptance by the council. This is a proposition that the United States would surely have vigorously resisted had it been invoked by any other nation on the seventy-six occasions on which it has itself used the veto. (Only the former Soviet Union has used the veto more frequently.) And when, despite great efforts from both Bush and British prime minister Tony Blair, it became apparent that there would not even be a majority for a resolution authorizing force, Bush acted as if a second resolution was not necessary anyway. Robin Cook, the leader of the House of Commons until he resigned to show his opposition to Blair's stance on Iraq, was surely correct when he said, in explanation of his resignation, "I applaud the determined efforts of the prime minister and foreign secretary to secure a second resolution. Now that those attempts have ended in failure, we cannot pretend that getting a second resolution was of no importance."

The United Kingdom's attorney general, Lord Goldsmith, issued a statement outlining a legal basis for the use of force against Iraq. He claimed that if the Security Council had, in passing Resolution 1441, intended that a further resolution was required to authorize the use of force against Iraq, it would have said so explicitly in 1441. The fact that it did not do so means that, in Lord Goldsmith's view, "all that resolution 1441 requires is reporting to and discussion by the Security Council of Iraq's failures, but not an express further decision to authorise force." Logically, however, one might just as well argue that if the Security Council had intended that no second resolution was required, it would have explicitly said this. But it didn't; therefore we should presume that a second resolution was required. In any case, Lord Goldsmith's interpretation suggests that the Security Council was asking the inspectors to report to it on Iraq's compliance, or failure to comply, and was planning to discuss the question, but at the same time was willing to leave the decision to use force to individual member nations acting on their own. Why would the Security Council intentionally turn itself into a mere talking-shop, while the decisions that matter are taken elsewhere? Vaughan Lowe, Chichele Professor of Public International Law at Oxford University, and several other leading British law professors took a different, and surely more plausible, view: "There is nothing in the resolution that gives anyone *apart from the Security Council itself* the right to decide when the final chance has been exhausted." Lord Goldsmith was valiantly attempting to find a legal basis for the actions about to be taken by Tony Blair's cabinet, of which he was a member, but as the British law professors point out, his interpretation makes no sense, and is inconsistent with the words of the UK's own representative at the UN on the day on which Resolution 1441 was passed.

As I have already indicated, there were other arguments for war with Iraq, apart from the claim that war was justified in order to enforce UN resolutions. Since we are still to consider these arguments, at this stage it would be wrong to decide whether the war was or was not ethically justified. Nevertheless, the record of the Bush administration in taking its case for the disarmament of Iraq to the United Nations, and then, when it could not get its way there, going ahead anyway, is not one that puts Bush in a good light. It looks very much as if Bush supported Resolution 1441 because he expected that Iraq would refuse to accept the stringent inspection requirements. That was a reasonable prediction, since Saddam had previously refused to accept more restricted inspections. Bush no doubt thought that Saddam's refusal to accept the inspectors would provide a justification for the U.S. to overthrow Saddam with the backing of the United Nations. Indeed, while Bush was going to the UN, the military forces under his command were already softening up Iraq for the war to come. From June 2002 into early 2003, the U.S. Air Force was striking at Iraq's command centers, radar, and fiber-optic networks, dropping more than 600 bombs on about 350 selected targets. Although these attacks were justified at the time as a reaction to Iraqi violations of a no-flight zone that the United States and Britain had established in southern Iraq, Lieutenant General Michael Moseley, the chief commander of the air war against Iraq, later admitted that this justification was at least partly spurious, since the Iraqis were responding to more aggressive American attacks that were consciously preparing the way for a military offensive against Iraq.

When, to the surprise of Bush and his advisers, Saddam accepted the inspectors, who then proved unable to find proof of the existence of weapons of mass destruction in Iraq, Bush became concerned that if the inspections continued in that manner, he would no longer have any grounds for attacking Saddam. So he switched to a different justification for an attack. Two weeks before the outbreak of war, CBS News journalist Mark Knoller asked Bush whether he was worried that the United States might be perceived as defying the UN, if it went ahead with military action without explicit authorization from that body. On that occasion Bush did not go into the details of past UN resolutions to claim that an attack would be lawful. Instead he replied:

> I'm confident the American people understand that when it comes to our security, if we need to act, we will act, and we really don't need United Nations approval to do so . . . as we head into the twenty-first century, Mark, when it comes to our security, we really don't need anybody's permission.

As this comment indicates, Bush's real justification for invading Iraq does not lie in his commitment to upholding international law. In going to the UN, he was not doing so in good faith. Like someone who accepts arbitration in a dispute because he hopes the decision will go his way, but has no intention of complying if it does not, Bush took his case to the UN but had already decided to act no matter what the UN decided.

Being in bad faith on so serious an issue at the United Nations is a grave ethical failing. But there is an even more serious charge to be considered. As I noted at the beginning of this chapter, Bush's claims about Saddam's "vast arsenal of deadly biological and chemical weapons" have turned out to be false. Probably at least some senior figures in the Bush administration knew all along that these claims were not well grounded. In February 2001, at a press briefing in Cairo after meeting Egyptian leaders, Colin Powell said:

> We had a good discussion . . . about the nature of the sanctions—the fact that the sanctions exist—not for the purpose of hurting the Iraqi people, but for the purpose of keeping in check Saddam Hussein's ambitions toward developing weapons of mass destruction . . . and frankly they have worked. He has not developed any significant capability with respect to weapons of mass destruction. He is unable to project conventional power against his neighbors.

Why did Powell speak so differently two years later? Was it because, at least by July 2002, a decision to attack Iraq had been made, and it was based on considerations other than a belief about the danger posed by Iraq's weapons of mass destruction? According to Richard Haass, then director of the policy-planning staff at the State Department, it was around that time that Condoleezza Rice told him that opposing the decision would be "a waste of breath." If the decision had already been taken by that time, it seems clear that afterward the administration was not seeking the truth about Iraq's weapons in an objective manner.

That conclusion is strongly supported by the evidence of Joseph C. Wilson, who served as an American diplomat both in Iraq and in several African countries. Wilson has told how in February 2002 he was asked by the CIA to look into a report that Iraq had been trying to buy uranium from Niger. The office of Vice President Cheney was interested in getting the facts straight, Wilson was told. He therefore traveled to Niger, investigated the question, and concluded that the reports were "highly doubtful." It was most unlikely that Iraq was seeking uranium from Niger. The U.S. ambassador to Niger agreed with this finding, and had already reported to Washington along those lines. Wilson, of course, provided a detailed briefing to the CIA, and later shared his findings with the State Department. In October, the National Intelligence Estimate on Iraq, a secret CIA document, included the following sentence: "Finally, the claims of Iraqi pursuit of natural uranium in Africa are, in [the assessment of the State Department's Bureau of Intelligence and Research] highly dubious." That month, the CIA sent two memos to the White House voicing doubts about the claims. One went to Bush's deputy national security adviser, Stephen J. Hadley, and the other to his chief speechwriter, Michael Gerson. CIA director George J. Tenet also phoned Hadley before the president was to make a speech in Cincinnati on October 7, asking that the allegation be removed. Nevertheless, in January 2003, in the most solemn and well-prepared speech he gives each year, the State of the Union address, Bush referred to Iraq's attempt to purchase uranium from Africa as a significant piece of evidence for his assertion that Iraq was trying to obtain nuclear weapons. According to *The Washington Post,* administration officials developing the speech originally wanted to refer specifically to Niger, but substituted the vague reference to "Africa," after being told by CIA officials that there were problems with the information relating to Niger. If the most specific information in support of this claim was not reliable, however, why did administration officials not reconsider the entire allegation about Iraq's attempt to purchase uranium? If they had inquired further, they would have been told of the various grounds for doubting that Iraq had recently attempted to purchase uranium from any African country.

Further suspicion is raised by the fact that only a few days after Bush's State of the Union address, Secretary of State Colin L. Powell reviewed the information about Iraq's alleged attempt to purchase uranium in Africa, and decided that it was not sufficiently reliable to use in the speech he gave to the United Nations a week after Bush's State of the Union address. If Powell formed this view, it is reasonable to suppose that he would have mentioned it to Bush, or to one of his aides. This was still six weeks before the United States attacked Iraq. Meanwhile, the claim that Iraq was trying to purchase uranium from Africa had been made not only by the president, but by National Security Adviser Condoleezza Rice, Defense Secretary Donald Rumsfeld, and Deputy Defense Secretary Paul Wolfowitz. The White House finally retracted the information in July, when the war was all over and Wilson had made public his trip to Africa. Why did Bush not acknowledge—when the nation, and the United Nations, were still in the process of deciding whether to go to war—that part of his case against Iraq rested on information that could not be substantiated?

As we have seen, the case that the Bush administration made to show that Iraq was in breach of its obligations included other shaky pieces of evidence. One was the claim that Iraq was trying to buy aluminum tubes with specifications suitable only for use in a centrifuge, the equipment used to enrich uranium. This assertion was made despite advice from the Bush administration's own Department of Energy that the tubes were the wrong specification to be used in a centrifuge, and an opinion from the State Department's Bureau of Intelligence and Research that the tubes were most probably intended for use in a multiple-rocket-launching system, which Iraq was not prohibited from possessing. Another claim later shown to be false was that "Iraq could launch a biological or chemical attack forty-five minutes after the order is given." This claim, originally made by the British government, was repeated twice by Bush without receiving CIA clearance, in a speech he made in the Rose Garden in September 2002, and in a radio address made in the same month.

Apart from the issue of weapons of mass destruction, the other allegation about Iraq made by the administration was that there was a link between Saddam Hussein and Al Qaeda. In presenting his case for war with Iraq to the American public, Bush repeatedly linked Saddam Hussein with Al Qaeda, but provided no real evidence of such a connection. Early reports that Mohamed Atta, one of the hijackers involved in the attacks on September 11, 2001, had met a representative of the Iraq regime in Prague were later repudiated by the Czech government. In his Cincinnati speech on October 7, 2002, Bush said "we've learned" that Iraq trained Al Qaeda members "in bomb-making and poisons and deadly gases." He also said that Al Qaeda leaders had fled from Afghanistan to Iraq, and in particular that a "very senior Al Qaeda leader" had received medical treatment in Baghdad earlier that year. Yet the National Intelligence Estimate on Iraq, the secret CIA document that had been completed shortly before Bush's Cincinnati speech, warned that reports by Iraqi defectors and captured Al Qaeda members about ties between Iraq and Al Qaeda were contradictory and unreliable. It also indicated that contacts with Iraq and Al Qaeda had occurred in the early 1990s, when Al Qaeda was in its infancy, and that those early contacts had not led to any known, continuing, high-level relationship between Iraq and Al Qaeda. As for the "very senior Al Qaeda leader" who had received medical treatment in Baghdad, the National Intelligence Estimate stated that although he had occasionally associated with Al Qaeda adherents, he was not an Al Qaeda member at all. Months after the war, no real evidence of cooperation between Iraq and Al Qaeda in terrorist activities had come to light. On the other hand, *The New York Times* revealed that two Al Qaeda leaders captured by the U.S. independently told the CIA that their organization did not work with Saddam Hussein. The Bush administration did not make these statements public. Four days after Bush made his Cincinnati speech alleging that there was a link between Iraq and Al Qaeda, Congress voted to grant him the authority to make war on Iraq.

The overall impression obtained from these and other revelations is that, instead of taking an objective view of the intelligence it was receiving about whether Iraq did or did not have weapons of mass destruction and contact with Al Qaeda, and then deciding what action was necessary, the Bush administration decided what action it wanted to take, and then selected and massaged the intelligence to make it support that action. After reviewing the fate of the information he provided, Joseph Wilson concludes, "a legitimate argument can be made that we went to war under false pretenses." There can hardly be a more grave charge against the president of the United States and his administration than that he misled Congress, his own citizens, and governments and people all over the world, in order to start a war that killed thousands of people, including at least 3,000 civilians, and maimed and wounded, or made homeless, tens of thousands more.

After the war was over, it became known that as the American buildup for war was reaching its peak, the Bush administration was informed by a Lebanese-American businessman that Saddam was willing to give the Americans much of what they wanted. The businessman had been told by the Iraqi chief of intelligence that Saddam had no weapons of mass destruction, and was willing to allow American troops to conduct a search. The Iraqis were also reportedly offering to hand over to the Americans a man wanted as a suspect in the 1993 attempt to blow up the World Trade Center. Most remarkable of all, they were pledging to hold elections. As a result of these overtures, Richard Perle, an adviser to the Department of Defense, flew to London to meet with the businessman. The businessman pressed for a direct meeting between Iraqi officials and Perle or another representative of the United States. Perle conveyed this message to officials in the Bush administration, but they rebuffed the Iraqi overture. According to Perle, "The message was, 'Tell them that we will see them in Baghdad.'"

Though it is impossible to know whether the Iraqis were genuine in their offer to negotiate, the Bush administration's response to the offer fits the pattern we have already observed. The administration was not interested in negotiations for the same reason that it was not interested in evidence casting doubt on the existence of

Saddam's weapons of mass destruction. It had already decided on war. This was very far from being a war of last resort.

Liberating the Iraqi People

In speaking to the United Nations in September 2002, Bush said, "Liberty for the Iraqi people is a great moral cause and a great strategic goal. The people of Iraq deserve it." Six months later, he used similar terms when he gave General Tommy Franks the order to attack Iraq. Saddam Hussein was a brutal dictator, responsible for the deaths of hundreds of thousands of Iraqis. That fact offers a straightforward ethical argument for overthrowing him, as long as the cost of doing so, in terms of Iraqi deaths, injuries, and destruction of property is not great, in comparison to the suffering that he would continue to inflict on his own people.

This ethical argument is not a legal justification for the attack on Iraq. Traditionally, international law has recognized the sovereignty of nations, independently of how their governments are constituted, and—almost—independently of the crimes they commit against their own people. The United Nations Charter confirms this, stating that apart from acts of aggression or threats to peace, "Nothing contained in the present Charter shall authorize the United Nations to intervene in matters which are essentially within the domestic jurisdiction of any state or shall require the Members to submit such matters to settlement under the present Charter." It is true that the UN itself has sometimes stretched this clause to the limit. One such earlier "stretching" involved Iraq. In 1991 the Security Council resolved that the repression of the civilian population had consequences that were a threat to international peace and security, and therefore justified intervention. Since the council mentioned the flow of refugees to other countries, this repression did have some consequences outside the borders of Iraq. In other cases, however—for example, in Haiti, where the council acted to restore to power the democratically elected president Jean-Bertrand Aristide—the claim that intervention was necessary to prevent a threat to international peace and security was highly tenuous.

In extreme cases, however, an ethically-based right of humanitarian intervention has been recognized. Many believe that intervention to stop the genocide in Rwanda in 1994 would have been ethically justified. Remorse at the failure to do so may have encouraged the leaders of the NATO powers to intervene in Yugoslavia to stop the killing of people in Kosovo. Many people from President Clinton down regarded that as the right thing to do, although at the time it lacked UN authorization and so was of dubious legality. It is possible to argue that international law is constantly evolving, and will eventually follow world opinion on ethical issues such as the right to humanitarian intervention.

Nevertheless, the situation of Iraq in 2003 was significantly different from Rwanda in 1994 and Kosovo in 1999. Saddam was not, at the time of the invasion, engaged in any form of genocide or widespread massacres. In his speech to the United Nations, Bush said:

> Saddam Hussein attacked Iran in 1980 and Kuwait in 1990. He's fired ballistic missiles at Iran and Saudi Arabia, Bahrain and Israel. His regime once ordered the killing of every person between the ages of fifteen and seventy in certain Kurdish villages in northern Iraq. He has gassed many Iranians and forty Iraqi villages.

The killing of the Kurds in northern Iraq took place in 1988, and the use of gas against Iranian and Iraqi villages was from the same period. Subsequently, in 1991, Saddam put down an uprising by Shia in the south with great brutality, and in the mid-1990s, he attacked Arabs living in the remote marshes near the Iranian border. A plausible ethical case for humanitarian intervention against Saddam could have been made at any of those times. Over the years immediately before Bush's decision to attack Iraq, however, while the torture and executions of people suspected of opposition to Saddam continued, there was nothing on the scale of the earlier atrocities. Con Coughlin, who chronicles Saddam's long record of brutality in *Saddam, King of Terror,* acknowledges that by 2002, "ordinary Iraqis were starting to recover from the appalling privations that they had endured for most of the 1990s." Thus, when

Bush was building his case for an attack on Iraq, it would have been difficult to show that the Iraqi government was committing greater crimes against its people than were other repressive regimes, like those of Burma, North Korea, and Turkmenistan.

For Bush to have made his case for war with Iraq exclusively on humanitarian grounds, his position would have had to undergo a dramatic turnaround from the one he professed during his campaign for the presidency. In the second of Bush's debates with Al Gore, the debate moderator, Jim Lehrer, stated that 600,000 people had died in Rwanda in 1994, and there was no intervention from the United States. Was it, he asked, a mistake not to intervene? Bush replied, "I think the administration did the right thing in that case. I do . . . I thought they made the right decision not to send U.S. troops into Rwanda." Those familiar with the situation in Rwanda at the time believe that a relatively small number of troops, certainly far fewer than the number necessary to overthrow Saddam, would have sufficed to stop the massacre. It is therefore curious that Bush should, in 2000, have believed it wrong to send a modest number of U.S. troops to Rwanda to save 600,000 lives, but by 2003 have changed his mind to such an extent that he was willing to send a much larger force to overthrow Saddam who, though undoubtedly oppressive and cruel, was not about to massacre 600,000 of his subjects. (Condoleezza Rice ignored Bush's earlier statement of his views on Rwanda when, after it became apparent that the UN Security Council was unlikely to support a resolution authorizing the use of force in Iraq, she sought to undermine the Security Council's authority. "The UN Security Council could not act," she said, "when in Rwanda there was a genocide that cost almost a million lives.")

We have seen that the case for humanitarian intervention against Saddam was much weaker when the war actually began than it would have been some years earlier. There are other repressive regimes, just as bad as his. And we have seen that Bush had previously opposed humanitarian intervention to stop a horrific massacre. Nevertheless, it is still possible that Bush's decision to get rid of Saddam was justified. At its most straightforward, the case for getting rid of Saddam in order to help the people of Iraq was a utilitarian one. All that it required was a demonstration that the benefits that could reasonably be expected outweighed the costs, including the cost in innocent human lives, that also could reasonably be expected. Arguably, it would have been best to get rid of Saddam earlier, but it was better to do so late than never. Perhaps it would be better still to get rid of the Korean dictator, Kim Jong Il, but that might not be achievable without an even greater loss of innocent life than was involved in getting rid of Saddam.

Although there is a possible utilitarian justification for getting rid of Saddam, Bush would be contradicting his professed moral views on other questions if he were to appeal to it. As we saw when considering his stance on the loss of innocent lives caused by bombing, and on detention without trial, it would be odd for Bush to become a utilitarian on these issues while rejecting the same ethical approach to the destruction of embryos to produce stem cells. If he is prepared to argue in utilitarian terms that a war that kills innocents is justified because it saves many more innocents from being murdered under Saddam, he should be prepared to accept the same calculus of costs and benefits for using a few embryos to save many more lives. Alternatively, if Bush denies that it is right to cause some innocents to die so that others can live, he will run into difficulties in justifying war to rid Iraq of Saddam's tyranny. For there was not a shadow of a doubt that this war would cost the lives of innocent Iraqis.

In addition to the general problem of showing how the humanitarian argument for war can be compatible with his stance on other ethical issues, Bush also faces a more specific problem in using that argument to justify his war with Iraq. Under the U.S. Constitution, only Congress can authorize war. Congress did, in a resolution passed on October 10, 2002, authorize the president to use force in Iraq. But that authority is given for a very specific purpose. The president may use force in order to:

(1) defend the national security of the United States against the continuing threat posed by Iraq; and
(2) enforce all relevant United Nations Security Council resolutions regarding Iraq.

The resolution contains no authorization for the use of force to liberate the people of Iraq from a tyrant. If that was the real reason for the war, it was unconstitutional.

Notwithstanding these serious problems of constitutionality and consistency, I shall put them aside in order to ask whether there really was a strong utilitarian case for a war of liberation. Whether Bush was justified in attacking Iraq depends, in utilitarian terms, on how reasonable it was for him to believe that the benefits would outweigh the human costs of war, and that these benefits could not be obtained by any less costly means. We have already seen that the Bush administration did not go to all possible lengths to find out if there was any other way of freeing Iraq from Saddam's tyranny. It did not follow up on the alleged offer to hold elections, relayed by the Lebanese-American businessman to Richard Perle. Improbable as that offer may have been, it was wrong to reject it without serious scrutiny, given the costs that were to result from the war. If dictators like Chile's Pinochet have yielded to pressure and allowed free elections, it is not beyond the bounds of possibility that Saddam, under even greater pressure, might have done the same. Many will scoff at the thought of such a sudden conversion by so brutal a dictator, but it remains true that, whether the war was fought to eliminate the threat of Iraq's alleged weapons of mass destruction, or to liberate the Iraqi people from Saddam's tyranny, it was not a war of last resort.

The human costs of the war are difficult to estimate, but we know that for many Iraqis, they were very great. As in Afghanistan, bombs and missiles fell in the wrong places. Civilian deaths during the war exceeded 3,000, and civilian injuries have been estimated at 20,000. Parents lost their children, children were orphaned, and both adults and children were maimed. Appalling conditions in hospitals were reported during the war. Beds became filthy and blood-soaked, but blackouts had closed down the laundry. Anesthetics ran out, but casualties of the bombing continued to arrive, often with shocking injuries. Overworked, exhausted doctors performed emergency surgery on patients who had no pain relief apart from 800 milligrams of ibuprofen—the dose an American would take for muscle pain.

Months after Bush proclaimed the end of major combat operations in Iraq, American troops were still killing civilians. The shooting of Mazen Dana on August 17, 2003, by a soldier who thought his video camera was a rocket launcher was widely publicized, because he was a Reuters cameraman. Other shootings, like that of Adel abd al-Kerim and three of his children just a week earlier, got less attention. But the al-Kerim family, who was inside their car when it was stopped at an American roadblock, were, like Dana, the innocent victims of panicking American troops who wrongly thought they were under fire.

Nor is there any sound reason for leaving the deaths of combatants out of the calculation. The number of American military personnel killed in Iraq since the beginning of the war passed 400 in November 2003, and has continued to rise since then. In addition, 52 British, and 16 Italian military personnel have been killed, as well as individual soldiers from Denmark, Spain, Poland, and the Ukraine. More than 2,300 members of the coalition forces have suffered injuries, many of them with severe permanent effects. Iraqi combatant deaths have been estimated to be approximately 10,000, and the number of Iraqi wounded may be, as it is for the coalition forces, four or five times the number killed. Because the U.S. used an upgraded form of napalm on certain Iraqi positions, some of these deaths and injuries would have been particularly agonizing. Napalm, widely used by American forces in Vietnam, is a mixture of jet fuel and a polystyrene-like gel that sticks to the skin as it burns. Initially the Pentagon denied that it had used napalm, but later acknowledged that the upgraded form of the weapon it was using was "remarkably similar." Colonel James Alles, commander of Marine Air Group 11, said of one attack: "We napalmed both those [bridge] approaches." "Unfortunately there were people there . . . you could see them in the [cockpit] video. They were Iraqi soldiers. It's no great way to die." Precisely because Saddam's regime was so brutal, most of those serving in the Iraqi army were conscripts rather than volunteers. Thousands of young men, forced to go out and fight for a regime they did not support, were killed. They had mothers, perhaps wives and children, and their deaths are part of the costs of the war.

In addition to the deaths and injuries, the war caused extensive damage to property. Thousands of people were bombed out of their homes and many more have, for long periods, been deprived of basic services like electricity and running water and police protection from crime. Factories and office buildings were destroyed, putting people out of work. There have been environmental disasters, like the looting of the Tuwaitha Nuclear Research Facility, a relic of Iraq's 1960s nuclear program, which before the war was being monitored by the International Atomic Energy Agency. Because U.S. forces failed to secure the site in April 2003, locals ransacked the site for anything useful, emptying sealed barrels of uranium ore in order to use the barrels for household purposes, and causing radioactive material to be dispersed. Levels of radioactivity 3,000 times normal have been found near a primary school in the area. In another environmental catastrophe, a refinery warehouse west of Baghdad was ransacked after the war, and 5,000 tons of hazardous chemicals were spilled, burned, or stolen. The surrounding area, to a radius of up to two miles, is believed to be heavily contaminated, and groundwater may also be affected.

Then there is the cultural loss. The National Museum of Antiquities and the Mosul museum were looted. Although some objects were later recovered, an estimated ten thousand ancient artifacts are, at the time of this writing, still missing. These include statues, jewelry, vessels, and coins, as well as entire collections of clay tablets with cuneiform writing that are among the earliest written documents in the world, but have never been read. Since the collections of tablets have been broken up and individual items are being sold illicitly for a few hundred dollars each, the inscriptions will now never be read in their proper context. Archeological sites that experts were delicately excavating by hand before the war have now been bulldozed in the search for objects that can be sold. The burning of the National Library and National Archives, as well as a special library of religious works, caused the loss of hundreds of thousands of documents, including more than 600 irreplaceable early Islamic manuscripts more than nine centuries old, and the bulk of the records documenting the social and political history of the country.

Despite all this, can we say that the Iraqi people are better off now than they were before the war? As of this writing, such a judgment would be premature. True, Iraqis are free from Saddam's tyranny, and free, too, of the hardship caused by the U.N. sanctions against Saddam, but instead they risk violence, not only at the hands of nervous American soldiers, but also from their fellow citizens. Saddam, for all the horrors he perpetrated, maintained order. In Baghdad, from mid-April 2003, when American forces had taken over the city, through the end of August, the city morgue recorded 2,846 violent deaths. Deducting those that would have occurred if the prewar rate of violent death had continued during this period, there were at least 1,519 additional violent deaths in four and a half months. Gunshot wounds, which used to account for 10 percent of violent deaths, were responsible for 60 percent of these deaths. U.S. forces caused some of the violent deaths, but the majority are the result of Iraqis attacking other Iraqis. They are a consequence of the failure of the occupying forces to maintain order, and so are part of the price Iraqis are paying for the war. So, too, is the fear and insecurity that this breakdown of public order brings to every Iraqi, whether or not they become one of its victims.

Whether Iraqis will, in the long run, be better off than they would have been if the war had not happened will largely depend on the nature of the future government of Iraq. If a stable, democratic state emerges and Iraq prospers, then it may be possible to say that the tragic human costs of the war were outweighed by the benefits to Iraqis as a whole. But that judgment alone would not be sufficient to show that the war was ethically justified. Since international law does not recognize the desirability of "regime change" as a ground for going to war, there would still be larger questions to consider, in particular, questions about the possible impact of the war on weakening the constraints of international law.

In a speech to the United Nations General Assembly in September 1999, Kofi Annan stated the ethical dilemma that this question raises. Some, he noted, believe that "the greatest threat to the future of international order is the use of force in the absence of a Security Council mandate." He asked those who take this view to imagine that, in the dark days leading up to the genocide in Rwanda, a coalition of states had been prepared to act in defense of the Tutsi population, but had not received prompt authorization from the Security Council. Should that coalition have stood aside and allowed the horror to unfold? Most of us would answer that it should not have stood aside. But then Annan asked those who think that states or groups of states are justified in acting outside the established mechanisms for enforcing international law whether there was not a danger of such interventions "setting dangerous precedents for future interventions without a clear criterion to decide who might invoke these precedents, and in what circumstances?" After Bush's attack on Iraq, that question seems more pertinent than ever.

It is noteworthy that even the secretary-general of the UN is not saying that there can never be a case for intervention without UN authorization. But the possible exceptions that he had in mind were situations like Rwanda, where without immediate action by other states, hundreds of thousands of lives might be lost. As has already been mentioned, in March 2003 there was no such urgency about the invasion of Iraq. The invasion therefore was not a case in which a humanitarian catastrophe was so urgent that there simply was not time to persuade the Security Council to change its mind.

Tragically, however, at the very time when Bush was causing the United Nations and the world to focus all its attention on Iraq, a much more urgent crisis was developing in the Ituri region of the Democratic Republic of the Congo. For the past five years the region had been in a state of civil war and near anarchy, with warring militia from different ethnic groups barely held in check by occupying armies from neighboring Rwanda and Uganda. At the end of February 2003, Human Rights Watch, the world's leading non-government human rights organization, warned the UN that the war in the Congo had sparked "a humanitarian crisis of catastrophic dimensions," and that more than two million people were currently displaced from their homes. It urged the UN Security Council to ensure that its peacekeeping mission in the Congo was able to fulfill its mandate to "protect civilians under imminent threat of physical violence." But with Bush's efforts to persuade the Security

Council to authorize the use of force in Iraq grabbing all the headlines, nothing was done. Less than two weeks later, Human Rights Watch again warned that civilians were at risk of being killed in Ituri, and again the warning went unheeded. The result has been graphically described by Philip Gourevitch, author of *We Wish to Inform You That Tomorrow We Will be Killed With Our Families*, a heartbreaking book on the Rwanda genocide:

> . . . seven hundred poorly armed U.N. peackeepers in the northeastern Ituri region have watched helplessly over the past few weeks as massacres by tribal militias have filled graves with fresh corpses at about the same clip that the dead of Saddam Hussein's reign of terror have been exhumed in Iraq.

When the war in Iraq began, most of Saddam's victims had been dead for several years. The victims of the fighting and ethnic killings that took place in Ituri in April and May, meanwhile—more than 400 around Bunia, the major city, in the last three weeks of May alone, according to a Reuters report—were still alive, and their lives could have been saved by far fewer troops than were needed to overthrow Saddam. At the end of May, after the Iraq war was over, the UN Security Council did turn its attention to the Congo, and authorized a French-led multinational peacekeeping force to go to Ituri to try to prevent further massacres. The Bush administration did not offer to send troops or any other form of support.

As Kofi Annan suggests, in considering the ethics of humanitarian intervention, it is important to consider the precedent that is being set. That is why the claim that the war with Iraq has produced benefits for the people of Iraq that outweigh the heavy casualties they suffered during the conflict, does not, even if true, settle the issue of whether the war was a good thing. Even if the war in Iraq turns out to have good consequences for people in Iraq, if it is in flagrant defiance of international law, and weakens the authority of the UN to resolve disputes peacefully, it is likely to increase the danger that other nations, less scrupulous in their choice of circumstances, will also go to war outside the framework of the United

Nations. When that additional factor is taken into account, the resort to war may have been not only illegal, but also unethical.

This judgment relies on the thought that the United Nations is, and should remain, the only source of lawful authority for resorting to force, except of course when a nation is defending itself from attack. Before accepting that idea we need to consider the broader framework of international relations that Bush is seeking to inaugurate, and of which his war with Iraq was a part. In one major speech and in a central policy document of his administration, Bush has put forward a new and radically different approach to achieving a peaceful world. We cannot reach a final judgment on the ethical case for the war with Iraq until we have examined this new approach.

Chapter 9

Pax Americana

We must take the battle to the enemy, disrupt his plans, and confront the worst threats before they emerge. In the world we have entered, the only path to safety is the path of action. And this nation will act. . . . America has, and intends to keep, military strengths beyond challenge—thereby making the destabilizing arms races of other eras pointless, and limiting rivalries to trade and other pursuits of peace.

—George W. Bush, Graduation Speech at West Point, June 1, 2002

The Bush Doctrine

On June 1, 2002, Bush visited West Point to address the graduating class of the U.S. Military Academy during its bicentennial year. Speaking to the young men from whom the future leaders of the U.S. Army are likely to be drawn, the president talked of the honor of serving one's nation, and told jokes based on his own poor record at Yale, and on the traditional rivalry between the army and the navy. After the levity came the serious part. In four succinct paragraphs, he spelled out a new view of when it is justifiable to take military action—a view that has come to be known as the "Bush Doctrine." Here it is:

> The gravest danger to freedom lies at the perilous crossroads of radicalism and technology. When the spread of chemical and biological and nuclear weapons, along with ballistic missile technology—when that occurs, even weak states and small groups could attain a catastrophic power to strike great nations. Our enemies have declared this very intention, and have been caught seeking these terrible weapons.
>
> For much of the last century, America's defense relied on the Cold War doctrines of deterrence and containment. In some cases, those strategies still apply. But new threats also require new thinking. Deterrence—the promise of massive retaliation against nations—means nothing against shadowy terrorist networks with no nation or citizens to defend. Containment is not possible when unbalanced dictators with weapons of mass destruction can deliver those weapons on missiles or secretly provide them to terrorist allies.
>
> We cannot defend America and our friends by hoping for the best. We cannot put our faith in the word of tyrants, who solemnly sign non-proliferation treaties and then systemically break them. If we wait for threats to fully materialize, we will have waited too long.
>
> Homeland defense and missile defense are part of stronger security, and they're essential priorities for America. Yet the war on terror will not be won on the defensive. We must take the battle to the enemy, disrupt his plans, and confront the worst threats before they emerge. In the world we have entered, the only path to safety is the path of action. And this nation will act.

Perhaps this should have been tagged "Bush Doctrine II," since the president's declaration immediately after September 11 that the United States would make no distinction between terrorists and those who harbor them was also called the "Bush Doctrine." But it is the new doctrine that better deserves the name, for unlike its more specific predecessor, it points to a fundamentally new era in international relations.

Bush's words at West Point were carefully chosen. They represent the considered conclusions, not only of the president, but of his entire national security team. That became evident with the release of *The National Security Strategy of the United States of America* in September 2002. Issued from the White House, this document reiterated that, to forestall hostile acts by adversaries, "the United States will, if necessary, act preemptively." It argued that preemption is not a new idea, but an old one that needs to be revamped for new circumstances. In international law, the National Security Strategy acknowledged, the standard view is that a preemptive strike is legitimate only against an attack that is clearly imminent—for example, if the adversary can be seen to be mobilizing its army and preparing to attack. But today it is possible to launch an attack without warning, and that attack may kill millions of people. This new situation, the National Security Strategy argues, forces us to modify our sense of what kind of threat can be a justifiable trigger for a preemptive attack.

Bush and his advisers are right to say that the world has changed since the Cold War. Then the balance of terror, of "mutually assured destruction," kept the peace, at least between the two nuclear superpowers. Now we have to concern ourselves with a new possibility. The hijackers who flew the planes into the World Trade Center and the Pentagon were not deterred by a threat to their own lives, and they were not acting as the agents of any state that might fear retaliation. The prospect of nuclear weapons finding their way into the hands of such people is a nightmare that poses a real problem for prevailing ideas of legitimate self-defense. The difficulty is to find the best solution.

Under current international law, preemptive strikes are not permitted unless they are in defense against an imminent attack. It was the U.S. secretary of state Daniel Webster who, in response to an 1837 incident in which British troops attacked and sank an American ship carrying supplies to Canadian rebels, spelled out the conditions for justified "anticipatory self-defense." He wrote that this could be justified only when the need for action is "instant, overwhelming, and leaving no choice of means, and no moment for deliberation." Contemporary textbooks on international law take essentially the same view, emphasizing that the threatened attack must be immediate, and the need to respond urgent, with no possible alternative. Chapter VII of the United Nations Charter—a treaty to which the United States is a signatory—sets out the role of the Security Council in dealing with threats to the peace and acts of aggression, and then states that nothing in the charter impairs the inherent right of a nation to defend itself "if an armed attack occurs"—thereby suggesting that the provisions of the charter do "impair" any possible "right of self-defense" when no armed attack has occurred.

In his preamble to the National Security Strategy, Bush takes a very different position from that taken by Daniel Webster and by the UN Charter. He says that "as a matter of common sense and self-defense, America will act against such emerging threats before they are fully formed." One problem with this view lies in the risk of a government manufacturing a case for a preemptive war when it actually has other motives for going to war. A second problem is that a government may overestimate the danger that another nation poses due to flawed intelligence or exaggerated fears, suspicions, or biases. The Bush administration's war with Iraq illustrates both these problems, given that it was based on unsubstantiated assertions that Iraq had weapons of mass destruction, and may well pass them on to Al Qaeda, and given that some influential members of the Bush administration had, as we shall see, reasons for overthrowing the government of Iraq that had nothing to do with terrorism or the need to preempt an attack. If a U.S. administration can massage evidence to strengthen its case for war, other governments will be no less adept at doing the same.

There is also a more fundamental problem with Bush's claim that a nation has a right to strike preemptively when an attack is not imminent. If he is proposing a new understanding of international law, then the most pressing question to ask is: when does a nation have this right? Moral rights do not adhere to particular nations. The United States does not, simply because it is the United States, have a special right to use force preemptively that other nations do not have. Admittedly, a right to use force preemptively might adhere to nations with particular characteristics, but if that is what Bush is claiming, we need to know what those characteristics are.

Let us start with the most obvious case in which another nation might believe that it is justified in striking preemptively. In January 2002 Bush named North Korea, along with Iraq and Iran, as part of the "axis of evil." A year later, after North Korea admitted that it had a program to produce enriched uranium suitable for nuclear weapons, U.S. military officials stated publicly that they were reviewing military options against that country. In March, B-52 and B-1 bombers were flown to the U.S. base in Guam, within easy striking distance of targets in Korea. In April 2003 Bush said the successful war with Iraq "made it clear that people who harbor weapons of mass destruction will be dealt with"—a remark North Koreans could reasonably construe as threatening the same action against them that Bush had taken against Iraq, even though the president went on to say that "hopefully" most of this task can be accomplished by diplomatic means. The United States, it is scarcely necessary to mention, "harbors" weapons of mass destruction. Hence, if it is a sound moral principle that when a nation in possession of weapons of mass destruction threatens another nation, the threatened nation is justified in making a preemptive strike, North Korea would, after these developments, have been justified in making a preemptive strike against the United States.

What's wrong with this argument? Of course, it would be pointless for North Korea to attack the United States, because it could not possibly hope to eliminate the capacity of the United States to strike back. In that sense, North Korea cannot preemptively strike against the U.S. But that still leaves open the ethical question: if North Korea did have the capacity to strike the U.S. in a manner that would effectively preempt a U.S. attack, would it be justified in doing so? Those who defend the right of the U.S. to make preemptive strikes against nations it perceives to be a threat must either say yes, North Korea would be justified in making a preemptive attack on the U.S., or they must find a morally relevant ground for distinguishing the two cases. It is a safe bet that few will take the first option, so the question becomes one of finding relevant differences between the two nations.

One might say that, as Bush himself has often said, the United States is "a peace-loving nation" and it is only peace-loving nations that can be justified in waging a preemptive war. That comes too close to satire to be put forward seriously, but it may not be far from thoughts that Bush and some of his advisers have of their country. Asked, after the Iraq war, what he thought of the French president Jacques Chirac, who had been the most forthright of European leaders in opposing American efforts to gain UN endorsement for the war, Bush said that Chirac needed to be reminded that "America is a good nation, genuinely good." Since Bush frequently portrays other nations as "evil," and says the United States wants nothing but peace, freedom, and prosperity for its own citizens and for those of every nation, perhaps the position he really has in mind is that good nations are justified in striking preemptively against evil ones, but not the other way around. But as a principle of international law, this criterion is hopeless. Granted, there are evil rulers, people who kill innocents without compunction to gain and hold on to power. But who is to decide what counts as an evil regime? No doubt there are a few regimes that almost everyone would agree are evil—those of Hitler, Stalin, Idi Amin, Pol Pot, and a few others, perhaps. But we have no clear and agreed-upon criteria for deciding which regimes are evil, or sufficiently evil for them to be subject to preemptive strikes. England's appeasers of the 1930s considered Hitler's nationalism a distasteful but understandable response to the harsh terms of the Treaty of Versailles. In Russia, there are still millions of older people who think back nostalgically to the Communist regime as a time of economic stability, little crime, and very low unemployment. At various times, the United States itself seems to have had difficulty in recognizing evil regimes for what they were. For a decade after Pol Pot's Khmer Rouge government was overthrown and replaced by the vastly better Vietnamese-backed Heng Samrin government, the U.S. continued to recognize the murderous Khmer Rouge as the lawful rulers of Cambodia. After Saddam Hussein had abused human rights, used chemical weapons on his own people, aspired to obtain nuclear weapons, harbored terrorists, and started an aggressive war against Iran, the Reagan administration helped him to avoid defeat in that war. (As Reagan's envoy, Donald Rumsfeld traveled to Baghdad to shake Saddam's hand and assure him of U.S. support.) If even the U.S. government sometimes finds it difficult to recognize as evil regimes that are as bad as these ones, it is evident that the principle that good regimes may strike preemptively at evil ones lacks the clarity needed for a useful international standard of acceptable conduct.

One clear difference between the United States and North Korea is that the United States is a democracy while North Korea is a dictatorship. To make this fact relevant to the justifiability of preemptive attacks would require a revolution in international law, which has always recognized governments because they were able to rule over their territory, irrespective of how they managed to do so. That is the case, for example, with the recognition of governments as eligible to take their place at the United Nations, or the World Trade Organization. They do not have to justify their right to represent their nation by showing that they were democratically elected. It is arguable that the world would be a better place if this were changed—if these global bodies became "unions of democracies" rather than open to any form of government. That proposal runs the risk of isolating some of the world's most dangerous nations and excluding them from the world's leading forum for resolving international disputes. If we were nevertheless to exclude undemocratic nations from global bodies, we would need some impartial body to judge which nations are democracies, and which are not. George W. Bush, after all, received fewer votes than Al Gore in the 2000 presidential election. Critics of American democracy could also question the fact that the voters of Wyoming elect as many senators as the voters of California. Then there is the cloud cast over American elections by the fact that the candidate who raises the most money usually wins. Do the democratic deficits of the United States mean that the United States is not a democracy? Americans, used to thinking of their country not only as a democracy, but as the most democratic nation in the world, would consider that suggestion laughable, but to outsiders it is not so funny. In any case, the fact that the question can even be raised about the United States shows that borderline decisions about which nation is and which is not a democracy will not be easy to decide.

Democracies, it is often said, pose less of a security risk than dictatorships. No war, it is claimed, has ever occurred between two democratic states. Therefore, it might be argued, there is no justification for a preemptive strike against a democracy. The thesis that democracies are less likely to go to war with each other than nondemocratic forms of government, however, is controversial. Much depends on the definitions of "war" and of "democracy." There are several borderline cases, including the American Civil War and the First World War, and these, together with the small size of the sample—since widespread democracy is a recent phenomenon—make it hard to be confident of its truth.

There can, furthermore, be no guarantee that a democratic nation will never elect leaders who decide to use nuclear weapons in an act of aggression, or to pass them on to others who will so use them. Especially in a nation in the grip of a militant religious ideology, this is always a possibility. When free elections were held in Algeria in December 1991, the first round of results suggested a decisive victory for the radical Islamic Salvation Front. Instead of allowing the second round of elections to proceed, the army intervened, established a regime more to its liking, and put thousands of its opponents in concentration camps in the Sahara desert. The United States did nothing to oppose this suppression of democracy, and today Algeria is still not democratic. Yet its current rulers may well be less of a concern to international security than the leaders supported by the majority of voters would have been. Many nondemocratic governments have not been internationally aggressive, regardless of their records at home. If the focus is on the right to use a preemptive strike against a perceived international threat, the issue is not whether the alleged threat comes from a government that is domestically good, bad, democratic, or undemocratic—it is on how much of an aggressive international danger it poses.

Yet another difficulty in placing limits on preemptive strikes is that a nation may interpret "self-defense" quite broadly. In its most recent *Quadrennial Defense Review,* the U.S. Department of Defense states that the development of the nation's defense posture should take into account the nation's "enduring national interests" and then gives a list of what these interests are. The list includes not only the obvious things, like ensuring U.S. sovereignty and the protection of U.S. citizens, but also a category of interests "contributing to economic well-being" that includes "access to key markets and strategic resources." Richard Betts, director of the Institute for War and Peace Studies at Columbia University, who has served on the staff of the National Security Council, has warned, "When security is defined in terms broader than protecting the near-term integrity of national sovereignty and borders, the distinction between offense and defense blurs hopelessly. . . . Security can be as insatiable an appetitive as acquisitiveness." The combination of belief in the justifiability of preemptive strikes with the Defense Department's view of the enduring interests that the U.S. needs to defend does indeed blur hopelessly the line between offense and defense, and makes each of these views much more dangerous than either of them would be alone.

The problem of preemption lies in the logic of rational choice. It was powerfully laid out by the seventeenth-century English philosopher Thomas Hobbes in his classic work *The Leviathan,* published in 1651. "In the nature of man," he wrote, "we find three principal causes of quarrel. First, competition; secondly, diffidence; thirdly, glory." By "diffidence" Hobbes meant what we would call insecurity. This in turn is, for Hobbes, a natural outcome of the fact that since there is competition for scarce resources, we must always fear others who would take from us what we have. Given this situation, Hobbes argues, "There is no way for any man to secure himself so reasonable as anticipation; that is, by force, or wiles, to master the persons of all men he can so long till he see no other power great enough to endanger him: and this is no more than his own conservation requireth, and is generally allowed." But since this right to take preemptive action is universal, the outcome is Hobbes's notorious war "of every man against every man." If I expect my neighbor to be likely to take preemptive action against me, it is rational for me to strike at him first; but since he knows that this is what it is rational for me to do, he has equal reason to do it to me. As a result, as Hobbes puts it, we all live in a state of "continual fear, and danger of violent death; and the life of man, solitary, poor, nasty, brutish, and short."

Hobbes's analysis indicates the nature of the problem with accepting the legitimacy of preemptive strikes when there are no clear criteria setting out the conditions in which they are to be used. Acknowledging a general right of preemption creates a situation in which it will be rational for any country that might be the victim of preemptive action to make a preemptive strike against a possible foe before the foe takes preemptive action against it. Accordingly, the problem of establishing when a nation may or may not use preemption, or which nations are entitled to use it, is insoluble within the framework of a world of fully sovereign, equally independent nations.

The way out of this dire situation, according to Hobbes, is for everyone to hand over his power to a sovereign, whether an individual or an assembly, and thereby to establish "that great LEVIATHAN," the state, which has a monopoly on the use of force. Although Hobbes has individuals in mind, he also points out that, since there is no global sovereign who rules over independent nations, the usual state of international relations is one of continual war, in which nations are either actually at war or have "their forts, garrisons, and guns upon the frontiers of their kingdoms, and continual spies upon their neighbours, which is a posture of war." Thus, for nations as for individuals, the knowledge that an enemy may attack is itself a reason for attacking first, and this spiral of hostile expectations is extremely dangerous. As already mentioned, during the Cold War the threat of massive retaliation between the two superpowers was enough to prevent an all-out attack. But the risk of a catastrophe was always present, and few will regret the passing of that tense era. In the absence of the "balance of terror," however, we need some reasonable equivalent of the "great leviathan" to keep the peace at the global level.

American Preeminence

After the end of the Cold War, there were only two plausible candidates for the role of global peacekeeper in international affairs: the United Nations, or the sole remaining superpower, the United States. In his West Point speech, Bush never mentioned the

United Nations. Instead he said, "America has, and intends to keep, military strengths beyond challenge, thereby making the destabilizing arms races of other eras pointless, and limiting rivalries to trade and other pursuits of peace." He was, in effect, declaring that the United States would, now and for the foreseeable future, be the world's chief of police.

Bush did not start out with that view. In the second presidential debate, he contrasted the "humble" foreign policy he planned to follow with the more interventionist one of the Clinton administration. He said that American intervention to restore democracy to Haiti was "nation-building" and a mistake. He was, he said, "worried about over-committing our military around the world" and he wanted to be "judicious" in using it. Above all, he was against arrogance. Asked how people around the world should view America, he said, "If we're an arrogant nation, they'll—they'll resent us. If we're a humble nation, but strong, they'll welcome us." Even after being elected president, he pursued the idea of America as "strong and humble," praising Colin Powell in May 2001 for doing such a good job of making the case for America in these terms.

While Bush was saying this, however, others who were close to him, or were to become members of his team, were developing very different views. In 1997, three years before his run for the presidency, a group of conservative thinkers centered on William Kristol, editor of *The Weekly Standard,* founded the Project for a New American Century. They made no secret of their goal. In a "Statement of Principles" they said: "We aim to make the case and rally support for American global leadership." They called on the United States to use the fact that it was now the world's preeminent power "to shape a new century favorable to American principles and interests." More specifically, the statement called for an increase in defense spending, a challenge to regimes hostile to American interests and values, and acceptance of "America's unique role in preserving and extending an international order friendly to our security, our prosperity, and our principles." The signatories to this statement included Bush's brother Jeb, his future vice president, Dick Cheney, Cheney's chief of staff, Lewis Libby, and five others who would later serve in the Bush administration.

Although such naked assertion of American power was unfashionable and unfavored during the Clinton administration, in January 1998 the Project organized a "Letter to President Clinton on Iraq." The letter is remarkable because—years before the events of September 11, 2001—it sets out a course of action that was acted upon only after those events, and has been widely seen as a response to it. The letter opens by urging the president "to enunciate a new strategy that would secure the interests of the U.S. and our friends and allies around the world. That strategy should aim, above all, at the removal of Saddam Hussein's regime from power." From that opening, the letter warns of the danger of Saddam acquiring weapons of mass destruction, and then adds, "It hardly needs to be added that if Saddam does acquire the capability to deliver weapons of mass destruction, as he is almost certain to do if we continue along the present course, the safety of American troops in the region, of our friends and allies like Israel and the moderate Arab states, and a significant portion of the world's supply of oil will all be put at hazard." The signatories to this letter included, in addition to most of those who had signed the "Statement of Principles" a year earlier: Donald Rumsfeld; the person who would later become his deputy in the Department of Defense, Paul Wolfowitz; Richard Armitage, subsequently deputy to Colin Powell at the State Department; John Bolton, later Undersecretary of State for Arms Control and International Security; and Richard Perle, later chair of the Defense Policy Board.

Two months before the election that brought Bush to power, the Project brought out a much more substantial statement of its views. *Rebuilding America's Defenses: Strategy, Forces and Resources for a New Century* is a seventy-six-page report put together by a team that includes Wolfowitz and Libby as well as Stephen Cambone, who has since become Rumsfeld's Undersecretary of Defense for Intelligence, and Abram Shulsky, who as director of the Pentagon's Office of Special Plans is credited with having produced the intelligence reviews that helped to shape American policy toward Iraq. In addition to reiterating the call for a substantial increase in defense spending "for maintaining global US pre-eminence, precluding the rise of a great power rival, and shaping the international security order in line with American principles and interests," the report explicitly acknowleges that the desirability of the United States having a permanent presence in the Persian Gulf goes beyond the danger posed by Saddam Hussein: "The United States has for decades sought to play a more permanent role in Gulf regional security. While the unresolved conflict with Iraq provides the immediate justification, the need for a substantial American force presence in the Gulf transcends the issue of the regime of Saddam Hussein."

For the first eight months after he took office, Bush was not strongly focused on foreign affairs, but with Cheney as his vice president and Rumsfeld as his secretary of defense, it was predictable that many of those involved with the Project would be appointed to influential positions in his administration. That the Bush administration would not be "humble" in world affairs was certain once these appointees were known. Nevertheless, without the devastating shock that September 11 gave to the American psyche, they may not have been able to persuade the president to pursue their policy on Iraq—a policy that simultaneously achieved three of their major goals: removing Saddam Hussein from power, establishing a substantial American force in the Gulf, and asserting American preeminence over the United Nations and the rest of the world.

By taking the advice of those who wish to use America's military supremacy "to shape a new century favorable to American principles and interests," and making the United States, rather than the United Nations, the "new leviathan," is Bush following a course that can be defended as the right thing to do? The case for saying that he is, made very briefly by Bush himself in his West Point speech, is more fully developed by Lawrence Kaplan and William Kristol in their book *The War Over Iraq*—a book that makes the case for America attacking Iraq, and that was published before the final decision to go to war was announced. Since Kristol has always been at the core of the Project for the New American Century, it is safe to assume that his views are widely shared by leading figures in the Bush administration and, directly or indirectly, have an influence on Bush himself.

A key element in Kaplan and Kristol's case for American preeminence can be summarized as: "Remember Munich, not Vietnam." The overriding desire to avoid another catastrophe like the American military involvement in Vietnam has, they argue, made American foreign policy and defense strategy too timid. As a result, we have forgotten the lessons of the 1938 Munich Conference, where Britain and France appeased Hitler instead of crushing him while he was still relatively weak. Rumsfeld is on record as saying the same thing—that Hitler could have been stopped at minimal cost if only action had been taken early enough. But the comparison between Hitler and Saddam Hussein in 2003 is misleading, in various ways. First, Hitler was the leader of a major world power; Saddam was not. (Iraq was much weaker in 2003 than it had been when it invaded Kuwait in 1991, for sanctions and forced disarmament had prevented it from replacing much of the military equipment it lost during the Gulf War, or modernizing its armed forces.) Second, Hitler was on an expansionist path; since 1991, Saddam had been contained to such an extent that he was unable to control even those areas of his own state in which Kurds had effectively established an autonomous region. Third, at Munich, Hitler made claims to part of the territory of an independent state, Czechoslovakia, which strenuously resisted those claims. Britain and France should have stood by Czechoslovakia, and, if Hitler had invaded it, declared war on Germany. That, obviously, would have been in full compliance with international law. The situation in 1991, when Saddam invaded Kuwait, had certain parallels to Hitler's claims on Czechoslovakia, but by 2003 there was no parallel at all.

Nevertheless, as Bush argued at West Point and as the National Security Strategy reiterates, given today's weapons of mass destruction, isn't it better to act early, rather than wait for an attack? If international law stands in the way of such action, doesn't that merely show that international law needs to change? But that question leads us back to the issue of who is to decide when one nation is a danger to other nations. Kaplan and Kristol's answer is clear: "America must not only be the world's policeman or its sheriff, it must be its beacon and guide." The alternative, they say, "is a chaotic, Hobbesian world where there is no authority to thwart aggression, ensure peace and security or enforce international norms."

This invites the obvious response: why isn't strengthening the authority and power of the United Nations an alternative to this Hobbesian world?

The United Nations is the concrete realization of an aspiration for a world body that was eloquently voiced by Woodrow Wilson, and later by Franklin D. Roosevelt. The United States played a key role in bringing it into existence, at a conference in San Francisco in 1945. After the delegates unanimously adopted the UN Charter, the new U.S. president, Harry Truman, told them, "You have won a victory against war itself." More than fifty years later, it is an institution to which virtually all the world's nations belong, and the only institution in which many of them feel they have a voice, and in which they place their hopes for a peaceful world. On September 12, 2002, Bush went to the United Nations to make his case against Iraq—a move that was hailed by the French foreign minister, Dominique de Villepin, as showing that he had resisted "the temptation of unilateral action." But the question that Bush put in his speech was "Will the United Nations serve the purpose of its founding, or will it be irrelevant?" That question implied that unless the Security Council agreed to an attack on Iraq, it would be irrelevant. Six months later, as the crisis over Iraq was drawing to a close, he said much the same thing: "The fundamental question facing the Security Council is, will its words mean anything? When the Security Council speaks, will the words have merit and weight?" But Bush's claim that the United Nations would be irrelevant if it did not agree to the use of force against Iraq showed that he had already decided that it was irrelevant—that is, that if it did not go along with what he wanted, he would ignore its decision. Someone who really thought that the judgment of the Security Council carries weight would acknowledge a strong—if not necessarily always overriding—obligation to abide by its decisions, whether one agrees with them or not. (Similarly, there is a strong, though not necessarily always overriding, obligation to obey a law passed by Congress, whether or not one agrees with it.)

In the end, it was Bush who made the United Nations irrelevant in regard to Iraq. The United Nations Charter, to which the United States is a signatory, says in Article 2, Section 3, that "all members shall settle their international disputes by peaceful means." Section 4 of the same article reads: "All members shall refrain in their international relations from the threat or use of force against the territorial integrity or political independence of any state." Bush's threats and subsequent military attack on Iraq were in clear violation of the UN Charter. The real irrelevance of the UN was shown by the fact that it could only stand on the sidelines while its most powerful member, with Britain and minor military support from Australia and Poland, attacked a virtually defenseless member state that was not itself, at the time, engaged in any aggressive activity beyond its borders. What adverse impact this action has had on the global peacekeeping role of the United Nations it is still too soon to say.

In rejecting the authority of the United Nations, Bush may have been influenced by the views of Richard Perle, who has called the idea of achieving security through international institutions and international law a "liberal conceit." Perle was, until a conflict-of-interest problem forced his resignation, chair of the Pentagon's Defense Policy Board, an advisory board that reports directly to Defense Secretary Donald Rumsfeld. (Even after the conflict of interest was exposed, Perle remained a member of the board, though no longer its chair.) In an article published in the conservative British magazine *The Spectator* while the fighting in Iraq was going on, Perle expressed the hope that Saddam Hussein would, in falling from power, "take the United Nations down with him" and that "What will die in Iraq is the fantasy of the United Nations as the foundation of a new world order." What seems to have particularly troubled Perle was the idea that the United Nations is the sole legitimizing institution when it comes to the use of force. In a similar vein, in *The War Over Iraq,* Kaplan and Kristol dismiss, in a single sentence, the idea that the United Nations should be the authority that keeps the peace: "The United Nations? Far from existing as an autonomous entity, the organization is nothing more than a collection of states, many of them autocratic and few of them as public-spirited as America—which, in any case, provides the UN with most of its financial, political and military muscle." They then quote John Muravchik, a resident scholar at the American Enterprise Institute: "A policeman gets his assignments from higher authority, but there is no authority higher than America." Some might think that is the ultimate expression of American arrogance, but Kaplan and Kristol comment that it is "not merely an assertion of national pride. It is a simple fact." But it is not a fact at all. Questions of ultimate authority raise moral issues, and are not purely factual. Putting aside, for the moment, the question of the United Nations, what gives America greater authority than any other nation? Some would say that all sovereign nations have equal authority. We might think that democracies have greater moral authority than dictatorships, but granting this does not give the United States more authority than other nations that have equal or better claims to be democratically ruled. Switzerland has been a democracy for much longer than the United States, India is a much larger democracy, and many countries have much fairer voting systems than the United States. What distinguishes the United States from other democracies is that it has the strongest military. Are Muravchik, Kaplan, and Kristol saying that might makes right?

Contrary to what Kaplan and Kristol say, the United Nations is no mere "collection of states" but an organization with decision-procedures to which the states can bring disputes, and through which these disputes can be resolved. It is true that many member states are dictatorships. That has not, in the past, been widely seen as diminishing the authority of the United Nations. Kaplan and Kristol suggest that few of the member states of the UN are as public-spirited as the United States, but that is debatable. As we have seen, in respect to foreign aid, global warming, and the International Criminal Court, the United States is the least public-spirited of all the major industrial nations. The assertion by Kaplan and Kristol that the United States contributes "most" of the UN's finances is false. It contributes 22 percent—or would do so, if it paid its contributions on time, which it rarely does. America's record in supporting UN peacekeeping is also weak. A study carried out by the magazine *Foreign Policy,* in conjunction with the Center for Global Development, scored developed nations on their contributions to peacekeeping during the year 2000–2001, in proportion to the size of their domestic economy. The score was based on financial contributions to the UN peacekeeping program, as well as personnel contributions to UN and NATO operations (valued at $10,000 per person). On that basis, the United States ranked eighteenth out of twenty-one countries.

Admittedly, the UN is an imperfect body. In the Security Council, where the real decisions are made, the victors of World War II—China, France, Russia, the United Kingdom, and the United States—are permanent members, with the right to veto any resolution. There is no sound reason why nations like the United Kingdom and France should have veto rights, while Brazil, India, Indonesia, and Japan do not. Nor does it seem reasonable that four of the five permanent members should be nations that have a Christian cultural history, while no Islamic nation is represented. When, in the buildup to the 2003 war with Iraq, it became clear that France, Russia, and perhaps China would veto a Security Council resolution authorizing the use of force against Iraq, the United States and the United Kingdom continued to lobby for votes, indicating that they would regard acceptance of a resolution by a majority of the Security Council as a moral victory, even if the resolution was vetoed. Prime Minister Blair spoke of being prepared to disregard an "unreasonable use of the veto." (In the end, of course, they did not put the resolution to a vote, because they knew that they would not even get a majority.) That should indicate that the United States and the United Kingdom also do not think that their own "no" vote should be enough to defeat a resolution that is favored by a majority of Security Council members. More generally, it suggests a willingness to reconsider the veto system, perhaps replacing the veto by a requirement for resolutions to be passed by a qualified majority, perhaps three-quarters or two-thirds of the members. The permanent membership of the council could then be increased and made more representative of the world's population.

In view of the rejection of the United Nations organization implied by the Bush administration's attack on Iraq, there was considerable irony in Bush's return to the UN General Assembly on September 23, 2003, six months after the war, to say that the United States is "committed" to the United Nations, and to call for UN support for the costly occupation of Iraq. That was a little like a wife who has recently had an affair (and has not renounced the prospect of further affairs) turning to her husband, saying she was committed to the marriage, and asking him for money to pay for bringing up the child she has had by her lover. More significant than Bush's speech on that day, however, was the one that preceded it. Secretary-General Kofi Annan told the General Assembly that the arguments of those who assert a right to strike preemptively against other nations are contrary to the United Nations Charter and represent a fundamental challenge to the principles on which the United Nations has worked for the past fifty-eight years. Hence, he said, we are facing a moment in time "no less decisive than 1945 itself, when the United Nations was founded." What was needed, he urged, was not simply a repudiation of unilateralism and the doctrine of preemption invoked by the United States in its attack on Iraq, but a reform of the United Nations that would make it more effective in responding to the threats that might lead some countries to act preemptively. Among the reforms he mentioned was a restructuring of the Security Council to make it more representative.

These reforms would not be beyond the bounds of possibility if the United States were to push hard for them. Even more far-reaching changes are possible. If governments were required to show, before being seated at the United Nations, that they have gained their authority from the consent of their people, perhaps the UN could be turned into an association of democracies. Once that were done, it would also be possible to weight the votes of member states in the General Assembly in order to reflect their populations, thus making the assembly a kind of global parliament. But such changes—if they are deemed desirable—are for the more distant future. The reform of the Security Council would be easier to achieve and is more urgent. Whether it is worth the effort it would take depends on whether there is a better way of achieving a peaceful world. As we have already seen, the alternative favored by influential figures in the Bush administration is "the American century," the idea of a Pax Americana, a global peace enforced by the United States—or, in two words, American dominance.

In his West Point speech, Bush claimed that "America has no empire to extend or utopia to establish. We wish for others only what we wish for ourselves—safety from violence, the rewards of liberty, and the hope for a better life." Kaplan and Kristol are more open in their support of American dominance. They ask, "Well, what is wrong with dominance, in the service of sound principles and high ideals?" But if America's sound principles and high ideals mean anything, they mean democracy. Advocates of democracy should see something wrong with the idea of a nation of fewer than 300 million people dominating a planet with more than six billion inhabitants. That's less than 5 percent of the population ruling over the remainder—more than 95 percent—without their consent. If America is dominant, then the U.S. Congress and the president of the United States dominate the world—but only American citizens get to vote for them. That isn't "wish[ing] for others only what we wish for ourselves."

After democracy, the other sound principle that America stands for is the idea, so important to its founding fathers, that checks and balances are needed to prevent any single branch of government from becoming a form of tyranny. But if America is supreme, what is to stop it from becoming tyrannical in the exercise of its power? There may be checks and balances within its own constitutional structure, but they are all internal—an American Congress acts as a check on the American president, and American courts are a check on both of the other branches of government. This is what made American government, in the words of Chief Justice John Marshall in his famous 1803 decision in *Marbury v. Madison,* "a government of laws, and not of men." There are no external checks on America's power over the rest of the world, and Bush has undermined the only organizations that could offer such checks and strengthen the rule of international law, the United Nations and the International Criminal Court. America's founding fathers would not have trusted Bush's pledge that America has no empire to extend. They would have replied that power will always tend to become tyrannical, if there is no opposing power. Moreover, in his West Point speech, Bush also said "America has, and intends to keep, military strengths beyond challenge." That, obviously, contradicts his claim that "we wish for others only what we wish for ourselves," since there cannot be more than one nation with military strengths beyond challenge.

The claim that America would only use its dominance "in the service of sound principles and high ideals" is therefore a contradiction from the outset, since such principles and ideals are incompatible with the imposed, unelected global dominance of any single nation. We should also recall that the "Statement of Principles" issued by the Project for a New American Century, and signed by Vice President Cheney, as well as by Bush's brother and several members of the present Bush administration, called on the United States "to shape a new century favorable to American principles and interests." That doesn't sound like ruling the world impartially for the benefit of all. Nor could the citizens of other nations be encouraged by Bush's statement on why he would not sign on to the Kyoto Protocol: "[F]irst things first are the people who live in America." Even without this explicit statement, Bush's refusal to sign on to the Kyoto Protocol looks to most of the world very much like national selfishness. It shows a preference for taking grave risks with the lives of people who are much worse off than most Americans, rather than imposing much more moderate sacrifices on Americans. Under Bush's leadership, America's record as a global citizen does not encourage the belief that it can be trusted to wield its global dominance in the interests of all the world's people, rather than just Americans.

More fundamentally, for Bush and his supporters to proclaim America as the world's policeman is effectively to reject the possibility that the world will be governed by just laws, rather than by power. As Jonathan Glover, the director of the Centre of Medical Law and Ethics at King's College, London, and the author of *Humanity: A Moral History of the 20th Century,* has pointed out, the Pax Americana assumes a Hobbesian ruler who has power but no moral authority, a world in which conflict is merely suppressed, not resolved. Glover prefers the vision of the world offered by the eighteenth-century German philosopher, Immanuel Kant, in his book *Perpetual Peace*. Kant advocated a system in which the states would give up, to a world federation, a monopoly on the use of force. The world federation would possess the moral authority of a body that was established by mutual agreement, and reached its decision in an impartial manner. In the modern world, that means a reformed United Nations, with adequate force at its command, and impartial procedures to decide when that force should be used.

Bush might respond by saying that since we are now standing at "the perilous crossroads of radicalism and technology," we do not have the luxury of working, over decades, to improve the United Nations and ensure that it works properly to stop this peril. Is it so clear, though, that the route Bush is taking is more likely to make us safe? International terrorism recognizes no borders, and to stop it will require international cooperation. The greatest danger is that weapons-grade uranium or plutonium will fall into the hands of terrorists. Russia has more than 1,000 metric tons of such materials, and the United States more than 800 tons. Other nations, including Pakistan and India, also have some. (Iraq, at the time of the American attack on it, had none, and was not about to get any, either.) According to the *Bulletin of Atomic Scientists,* it takes just fifty-five pounds—twenty-five kilograms—of weapons-grade uranium, or 17.6 pounds of plutonium—eight kilograms—to construct a rudimentary nuclear weapon. Since the fall of the Soviet Union, hundreds of attempts to smuggle radioactive materials have been detected, including eighteen involving weapons-grade uranium or plutonium. Probably the most effective action that can be taken to prevent terrorists from getting hold of nuclear weapons is to ensure that all fissile material, whether from weapons programs like those in Russia or Pakistan, or from nuclear power programs, is rendered harmless, or safely stored and protected. That requires the cooperation of all countries that have or may produce such material. Similarly, we can only be secure against biological weapons if we have the cooperation of all countries that have the expertise to produce them. This seems more likely to be achieved by working together with other nations, through respected international institutions, than by attempting to dominate them.

After September 11, 2001, there was an unprecedented degree of international solidarity with the United States. Within twenty-four hours of the attacks NATO had, for the first time in its history, invoked Article 5 of the Washington Treaty, which states that an armed attack against one or more NATO member countries will be considered an attack against all. NATO also adopted a series of practical measures for fighting terrorism. All twenty-seven member nations accepted these measures, and Russia, which is not a NATO member, actively entered into cooperation with NATO on issues concerned with terrorism. The UN Security Council unanimously adopted a wide-ranging antiterrorism resolution calling for international cooperation in suppressing terrorism and cutting off financial support for terrorists, and set up a committee to monitor its implementation. Instead of using this atmosphere of cooperation as a means of achieving security, the Bush administration has provoked anti-American sentiment. John Brady Kiesling, a career diplomat serving in Greece, felt so strongly that this course of action was wrong that he gave up his lifelong career. In his letter of resignation, he told Colin Powell: "We have begun to dismantle the largest and most effective web of international relationships the world has ever known. Our current course will bring instability and danger, not security."

Undoubtedly, Bush is right to say that the conjunction of radicalism and technology has made the world a more dangerous place—so dangerous, in fact, that it may undermine the Hobbesian idea that a sovereign with overwhelming military supremacy can ensure the security of his or her subjects. In a Hobbesian world, in which a dominant nation is liable to attack and overthrow weak governments that are not to its liking, the most sensible response for a government that fears it may be attacked is to obtain nuclear weapons as rapidly as possible. Only then can it deter an attack by threatening to inflict intolerable losses on the dominant nation or its allies. Overwhelming military superiority is less significant when the militarily inferior nation possesses and is prepared to use nuclear weapons.

Whether the danger posed by the combination of new weapons technologies with radical religious and political ideas can be controlled at all is something that only time will tell. In the long run, however, we are more likely to succeed in meeting this threat by international cooperation than by one nation acting unilaterally and in defiance of international law. American preeminence may well prove to be not only unjust, but a tragic mistake with catastrophic consequences.

Chapter 10

The Ethics of George W. Bush

> *I think what this country needs to do is to usher in what I call "the responsibility era"—where you are responsible for the decisions you make. But we can't usher in the responsibility era when a figure that is on your TV screen on a daily basis has behaved irresponsibly. It sends a mixed message. What's needed in a president is a consistent message.*
>
> —George W. Bush, in an interview published in *Charisma*, November 2000

We have now examined Bush's words and deeds on the key ethical issues he has addressed during his presidency. We have seen how he frequently defends his actions in terms of right and wrong. Yet it still isn't obvious what kind of ethic the president holds. He insists that right and wrong are universal, and provides specific examples of good and evil, but offers no broad ethical principles or framework for thinking about what makes something good or evil. In several speeches there is an implicit appeal to one kind of ethic, but then other speeches or other decisions appear to be based on a quite different, and even contradictory, ethical stance.

Is Bush's Ethic Based on Individual Rights?

Individual rights have an important place in American ethics—not surprisingly, since the Declaration of Independence begins with the ringing statement that the rights to life, liberty, and the pursuit of happiness are self-evident. The Bill of Rights incorporates strong statements about rights into the Constitution of the United States. Belief in the importance of individual rights is part of the American conservative tradition from which Bush draws his support, for individual rights are seen as a barrier against the tyranny of the majority and the power of the state, and thus a necessary bulwark for a free society.

Bush's rhetoric often emphasizes individual rights. In his commencement address to the U.S. Coast Guard Academy in May 2003, he said that the advance of freedom is "our calling" and added, "If the self-evident truths of our founding are true for us, they are true for all." From there he went on to assert that America is "a people dedicated to civil rights" and is "driven to defend the human rights of others." We have seen Bush—consistent with his belief that individual rights are inviolable, and that human beings have a right to life from the moment of conception—refuse to provide federal support for research that would destroy a small number of human embryos in the hope of developing medical techniques that could save the lives of many more children and adults. His statements on taxation can also be seen as consistent with a philosophy based on individual rights, including the right to property. For when he says "It's your money," he implies that taxation, at least beyond what the state needs for some basic functions, is a violation of the property rights of citizens. He has also suggested, as many defenders of individual rights do, that the scope of the state's power should be reduced.

To hold a workable ethic based on rights, however, it is not enough to make broad statements expressing general support for individual rights. The difficult part is defining the scope and limits of those rights, and the circumstances, if any, in which they may be overridden. One way of doing that was taken by the Harvard philosopher Robert Nozick in his book *Anarchy, State, and Utopia.* Nozick begins with a firm statement of a rights-based ethic: "Individuals have rights, and there are things no person or group may do to them. . . ." So strong and far-reaching are these rights, Nozick argues, that they lead to a libertarian ethic. The only state that is compatible with respect for individual rights is a minimal one. It must limit its functions to defending its citizens from attack, whether from their fellow citizens or from outside forces. Beyond that, the state has no right to tax its citizens, and must leave people alone to get on with their lives as they see fit (and as best they are able, without any other government assistance).

Bush evidently rejects the libertarian view. His tax cuts have been large, but they do not go so far as to challenge the modern state as we know it, which funds a host of government programs beyond providing law and order and national defense. The modern state can be justified, consistently with a moral framework based on rights, by saying that while some rights are inviolable, the right to property is not one of them—it is not, after all, mentioned in the opening sentences of the Declaration of Independence. But then, what rights does Bush take to be inviolable? He appears not to think that the right to liberty—which is part of the Declaration of Independence's trinity of "life, liberty and the pursuit of happiness"—is inviolable. If he did, how could he have detained hundreds of people—both American citizens and others—for more than two years as of this writing without charging them with any offense? Nor can he hold that the right to life is inviolable for all human beings, for that would be incompatible with the conduct of wars he has ordered. But if Bush does not take the rights to life and liberty as inviolable, it is difficult to say what rights he does consider inviolable.

Is Bush a Utilitarian?

Utilitarianism is the view that the right action is that which is expected to have the best consequences for all those affected by our actions, now and in the future. Typically, utilitarians focus on consequences like pleasure and pain, happiness and misery, or the satisfaction and frustration of preferences. They seek to maximize the net surplus of the good consequences, after subtracting the bad ones. Individual rights have, at most, a derivative role to play in utilitarian thinking. (Utilitarians will support individual rights only if recognizing such rights will, in the long run, have better consequences than not recognizing them.) In the aftermath of the September 11 attacks, John Ashcroft and other senior officials in the Bush administration gave a classic utilitarian argument for overriding individual rights. They said that the indefinite detention of suspected terrorists was justified by the risk of much greater harm if a suspect was allowed to go free and later carried out a terrorist attack. Bush seemed to use a utilitarian argument in justifying the war in Iraq. Along with his argument about America's right to take preemptive action in its own defense, he suggested that the great good of liberating millions of Iraqis from Saddam's brutal tyranny justified the harm inflicted on a smaller number of Iraqis, even though many of them were innocent of any wrongdoing. In a different way, when Bush said, before his trip to Africa in July 2003, "We believe that human suffering in Africa creates moral responsibilities for people everywhere," he might have been reading from a utilitarian textbook. Utilitarians would want to go much further than the limited amounts Bush has agreed to spend on relieving human suffering and assisting those at risk from AIDS, but from a utilitarian perspective, he has moved in the right direction on these issues.

Within a utilitarian framework, there is scope for disagreement about how the prospective good and bad consequences are to be assessed, and of course the probabilities of achieving these consequences are also relevant. Utilitarians would accept the ethical framework that Ashcroft and Bush are using when they justify detention without trial and the war on Iraq. But many utilitarians would disagree with the calculations that Ashcroft and Bush used in order to justify the detentions and the war. They would point to the risk of abuse when basic rights are not protected, and to the virtual certainty that war will bring great suffering, without any comparable assurance that it will also bring about the desired good consequences. Utilitarians might suspect that Ashcroft and Bush's calculations are not truly utilitarian, but simply biased toward protecting American lives and American interests, rather than impartially protecting the lives and interests of all those affected by what they do.

On other issues, however, Bush firmly rejects utilitarian ethics. It is hard to see what utilitarian grounds there are for denying terminally ill people the assistance of a physician in ending their lives, as long as such decisions are carried out under strict guidelines like those required by Oregon's physician-assisted suicide legislation. The same can be said about the medical use of marijuana. Most notably, though, as we have seen, Bush's decision on the use of stem cells derived from embryos fits much better within a rights framework than within a utilitarian one.

Is Bush's Ethic Christian?

Some will say that Bush's ethic is based neither on rights, nor on utility, but on his Christian religious beliefs. As we have seen, Bush's speeches include many religious, sometimes specifically Christian, references. But Christians hold a wide range of ethical views. Christian ethics has been, in the teachings of different Christians, neo-Platonic, Aristotelian, Kantian, Marxist, and existentialist. Some Christian ethicists, pointing to what they claim to be "natural law," say that it is always wrong to violate moral rules like "do not kill innocent human beings" and "do not tell a lie." Others say that Christianity is love, and develop forms of "situation ethics" that are very close to utilitarianism. Protestant Christians often look to the Bible, but cannot agree on how to interpret it, nor what priority to give its varying suggestions. To see to what extent Bush's Christian faith explains his ethical views, it is necessary to take a more detailed look at some of his views and their relationship to Christian scriptures or teachings.

Anyone seeking to show the Christian origins of Bush's values would be most likely to start with his professed reverence for human life. In his second inaugural speech as governor of Texas, he said, in words he quotes in *A Charge to Keep,* "All of us have worth. We're all made in the image of God. We're all equal in God's eyes." Elsewhere in that book he writes, "my faith teaches that life is a gift from our Creator," and that "In a perfect world life is given by God and only taken by God." Subsequently, in his August 2001 speech on federal funding for stem-cell research, he says that his belief that "human life is a sacred gift from our Creator" influences his position on whether the federal government should fund research on human stem cells. A year later he used similar language when signing the Born Alive Infants Protection Act: "Today, through sonograms and other technology, we can clearly—see clearly that unborn children are members of the human family, as well. They reflect our image, and they are created in God's own image."

Does it follow from acceptance of the Christian faith that frozen human embryos are precious and need to be protected, even when destroying them could save many more lives? Obviously the Bible says nothing about how frozen embryos should be treated, because the idea that a viable embryo could survive outside the human body—let alone be frozen—was beyond the comprehension of the Bible's authors. The Bible doesn't even have anything directly to say about abortion, and what it does say suggests that the death of a fetus is not to be thought of as equivalent to the death of a normal adult human. (For example, in Exodus we read that the penalty for hitting a pregnant woman and causing her to miscarry is a fine; but if the woman is injured, the principle of a life for a life, an eye for an eye, and so on, is to be applied.) Many Christians support the use of embryos for research and consider that a woman's right to control her body overrides any right to life that an embryo or fetus may have. So a Christian can come to different conclusions from those that Bush comes to, and his view on these issues is not inescapably implied by his Christian belief.

The difficulty of resolving what is a distinctively Christian view emerges even more sharply when we contrast Bush's opposition to abortion and embryo research—on which Jesus, the founder of Christianity, and Paul, the first great exponent of Christian teachings, are silent—with his readiness to strike out at his adversaries, which they both quite explicitly oppose. Jesus famously said "Do not resist one who is evil. But if any one strikes you on the right cheek, turn to him the other also." Paul reinforced this message: "Do not repay anyone evil for evil. . . . Be not overcome by evil, but overcome evil with good." The early Christians took these texts seriously and were pacifists. Tertullian, Origen, and Clement of Alexandria—leading thinkers of the early church—all agreed that a Christian could not be a soldier. If one of the faithful becomes a soldier, Clement said, he must be cast out of the church, for he has "scorned God." It was not until 312, when Constantine, the Roman Emperor, became a Christian, that this attitude changed, and Christian thinkers like Augustine began to develop the doctrine of the "just war." Accepting that war could be justifiable was a smart political move—without it, Christianity could hardly have become the official religion of the Roman Empire—but it is flatly against the explicit teachings of Jesus and Paul. Yet after September 11, Bush did not turn the other cheek—and from the account given by Bob Woodward in *Bush at War,* he never seriously contemplated doing so.

On Iraq, Bush's pro-war view was opposed by most Christian religious leaders. The pope spoke out forcefully against the war, and so, too, did the leaders of most, though not all, American Christian denominations, as well as most leading Christian theologians. When the leaders of the National Council of Churches, and of Bush's own church, the United Methodists, asked for the opportunity to present their objections to the war, Bush refused to meet with them. On any reasonable interpretation of the Christian message, there was nothing especially Christian about his decision to go to war, and there is a strong case for saying that it was distinctly un-Christian.

The clearest sign of a Christian, and, more specifically, evangelical, influence on Bush's ethics is his repeated invocation of a conflict between good and evil. We have seen that Bush often talks of "the evil ones" and even occasionally of those who are "servants of evil." He urges us to "call evil by its name," to "fight evil," and tells us that out of evil will come good. This language comes straight out of apocalyptic Christianity. To understand the context in which

Bush uses this language, we need to remember that tens of millions of Americans hold an apocalyptic view of the world. According to a poll taken by *Time,* 53 percent of adult Americans "expect the imminent return of Jesus Christ, accompanied by the fulfillment of biblical prophecies concerning the cataclysmic destruction of all that is wicked." One of the signs of the apocalypse that will precede the Second Coming of Christ is the rise of the Antichrist, the ultimate enemy of Christ, who heads Satan's forces in the battle that will culminate in the triumph of the forces of God, and the creation of the Kingdom of God on Earth. Projecting this prophecy onto the world in which they live, many American Christians see their own nation as carrying out a divine mission. The nation's enemies therefore are demonized. That is exactly what Bush does. When, during a discussion about the looming war with Iraq with Australian prime minister John Howard in February 2003, Bush said that liberty for the people of Iraq would not be a gift that the United States could provide, but rather, "God's gift to every human being in the world," he seemed to be suggesting that there was divine endorsement for a war to overthrow Saddam Hussein. David Frum, Bush's speechwriter at the time of his "axis of evil" speech, says of Bush's use of the term "evil ones" for the people behind 9/11: "In a country where almost two-thirds of the population believes in the devil, Bush was identifying Osama bin Laden and his gang as literally satanic."

Frum has given an account of how Bush came to use the phrase "axis of evil" to refer to Iraq, Iran, and North Korea. In his initial draft, he compared America's enemies today with those in World War II, and referred to them as the "axis of hatred," but Michael Gerson, who had overall responsibility for the speech and is an evangelical Christian, changed "hatred" to "evil" because he "wanted to use the theological language that Bush had made his own since September 11." Despite being criticized, especially in Europe, for introducing such heavily moralistic language into international relations, Bush used it again and again until, in Frum's words, it "ceased to be a speechwriter's phrase and became his own."

Don Evans, who is not only Bush's commerce secretary but also his close friend, says that Bush's religious faith gives him "a very clear sense of what is good and what is evil." Seeing the world as a conflict between the forces of good and the forces of evil is not, however, the orthodox Christian view, but one associated with the heresy of Manichaeanism. The Manichaeans were ferociously attacked by Augustine, who thought that seeing some kind of evil force as the source of all that is bad is a way of masking one's own failings. Centuries of suppression and frequent persecution, however, did not eradicate the Manichaean way of looking at the world. After the Reformation, the Manichaean view appeared in some Protestant sects and was brought by them to America, where it flourished. Writing at a time when America entered World War I, the commentator and critic Walter Lippmann called the idea of a war betweeen good and evil forces "one of the great American traditions." Bush's readiness to see America as pure and good, and its enemies as wholly evil, has its roots in this American-Manichaean tradition.

That Christian teachings have influenced Bush's ethics is highly probable. They support Bush's professed concern for the world's poor. In promoting his initiative against AIDS, he spoke of the "wounded traveler on the road to Jericho." His support for the "sacred institution" of marriage and for faith-based organizations also very probably derives from his religious beliefs. But his readiness to go to war suggests that he does not simply derive his ethics from his reading of the Bible. There has to be some other basis on which he sometimes chooses to follow the path more compatible with Christian teachings and Christian scripture, and sometimes chooses not to do so.

An Intuitive Ethic

If Bush's ethics do not fit into any of the three frameworks that seem likely to be compatible with the positions he has taken, from where does he derive his ethical views? A clue can be found in what Bush said to Bob Woodward during an interview he gave for *Bush At War:* "I'm not a textbook player. I'm a gut player." When Bush spoke about the North Korean president, Kim Jong Il, he twice said that his reaction was "visceral." During the interview, "the president spoke a dozen times about his 'instincts' or his 'instinctive reactions.'" As Woodward comments, "Bush's role as politician, president and commander in chief is driven by a secular faith in his instincts—his natural and spontaneous conclusions and judgments. His instincts are almost his second religion."

Bush's views do not fit within a coherent ethical framework, because he reacts instinctively to specific situations. He feels that he knows what to do on any given occasion, but because he is not a reflective kind of person, he makes no attempt to put his judgments on specific issues together and see how coherently they fit with each other. David Frum describes the president as "a politician of conservative instincts rather than conservative principles. He knew in a general way what he believed and what he did not. But on any specific issue, nobody could ever be sure where the line was beyond which he could not be pushed."

We can see the limitations of Bush's instinctive approach to ethical issues in his failure to resolve the inherent conflict between his own two ethical imperatives of building "a single nation of justice and opportunity" and returning to the taxpayers what he saw as "their money." For Bush, each of these was no doubt self-evidently right, but he never made a serious attempt to work out to what extent the government should tax its citizens in order to provide the resources for creating a single nation of justice and opportunity. The same is true of the conflict between protecting the liberty of the individual and fighting the "war against terror." Obviously Bush thinks both are right; but there is no sign, in his pronouncements or his actions in detaining those he has designated "enemy combatants," that he has tried to reach a considered judgment on how to balance the two. Only in his speech on stem-cell research does Bush make an explicit attempt to reconcile two conflicting values. John DiIulio, who was at the White House at the time, regarded this decision as showing "unusual depth of reading, reflection, and staff deliberation." In the Bush White House, that is, indeed, lamentably unusual.

We all draw on our intuitions to decide what is right and what is wrong. In the hustle of everyday life it would be impractical to go back to first principles every time we need to make rapid moral decisions, or to pass judgment on what someone else has done. So we rely on a general intuitive sense that works most of the time. Usually our intuitions fall back on simple principles, like "Don't lie," "Keep your promises," "Do good to those who do good to you," "Do no harm," and so on. Following these simple intuitive rules produces the right answer most of the time—that is, the answer that we would have reached had we had the time and capacity to go back to fundamental principles and work out what they would imply in our particular situation. So intuitive thinking about ethics is usually a good thing. But in any complex situation, we are likely to have clashing intuitions, and then an appeal to intuition alone does not help. To take a famous example discussed by philosophers down the centuries: if a man seeking to kill another comes to my door and asks if I have seen his intended victim, must I tell the truth, and say, "Yes, he is hiding in my closet"? Here the intuitive judgments "Tell the truth" and "Do no harm" are in conflict, and we must think about which is more important. That requires us to consider what ethical principles we take as ultimate.

For someone in Bush's situation, called upon to decide important and complex issues on a daily basis, relying on moral instincts or intuitions is not enough. Reflection and critical thought are needed as well; but that is not something that Bush relishes. *New York Times* columnist Nicholas Kristof has described Bush as "less interested in ideas than perhaps anybody I've ever interviewed" and added, "Nuance isn't his natural state."

Here we return to Bush's tendency to see the world in the stark terms of good and evil. We've already read Greg Thielmann, of the State Department's Bureau of Intelligence and Research, saying that the Bush administration had "a faith-based intelligence attitude: 'We know the answers, give us the intelligence to support those answers.'" We can now add to this account. It seems probable that it was not faith in general that gave Bush and his aides a misplaced confidence that they knew the answers. It was the idea that Saddam was evil. Writing in *Newsweek* on how Bush justified going to war with Iraq, Howard Fineman observed, "He decided that Saddam was evil, and everything flowed from that." That alone made it intuitively obvious that Saddam must be building weapons of mass destruction. But it is a mistake to divide the world neatly into good and evil, black and white without shades of gray, in a manner that eliminates the need to learn more about those with whom one is dealing. For an unreflective person, having a sense of "moral clarity" that disregards the shadings in human motivation and conduct can be a vice, not a virtue. When it is coupled with a firm belief that the nation you lead is on the right side of history, pursuing "God's justice," and even that there is some divine plan that has put you in the position of leader of that nation, what you see as moral clarity, others will see as self-righteousness. When that self-proclaimed moral clarity is coupled with actions that fail to live up to the rhetoric, others will see it as hypocrisy. In the president of the most powerful nation on earth, self-righteousness and hypocrisy are dangerous vices.

An Honest Man?

Many people believe that George W. Bush is fundamentally a morally good person. John DiIulio, who Bush appointed to head the White House Office of Faith-Based and Community Initiatives, wrote after he had left the White House: "In my view, President Bush is a highly admirable person of enormous personal decency. He is a godly man and a moral leader." David Frum, also writing after he had ended his employment at the Bush White House, described Bush as "a good man" with the virtues of "decency, honesty, rectitude, courage, and tenacity." Frum, himself very much a conservative, offers us an extraordinary glimpse of what he calls "the moral fervor of the Bush White House." But the moral fervor of the White House could be extraordinarily petty. Ethics rules for staff behavior were enforced, in Frum's words, to "every last absurdity." At a meeting, Frum was asked if he was sure about something, and he replied, "Yes, I am damn sure." There was a prolonged silence and the atmosphere suddenly turned chilly. Eventually Frum realized what he had done wrong, and amended his reply to, "I am quite sure." This kind of moral fundamentalism—that is, a tendency to take simple moral rules in an absolute and literal fashion—appears to have been set by Bush himself. Frum tells us that Bush "scorned the petty untruths of the politician" and insisted so strictly on not departing from the truth that when, a day before departing for a trip to California, he was asked to make a radio address to be broadcast the following day, he would begin reading, "Today I am in California . . ." Then he would break off, saying with exasperation, "But I'm not in California."

Taking the obligation to be truthful so literally suggests an arrested moral development. The Harvard psychologist Lawrence Kohlberg studied moral judgment in children, adolescents, and adults from the United States and other countries, and concluded that, across a wide range of cultures, we pass through the same stages of moral growth in the same order. (Kohlberg would agree with Bush in rejecting ethical relativism and believing that we can educate our children in terms of universally valid standards of moral development toward a higher stage of moral reasoning.) As young children, Kohlberg says, we are at the preconventional level, concerned only about doing what is in our own interests and not being punished for what we do. Then we reach a conventional level, where we obey social conventions for their own sake. Kohlberg describes the higher of the two stages within the conventional level as "an orientation toward authority, fixed rules, and the maintenance of the social order." He found this to be the dominant conception among thirteen-year-old boys. By the age of sixteen, many had moved beyond the conventional level to the postconventional, or principled level. A person at the postconventional level can see the possibility of altering rules on the basis of larger considerations of social utility, or on the basis of ethical principles one has chosen for oneself, not in an arbitrary manner, but "in accord with self-chosen ethical principles appealing to logical comprehensiveness, universality, and consistency." Kohlberg stresses that the principles chosen at the postconventional level are not concrete moral rules, like the Ten Commandments (or the simple rule "Do not lie") but broader ethical principles like the Golden Rule or Kant's categorical imperative ("act always as if the maxim of your action were to be a universal law"). Frum's account of Bush's appeal to "fixed rules" and his apparent inability to assess the simple rule against lying in terms of larger considerations about why we have such a rule, suggests that Bush has not progressed beyond Kohlberg's conventional level of moral reasoning. This is the stage typically reached by early teenage boys, although Kohlberg notes that many develop no further, and hence it is not unusual for an adult to be at this stage.

Frum concludes, after describing Bush's moral character, that "The country could trust the Bush administration not to cheat and not to lie." But events have proven Frum wrong about that, and the Bush White House has provided us with a textbook example of what is wrong with an ethic based on rigid adherence to fixed moral rules, literally interpreted. While Bush may naively consider that it would be lying, and therefore wrong, to say that he is in California when he is recording a speech in Washington, he has failed to see that he did something gravely wrong when he created false impressions in his worldwide audiences about Iraq's alleged possession of weapons of mass destruction. These false impressions were fostered by the White House on the basis of a highly selective dossier of evidence. Bush included in his own State of the Union address statements about Iraq's attempt to purchase uranium from Africa that either he or his staff—or perhaps both—knew to be highly doubtful, if not false. In July 2003, when questions were raised about how the statement was allowed to remain in Bush's State of the Union address, both Condoleezza Rice and Donald Rumsfeld tried to argue that the statement was accurate. The way in which they did so suggests that Bush's childishly literal notion of what it is to be truthful has set the tone for his entire administration.

Bush's actual words, in the State of the Union address, were "the British government has learned that Saddam Hussein recently sought significant quantities of uranium from Africa." Bush's statement took this form because the CIA had objected to an original version, which flatly stated that Saddam Hussein had sought to buy uranium from Africa. The White House staff member involved in that discussion with the CIA then suggested changing the sentence so that it stated that the British had reported that Saddam Hussein had sought to buy uranium from Africa. This would have been literally true, because the British had indeed made such a report. It was nevertheless misleading, because the CIA had earlier informed the British that their information was not reliable. The fact that Bush only referred to a British statement is the basis for Rice and Rumsfeld's defense of the statement. Rice said that "the statement that [Bush] made was indeed accurate. The British government did say that." Rumsfeld said that Bush's statement was "technically accurate." In fact, even in the most literal interpretation of Bush's statement, it was not accurate. Bush did not merely say that the British had "reported" that Iraq had sought to buy uranium from Africa, he said that the British had "learned" this. To say that someone has learned something is to endorse what they say they have learned as true. (Imagine that the British had said that Saddam Hussein was a peace-loving man about to bring democracy to his country. Would Bush have said that the British had "learned" that?) But quite apart from these weak attempts to justify what Bush said as "technically accurate," the more serious charge is that even if what Bush said really were technically accurate, it still would have been designed to mislead the world into thinking that Iraq had been trying to buy uranium from Africa, when Bush's staff had good reason to believe that this was not true.

If Bush's staff knew that the information in his speech was not reliable, then Bush himself should have known. And if he knew, then he is, of course, as culpable as they are. If he did not know, then either he had not properly instructed his staff on the importance of passing such information on to him, or he had properly instructed them, and they failed to follow his instructions. If they had failed to follow his instructions, then a president who was sensitive to the seriousness of misleading the Congress and the American people on so vital a matter as the basis for starting a war would, on first learning of the possibility that his staff had acted improperly, have seen that whoever was responsible for this serious error of judgment suffered the usual consequences that befall senior officials or political leaders who make such mistakes. Bush, however, did nothing of the sort. When the issue became public, instead of launching an investigation into what went wrong and why,

Bush's initial response was to condemn his critics as "revisionist historians" and to evade questions about the credibility of the information he had provided by asserting that the war has had, in the removal of Saddam, a good outcome. Then Bush said that his speech had been cleared by the CIA, as if that absolved him of all responsibility for it. After CIA director George Tenet took responsibility for the inclusion of the misleading material, Bush said that he "absolutely" had confidence in Tenet and the CIA, and that he considered the matter closed. When asked at a press conference why Condoleezza Rice was not being held responsible for the mistaken inclusion of the statement about African uranium, he simply said: "Dr. Condoleezza Rice is an honest, fabulous person and America is lucky to have her service. Period." There was no further explanation of her role in the matter. (Rice later admitted that she feels "personal responsibility for this entire episode.") Then, asked directly if he takes personal responsibility for the inaccuracy, Bush said, "I take personal responsibility for everything I say, of course, absolutely." But Bush seems to think that "taking responsibility" is a mere matter of words, for neither Tenet nor Rice lost their jobs for the mistakes for which they took responsibility—nor were they even reprimanded—and Bush himself made no admission of error, nor did he apologize to Congress and the American people for having misled them.

When Senator Jon Corzine, a Democrat from New Jersey, moved to establish an independent twelve-member commission with a broad mandate to examine questions like whether Iraq possessed so-called weapons of mass destruction, had links to Al Qaeda, or had tried to buy uranium in Africa, the Republican-controlled Senate, voting along party lines, killed the proposal. A word of support from Bush would have cleared the way for it. But he was evidently more interested in protecting his own position than in establishing the truth about these matters, or in preventing something similar from happening again.

That Bush had something to hide is suggested by the fact that in October 2002 the CIA had already removed a reference to Iraq's attempts to purchase uranium from Africa—specifically, from Niger—from a speech that Bush was to give. If Bush was aware of that, then he should have known that he was on dangerous ground in repeating a similar claim in his State of the Union address the following January. And since he receives a daily briefing from the CIA, it seems that he would have known that. On July 14, 2003, Bush said that doubts were only raised about the intelligence underlying the African uranium claim after his State of the Union address, but this was contrary to earlier statements from both the CIA and Bush's own White House staff, including Condoleezza Rice. At a press conference the following day, a reporter asked Scott McClellan, the White House spokesperson, why the president had made an inaccurate statement on this matter, but McClellan evaded the question. Another reporter then asked whether the president was aware that the CIA had insisted on removing the reference from his earlier speech. McClellan evaded that question, too. The reporter tried four more times to get a definite answer from McClellan to his question, but eventually gave up in frustration, the question still unanswered.

The way in which the Bush administration handled the issue of misleading information about Iraq offers the clearest demonstration of its gross misunderstanding of the moral requirements of honesty, but there are many other instances in which Bush has made rhetorically powerful statements and then failed to live up to the expectations he has created. John DiIulio has written:

> Remember "No child left behind"? That was a Bush campaign slogan. I believe it was [in] his heart, too. But translating good impulses into good policy proposals requires more than whatever somebody thinks up in the eleventh hour before a speech is to be delivered.

After a White House spokesperson described DiIulio's charges as "baseless and groundless," DiIulio subsequently apologized, saying his criticisms were "groundless and baseless due to poorly chosen words and examples." But the original statement reads as if it were well-considered, and the apology appeared to have been made under pressure.

As a candidate, Bush led people to believe that it was important to him that no child should be left behind. As president, he did not make a genuine effort to do something to prevent millions of children from being left behind—in fact, his tax cuts deprived the state of the resources it would need to tackle this problem. Similarly, he says that he supports free trade, but when there is a political advantage to be gained by protecting the American steel industry or granting unprecedented subsidies to wealthy farmers, he does not stick to his free-trade principles. He speaks of America's calling to promote democracy around the world, but his administration reacted positively to the first reports of an apparently successful coup against the left-leaning, but democratically elected, Venezuelan government of Hugo Chávez. Following the Enron scandal, he pledged to increase enforcement against corporate rip-offs, but his 2003 budget actually reduced funds for such enforcement by $209 million. We may take these deceptions lightly because we have come to expect them of politicians, but if a candidate campaigns by stressing his moral character and his honesty, and then fails to make even a serious attempt to implement his campaign promises, he has damaged the moral fabric of democracy.

Belief in Bush's honesty led many voters to prefer him to Gore in the 2000 presidential election. Among voters who rated "honesty" as an important factor influencing their choice of candidate, 80 percent said that they voted for Bush. These voters were disgusted with Clinton, not only for his sexual relationship with White House intern Monica Lewinsky, but for lying about it. That Clinton did lie about his private life is clear, and he was wrong to do so. But his lies did not lead his country into a war that cost thousands of lives. The false impressions created in the mind of the American public by Bush have had far more serious consequences.

Taking a Cynical View

In ancient Athens, if we can believe the account given by Plato in *The Republic,* the sophist Thrasymachus argued that whatever is in the interests of those who are strongest is just. Thrasymachus didn't mean that we should really do whatever is in the interests of the strongest. He was suggesting that the very idea of justice is a kind of fraud perpetrated on the weak by the strong, the better to further their own interests. Some people take this view of Bush's ethics. His real motive, these cynics suggest, is to please his wealthy friends and supporters. His many speeches and comments on ethics camouflage decisions that are just as self-serving as those of any other politician, perhaps more so. Even his religious conversion was so conveniently timed—shortly before he revived his long-abandoned political career with the Republican Party, then increasingly coming under the influence of evangelicals, especially in the South—that it gave rise to doubts about how genuine it was. To take Bush's ethical views seriously, to subject them to a reasoned critique and try to fit them into a coherent ethical framework, is therefore to treat them more seriously than they deserve. Instead, we should expose the naked political and economic interests that lie behind them.

Among the cynics, none has been more forceful than the Princeton economics professor and *New York Times* columnist Paul Krugman. "We are well advised," Krugman tells us, "not to trust anything the administration says about the goals of its domestic policy." The real interest of the Bush White House, in Krugman's analysis, is not to achieve social objectives, but to win political support. On free trade: "The Bush administration is all for it—unless there is some political cost, however small, to honoring its alleged principles." Bush's plan on global warming is "a sham, relying on the kindness of corporations." On tax cuts, the administration "knows exactly what it's doing" and what it's doing is "shamelessly misrepresenting the content of its own policies" to disguise how much of the cut is going to the rich. Even before it began to look as if no weapons of mass destruction would be found in Iraq, Krugman pointed to Bush's "credibility problem," saying that his mendacity "has reached almost pathological levels." Nor does Krugman spare Bush's personal character, pointing to the many unanswered questions about his business dealings before he became governor of Texas and his history of taking "institutions traditionally insulated from politics" and turning them into "tools for rewarding your friends and reinforcing your political control."

The case for taking a cyncial view of Bush's talk of ethics cannot be lightly dismissed. There are two distinct versions of it. One is that Bush himself is carrying off this sham, consciously deceiving his audience every time he speaks of morality, of right and wrong, and even of his religious faith. The real Bush is not interested in living a morally good life at all, he's motivated by personal ambition and the desire to help his rich friends. Though it is difficult to disprove such a hypothesis, I do not find it plausible. No one who has known Bush personally, at least not since he became a Christian, has suggested that he is so shameless, nor so good an actor. The standard view, even from those who, like John DiIulio, are prepared to speak critically of the Bush administation, is that Bush is a "decent" man, though one with intellectual limitations. It is difficult to believe that Bush could be so successfully living a lie.

There is also a more intriguing possibility that will appeal to those who enjoy speculating about secret cliques that rule the world. We might attribute cynical motives not to Bush himself, but to those who manipulate him for their own purposes. Several magazine and newspaper reports have highlighted the fact that followers of the political philosopher Leo Strauss play an important role in the Bush administration. A less likely person than Leo Strauss to have a major influence on the Bush administration is hard to imagine. Born in Germany in 1899, his ideas were shaped by the failure of the liberal, tolerant Weimar Republic to deal with the dual threat of Communism and Nazism. That failure meant that Strauss, who was Jewish, had to flee his native country in 1938. He came to America and spent most of his remaining years, until his death in 1973, at the University of Chicago. There he lived quietly and without gaining much public attention, writing difficult and often obscure academic essays on the thought of philosophers like Plato, Maimonides, Machiavelli, and Hobbes. Yet through his teaching Strauss gathered a band of followers devoted to his view of the world. They in turn attracted their own disciples, so that Strauss's influence spread to a third generation.

Strauss's ideas lend themselves well to a conspiracy theory. Central to all his writings is the doctrine that there is one kind of truth for the masses, and another for the philosophers—that is, for those in the know. Strauss claimed that all the great philosophers wrote in a kind of code, so that the masses could read them in a way that would not disturb necessary social conventions, while the philosophers could grasp the more radical meaning hidden in their texts. One of these not-to-be-revealed-to-the-masses truths is that the existence of God is, at best, unprovable in any rational, scientific view of the world. Strauss himself is widely regarded as having been an atheist. But this truth should not be revealed to the masses, because religion "breeds deference to the ruling class," and without that, the masses may rise up and destroy the higher culture that is at the apex of Straussian values. Thomas Fleming, editor of the right-wing journal *Chronicles,* puts it more bluntly. Straussians, he says, "believe that religion may be a useful thing to take in the suckers with." Something similar is true, in Fleming's view, of the attitude of the Straussian inner circle to democracy and liberty. They don't themselves believe in them, but they teach others to believe in them. The conservative Robert Locke, who counts himself as a Straussian, would add equality to this list: "Civic equality may be salutary for the functioning of society, but men are not truly equal in value." Indeed, we have "no higher duty, and no more pressing duty," Strauss thought, "than to remind ourselves and our students, of political greatness, human greatness, of the peaks of human excellence."

The fact that Straussians are cultish and network to find one another jobs in Washington has taken them to a position of extraordinary influence in the Bush administration. Adding to the sense of a conspiracy is the fact that, to quote Locke once more, "Straussians talk in a kind of code to one another." One of these Straussian code words is "gentleman," which refers to someone who lacks the intellect required for philosophy, but is nevertheless in some ways morally admirable. These "gentlemen" have a special role to play in the Straussian scheme. In 1985 Miles Burnyeat, a scholar of classical philosophy, published an article on Strauss in the *New York Review of Books* that included this paragraph, which some might now consider prophetic:

> The leading characters in Strauss's writing are "the gentlemen" and "the philosopher." "The gentlemen" come, preferably, from patrician urban backgrounds and have money without having to work too hard for it. . . . Such "gentlemen" are idealistic, devoted to virtuous

> ends, and sympathetic to philosophy. They are thus ready to be taken in hand by "the philosopher," who will teach them the great lesson they need to learn before they join the governing elite.

The picture will now start to look familiar. So who are the Straussians around Bush? Paul Wolfowitz, Rumsfeld's deputy and the man often credited with being the chief architect of the war on Iraq, is one. So too is Abram Shulsky, who headed the Office of Special Plans, a unit set up by Rumsfeld because he wasn't getting the kind of information he wanted from the CIA and the Defense Department's own intelligence service, the Defense Intelligence Agency. Shulsky was responsible for analyzing intelligence in a manner that selectively highlighted dubious evidence pointing to Saddam Hussein's supposed arsenal of weapons of mass destruction. In the previous chapter I discussed the influential case made by William Kristol, the founder of the Project for a New American Century, for going to war with Iraq. Kristol is a Straussian. In a different area, bioethics, Bush listens to another Straussian, Leon Kass, who now heads the President's Council on Bioethics.

If we are persuaded that there is a Straussian conspiracy, we will view Bush as the "gentleman" of suitably patrician background, being used by Straussians for their own political purposes. Bush's frequent talk of God and faith keeps the masses in line. His rhetoric about "leaving no child behind" and building "a single nation of justice and opportunity" is helpful because belief in equality is "salutary for the functioning of society." Naturally, the powers behind the president make sure that his actions are the very opposite of what would be needed to bring about a nation of equals, for in their eyes true equality is impossible and the attempt to approach it more closely is dangerous. It could imperil what is much more important: protecting from the multitude those who are truly great, the "philosophers" and others who can aspire to "the peaks of human excellence."

I'm not particularly keen on conspiracy theories myself, but I have to admit that, as an explanation of why the Bush administration was so determined to go to war with Iraq, this one has some plausibility. Wolfowitz, Kristol, and Shulsky were key players in driving the United States into this war. Years before September 11, 2001, they wanted to overthrow Saddam Hussein, to secure America's oil supplies and to change the political complexion of the Middle East. They seized the opportunity of the "war on terror" to do so, despite the absence of any meaningful link between Saddam and the attacks on the World Trade Center and the Pentagon.

Could it really be the case, though, that Bush was a dupe in this situation? It is possible that he was given lines to speak—like the famous sentence about Iraq's attempt to purchase uranium in Africa—and not told how weak the basis for believing them was. The possibility that Bush did not really understand everything he was saying may provide an explanation of the utterly bizarre account of the reasons for attacking Iraq that he gave to reporters three months after the war ended. Speaking in the White House's Oval Office, in the presence of UN secretary-general Kofi Annan, Bush said, of Saddam Hussein, "we gave him a chance to allow the inspectors in, and he wouldn't let them in. And, therefore, after a reasonable request, we decided to remove him from power. . . ." Anyone who can, in all seriousness and sobriety, offer such a totally fictitious account of events of global significance that took place only three months earlier, and in which he has been the central figure, can hardly have had a firm grasp of the situation that he was supposedly directing. Perhaps Bush was not sober, or had ingested mind-altering substances, or was having a psychotic episode. None of those explanations is at all likely, but in the absence of some such explanation, Bush's astonishing statement makes it seem possible that on Iraq, he really was someone's puppet.

If the president was someone's puppet on Iraq, he might be someone's puppet on other issues, too. Not, presumably, Straussians—they are less well placed to influence Bush's domestic agenda. In the early days of the Bush presidency, it was suggested that Vice President Cheney was the controlling influence—when Cheney had heart problems, comedians joked that now Bush was "only a heartbeat away from the presidency." More recently, the finger has been pointed at Karl Rove, the president's chief political strategist. According to *Time* magazine, Rove "ranks among the most influential staff members ever to advise a President." There is no doubt that when Bush abandoned free-trade principles to protect America's steel industry, mostly located in key midwestern states, he was following Rove's advice. But some see Rove's hand in much more than that. Tom Daschle, leader of the Democrats in the Senate, accused him of trying to gain political advantage for the Republicans out of the national security debate. Rove himself admitted making use of the war on terror to benefit Republican candidates at the mid-term elections. That is, of course, not the same thing as waging the war on terror in order to benefit Republican candidates. But some find it hard to determine the limit of Rove's influence.

Bush's Ethical Failure

Whether he really believes in the fine phrases and lofty rhetoric that he uses, or is consciously using it to win public support, it is clear that Bush has no real interest in the policy details needed to achieve the aspirations he has voiced. He has failed to follow through on most of the commitments he has made to work for a better, more just society. He has said that deep, persistent poverty is unworthy of America's promise, but the number of Americans living in poverty increased in both 2001 and 2002. Instead of combating that increase, he has pressed for tax cuts that hobble the government's capacity to do anything about it. Rather than ensure that the nation he leads is a good global citizen, Bush has spurned institutions for global cooperation and set back the task of making the rule of law, rather than force, the determining factor in world affairs. He has launched an unnecessary war, costly in human lives and in dollars, with a final outcome that is still uncertain. His protection of the steel industry and his signature on a law authorizing the largest-ever subsidies to American farmers shows his strong rhetoric about free trade to be a brutal hypocrisy that is driving millions of impoverished farmers in other countries deeper into poverty. A comparison between the size of these subsidies and Bush's proposed increase in foreign aid makes his compassion look stingy.

Nor has Bush's own moral character stood up well to the test of high office. Handicapped by a naive idea of ethics as conformity to a small number of fixed rules, he has been unable to handle adequately the difficult choices that any chief executive of a major nation must face. A person of good moral character who takes a false step will admit it, seek to understand what went wrong, and try to prevent something similar from happening again. When Bush's use of misleading intelligence about Iraq was exposed, however, he blocked an open investigation into how he and his staff came to mislead the American public and the world about the basis on which he went to war. Instead, he made further inaccurate statements about when the intelligence was first known to be unsubstantiated and about the events that led to the decision to go to war. This may be the kind of behavior we expect from a politician more concerned about protecting his reputation than doing what is right. They are not the actions of a person of good moral character.

In the end, it is impossible to be sure how genuine Bush and those who advise him are about the ethics that he advocates. This book can therefore be seen as an attempt to cover all the possibilities. When Bush speaks about his ethics, he is either sincere or he is insincere. If he is insincere, he stands condemned for that alone. I have started with the opposite, more generous assumption: that Bush is sincere, and we should take his ethic seriously, assessing it on its own terms, and asking how well he has done by his own standards. Even if that assumption should be false, the task has been worth undertaking, for we now know that, sincerely held or not, Bush's ethic is woefully inadequate. He now trails behind him a string of broken promises and reversed policies, from his claim that he would champion the rights of states against the power of the federal government, to his pledge to bring the American dream to the poor, and his opposition to "nation-building." Instead of ushering in "the responsibility era" of which he often spoke, his tax cuts have pushed the budget further into the red, piling up problems for future generations. If what's needed in a president is, as Bush himself said in November 2000, a consistent message, then George W. Bush is a conspicuous failure.

Sources

Chapter 1: Introduction

1. Bush used the term "axis of evil" in his State of the Union address, Washington, D.C., January 29, 2002, *www.whitehouse.gov/news/releases/2002/01/20020129-11.html.* For his account of the U.S. as a moral nation, see Todd Purdum, "Bush's Moral Rectitude is a Tough Sell in Old Europe," *The New York Times,* January 30, 2003. His comment on free trade is from "A Distinctly American Internationalism," speech delivered at the Ronald Reagan Presidential Library, Simi Valley, California, November 19, 1999, available at *www.reagan.utexas.edu/resource/speeches/1983/30883b.htm,* see also "President Bush Addresses Council of the Americas," May 7, 2001, *www.usemb.gov.do/IRC/speeches/bush8.htm.* On the moral imperative of alleviating hunger, see "Statement by Secretary of Agriculture Ann M. Veneman Regarding World Food Day," October 16, 2002, USDA Release No. 0443.02, *www.usda.gov/news/releases/2002/10/0443.htm.* The statement about America's economic need for higher ethical standards is from "Remarks by the President on Corporate Responsibility," New York, July 9, 2002, *www.whitehouse.gov/news/releases/2002/07/print/20020709-4.html.* Finally on the universality of moral truth, see "Remarks by the President at 2002 Graduation Exercise of the United States Military

Academy," West Point, June 1, 2002, *www.whitehouse.gov/news/releases/2002/06/20020601-3.html.*

2. I thank Campbell Goodloe Hackett for her assistance in compiling the figures on Bush's use of the term "evil." They are based on a search of all Bush's speeches listed on the White House website, *www.whitehouse.gov,* up to June 16, 2003.

3. Bush's endorsement of using moral terms is from his *A Charge to Keep,* William Morrow, New York, 1999, p. 11.

4. The quotes from Bush's second inaugural speech as governor of Texas are from *A Charge to Keep,* p. 11. For his conversation with Billy Graham, see the same source, p. 136, and Molly Ivins and Lou Dubose, *Shrub: The Short but Happy Political Life of George W. Bush,* Random House, New York, 2000, p. 59.

Chapter 2: A Single Nation of Justice and Opportunity

11. The "It's your money" quote is from "Remarks by the President at Tax Family Event," Kirkwood Community Center, St. Louis, Missouri, February 20, 2001, *www.whitehouse.gov/news/releases/2001/02/20010220-5.html.* The other two quotes in the same paragraph are from a speech Bush gave in Michigan on November 4, 2000, and from his message to Congress outlining his budget, February 27, 2001.

12. The figures for the cuts enacted by the Economic Growth and Tax Relief Reconciliation Act of 2001 come from: Joint Committee on Taxation, Estimated Budget Effects of the Conference Agreement for H.R. 1836 [1]: Fiscal Years 2001–2011 (May 26, 2001).

12–13. The estimated cost of the 2003 tax cut is from David Rosenbaum, "A Tax Cut Without End?" *The New York Times,* May 23, 2003. The *Financial Times* comment is from "Tax Lunacy," *Financial Times,* May 23, 2003.

13. David Frum's term "folk libertarianism" occurs on p. 58 of his book *The Right Man: The Surprise Presidency of George W.*

Bush, Random House, New York, 2003. Robert Nozick's more sophisticated argument for libertarianism can be found in his *Anarchy, State, and Utopia*, Basic Books, New York, 1977. On Bush's support for education spending, see his remarks at the presentation of National Teacher of the Year Awards, April 23, 2001, *www.whitehouse.gov/news/releases/2001/04/2001042316.html,* where he said "I support historic new levels of education funding," and his speech on the "No child left behind" legislation, January 8, 2002, *www.whitehouse.gov/news/releases/2003/01/20030108-4.html.* He refers to "priorities" and "needs" in his budget outline message to Congress on February 27, 2001.

14–15. I am indebted here to Liam Murphy and Thomas Nagel's fine work, *The Myth of Ownership,* Oxford University Press, New York, 2002, especially pp. 8–10, 31–37.

16. For Herbert Simon's argument about the minor role played by individual effort, see his "UBI and the Flat Tax," in Philippe Van Parijs, *What's Wrong With a Free Lunch?,* Beacon Press, Boston, 2001, pp. 35–366. Thanks to Brent Howard for directing my attention to this point.

17. The quote from Murphy and Nagel is from *The Myth of Ownership,* pp. 32–34.

18. The quote from the presidential debate in St. Louis, on October 17, 2000, can be found at *www.newsminute.com/bushgoredebate3.htm.* The first post-election quote is from "Remarks by the President on Tax Cut Plan," February 5, 2001, *www.whitehouse.gov* and the second from "Remarks by the President at Tax Family Reunion," February 7, 2001, *www.whitehouse.gov.*

19. The Bush spokesman, Scott Lindlaw, was quoted by Associated Press, February 5, 2001. The analysis of the impact of the 2001 tax cuts is from William Gale and Samara Potter, "An Economic Evaluation of the Economic Growth and Tax Relief Reconciliation Act of 2001," *National Tax Journal* 55 (2002), p. 147 and from Citizens for Tax Justice, *Year-by-Year Analysis of the Bush Tax Cuts Shows Growing Tilt to the Very Rich,* June 12, 2002,

www.ctj.org/html/gwb0602.htm. The analysis of the 2003 tax cut is from David Rosenbaum, "A Tax Cut Without End?" *The New York Times,* May 23, 2003, drawing on the graph, "How the Tax Breaks Would Fall," based on research by Deloitte and Touche; and from Paul Krugman, "A Radical Tax Cut," *The New York Times,* May 27, 2003.

21. On the proportion of the estate tax collected from the top 1 in 700 Americans, see Leonard Burman and William Gale, "The Estate Tax is Down, But Not Out," *Tax Policy Issues and Options,* 2 (March 2002), The Urban Institute, Washington, D.C., p. 3. The quote from Paul Krugman is from his "For Richer," *The New York Times Sunday Magazine,* October 20, 2002, p. 77. Bush made his "double taxing" objection to estate taxes in the October 17, 2000, presidential debate: *www.newsminute.com/bushgoredebate3.htm.* He used a similar argument against taxing dividends in his State of the Union address, January 28, 2003, *www.whitehouse.gov/news/releases/2003/01/20030128-19.html.*

21. On the proportion of stocks and bonds held by those with the highest incomes, see Richard Stevenson, "The Politics of Portfolios: Bush Bets on an Investor Class," *The New York Times,* January 7, 2003, and see also Richard Stevenson, "In Bush Math, Economy Equals Votes," *The New York Times,* May 25, 2003.

23–24. On comparisons of poverty and longevity in the U.S. and Europe, see Will Hutton, *The World We're In,* Little, Brown, London, 2002, p. 149, citing Lawrence Mishel, Jared Bernstein, and John Schmitt, *The State of Working America, 2000–2001,* Cornell University Press, Ithaca, 2001, p. 293; and *The World We're In,* p. 274, citing Timothy Smeeding, *Financial Poverty in Developed Countries: The Evidence from the Luxembourg Income Study* (UNDP 1997). See also Richard Freeman, "The U.S. Economic Model at Y2K; Lodestar for Advanced Capitalism," Working Paper 7757, National Bureau for Economic Research, June 2000, p. 28, Exhibit 4 (*http://papers.nber.org/papers/W7757*); Marque Miringoff and Marc Miringoff, *The Social Health of Nations,* Oxford University Press, New York, 1999; Organization for

Economic Cooperation and Development (OECD), *Health at a Glance,* Paris, 2001, pp. 66–67, Tables 1.1 and 1.2; and Paul Krugman, "For Richer," *The New York Times Sunday Magazine,* October 20, 2002, p. 67.

23–24. On comparisons of the concentration of wealth in America and other nations, see Will Hutton, *The World We're In,* p. 149; Congressional Budget Office, *Effective Federal Tax Rates, 1979–97,* Washington, D.C., October 2001, Table 1.2c, p. 134, cited by Kevin Phillips, *Wealth and Democracy,* Broadway, New York, 2002, p. 396; Paul Krugman, "For Richer," *The New York Times Sunday Magazine,* October 20, 2002, p. 64; U.S. Census Bureau, "Historical Income Tables—Income Equality," Table IE-3, available at *www.census.gov/hhes/income/histinc/ie3.html*; and Geoffrey Colvin, "The Great CEO Pay Heist," *Fortune,* June 11, 2001.

24. Bush's "what America is all about" statement is from the presidential debate in St. Louis, on October 17, 2000, *www.newsminute.com/bushgoredebate3.htm* and his "equal place at the starting line" is quoted by David Sanger, "Bush Touts Education Plan in Pennsylvania," *The New York Times,* April 2, 2002.

25–26. On the relationship between family earnings and getting a college degree, see Will Hutton, *The World We're In,* p. 155; see also the Educational Testing Service Policy Information Center report, "Toward Inequality: Disturbing Trends in Higher Education," *www.ets.org/research/pic/twtoc.html.* On the likelihood of rising—and staying—out of poverty, see Will Hutton, *The World We're In,* p. 152, citing Lawrence Mishel, Jared Bernstein, and John Schmitt, *The State of Working America, 2000–2001,* Cornell University Press, 2001, p. 395, table 7.16. Warren Buffett's "food stamps" remark is from Roger Lowenstein, *Buffett: The Making of An American Capitalist,* Random House, New York, 1995, p. 342. I owe this reference to John Grote. See his "Is Unlimited Inheritance Un-American?" *Responsible Wealth, www.responsiblewealth.org/tax_fairness/Estate_Tax/Estate_Tax_History_Grote.html.* For studies of the impact of inherited wealth on consumption and motivation, see Douglas Holtz-Eakin, David Joulfaian, and Harvey Rosen,

"The Carnegie Conjecture: Some Empirical Evidence," *Quarterly Journal of Economics,* 198 (1994) pp. 413–35, and David Joulfaian, "Taxing Wealth Transfers and Its Behavioral Consequences, *National Tax Journal,* 53 (2000) pp. 933–57; both cited in Leonard Burman and William Gale, "The Estate Tax is Down, But Not Out," *Tax Policy Issues and Options,* 2 (March 2002), The Urban Institute, Washington, D.C., p. 3.

26. The Buffett quote about repealing the estate tax is from David Cay Johnston, "Dozens of Rich Americans Join in Fight to Retain Estate Tax," *New York Times,* February 14, 2001. The quote from William Gates, Sr., is from his testimony to the Senate Committee on Finance, Subcommittee on Taxation and IRS Oversight, *www.senate.gov/~finance/031501wgtest.pdf.*

27. George W. Bush, "Foreword," in Melvin Olasky, *Compassionate Conservatism: What It Is, What It Does, and How It Can Transform America,* Free Press, New York, 2000, p. xi.

27. On the impact of redistribution on poverty, see Timothy Smeeding, Michael O'Higgins, and Lee Rainwater, eds., *Poverty, Inequality and Income Distribution in Comparative Perspective,* Harvester Wheatsheaf, Hemel Hempstead, 1990, pp. 31, 67. For the statement that, among the twenty-three higher-income OECD nations, the more equal ones have, on average, a higher income per capita, I am indebted to calculations by Brent Howard, based on OECD figures for per-capita GDP and GINI inequality estimates available from the Luxembourg Income Study website, *www.lisproject.org.*

28–29. For the passages cited from Melvin Olasky, see his *Compassionate Conservatism: What It Is, What It Does, and How It Can Transform America,* Free Press, New York, 2000, pp. 27, 30, 60, 69, 131, 133.

29–30. For Bush's positive response to the news of a shrinking surplus, see David Sanger, "President Asserts Shrunken Surplus May Curb Congress," *The New York Times,* August 25, 2001. On the cut in education spending, and the impact of Bush's tax changes on allowing tax deductions for charitable donations, see Dana Milbank, "President's Compassionate Agenda Lags," *The Washington Post,* December 26, 2002, p. A1.

30. John DiIulio is quoted in Elizabeth Becker, "A Bush Aide Faults Plan to Repeal Estate Tax" *The New York Times,* February 10, 2001.

31. For Bush's 2003 State of the Union address, see *www.whitehouse.gov/news/releases/2003/01/20030128-19.html.* On the increase in poverty, see Lynette Clemetson, "More Americans in Poverty in 2002, Census Study Says," *The New York Times,* September 27, 2002.

For Bush's switch to arguing that the tax cut was necessary to increase employment, see Richard Stevenson, "Job Report Leads Bush to Defend Reliance on Tax Cuts," *The New York Times,* September 6, 2003. A chart on losses and gains in each term of every president from Hoover to Bush appears as part of David Rosenbaum, "Bush Wants to Create More Jobs, but How?" *The New York Times,* September 28, 2003. Bush's statement about making the tax cut permanent is from "President Bush Discusses the Economy in Indianapolis," September 5, 2003, *www.whitehouse.gov/news/releases/2003/09/20030905-1.html.* Greenspan's comment was reported at *CNN Money,* "Warning of growing budget deficits, Fed chairman undercuts Bush, GOP arguments for tax cuts," February 11, 2003, *http://money.cnn.com/2003/02/11/news/economy/greenspan/.*

32. Bush's rejection of a "little bitty" tax cut is quoted in Elisabeth Bumiller, "With Help from a Democrat, Bush Pitches Tax Cut Plan," *The New York Times,* February 21, 2003, and Anon., "Bush in Push for Deep Tax Cuts," April 24, 2003, CBS News, *www.cbsnews.com/stories/2003/04/26/politics/main551230.shtml.* For Akerlof's comment on the budget deficit, see *"Das Akerlof-Interview im englischen Orginal," Der Spiegel,* July 29, 2003, online edition, *www.spiegel.de/wirtschaft/0,1518,258983,00.html.* For the *Financial Times* speculation, see "Tax Lunacy," *Financial Times,* May 23, 2003.

Chapter 3: The Culture of Life

34. The White House Fact Sheet on Stem Cells is available at *www.whitehouse.gov/news/releases/2001/08/20010809-1.html.*

36–37. For Specter's proposal and doubts about the availability of stem-cell lines suitable for research, see Nicholas Wade, "Specter Asks Bush to Permit More Embryonic Cell Lines," *The New York Times,* April 23, 2003; Elias Zerhouni, Testimony before the Senate Committee on Appropriations, Subcommittee on Labor, Health and Human Services, and Education, *Federal Funding for Stem Cell Research,* 108th Cong. (May 22, 2003). Gerald Schatten's comment is quoted in Sheryl Stolberg, "Stem Cell Research Is Slowed by Restrictions, Scientists Say," *The New York Times,* September 26, 2002.

39. For Bush's exhortation to young people against becoming parents, see Frank Bruni, *Ambling into History: The Unlikely Odyssey of George W. Bush,* HarperCollins, New York, 2002, p. 46.

42. For further discussion of when it is wrong to take the life of the developing human being, see Peter Singer, *Rethinking Life and Death,* St. Martin's Press, New York, 1995.

44. Hatch's comment is quoted in Jane Brody, "Weighing the Rights of Embryo Against Those of the Sick," *The New York Times,* December 18, 2001.

44–45. International statistics on the use of the death penalty are available from Amnesty International, *The Death Penalty Worldwide: Developments in 2002,* April 11, 2003, *www.amnestyusa.org/abolish/reports/dp_worldwide.html.* On Bush's use of the death penalty, see Molly Ivins and Lou Dubose, *Shrub: The Short but Happy Political Life of George W. Bush,* p. 142; Alan Berlow, "The Texas Clemency Memos," *The Atlantic,* July/August 2003; and Reuters, "Bush Unlikely to Soften Death Penalty Support," *The New York Times,* January 12, 2003. For Bush's comments in the presidential debates, see *www.newsminute.com/bushgoredebate2.htm* and *www.newsminute.com/bushgoredebate3.htm.*

45–47. The quote on the difference between abortion and the death penalty is from *A Charge to Keep*, p. 147. Bush used almost identical language on other occasions, for example, in an interview with *Catholic News Service* and *Our Sunday Visitor,* September 20, 2000, reported in Anon., "Bush opposes abortion, supports capital punishment," *America Press,* 183 (4), p. 4 (October 28, 2000). On people wrongly sentenced to death, see Death Penalty Information Center, "Innocence and the Death Penalty," *www.deathpenaltyinfo.org/innoc.html;* Michael Radelet and Hugo Bedau, *In Spite of Innocence,* Northeastern University Press, Boston, 1992; Steve Mills, Maurice Possley and Ken Armstrong, "Shadows of Doubt Haunt Executions: 3 Cases Weaken under Scrutiny," *Chicago Tribune,* December 17, 2000, and Steve Mills, "Questions of Innocence: Legal Roadblocks Thwart New Evidence on Appeal," *Chicago Tribune,* December 18, 2000; Associated Press, "Fla. Judge has 'Grave Doubts' on Guilt of Some Convicts Executed," *Washington Post,* December 25, 1998, p. A19. The critical study of the Death Penalty Information Center's list is by Ward Campbell, "'Innocence' Critique," *www.prodeathpenalty.com/DPIC.htm.* On Governor Ryan's actions, and the response, see Jodi Wilgoren, "Governor Assails System's Errors as He Empties Illinois Death Row," *The New York Times,* January 12, 2003; Reuters, "Bush Unlikely to Soften Death Penalty Support," *The New York Times,* January 12, 2003; Bill Heltzel, "Students Recount Freeing Innocent from Death Row," *Post-Gazette,* February 7, 1999, *www.post-gazette.com/regionstate/19990207cara3.asp.*

47–48. Bush claims that the death penalty is a deterrent in *A Charge to Keep,* p. 147. He repeated the claim in the third presidential debate *www.newsminute.com/bushgoredebate3.htm.* For studies indicating that the death penalty is not a deterrent, see Raymond Bonner and Ford Fessenden, "Absence of Executions: A Special Report," *New York Times,* September 22, 2000; Ernie Thompson, "Effects of an Execution on Homicides in California," *Homicide Studies,* vol. 3, pp. 129–50 (1999); William Bailey, "Deterrence, Brutalization, and the Death Penalty: Another Examination of Oklahoma's Return to Capital Punishment," *Criminology,* vol. 36, pp. 711–33 (1998); Keith

Harries and Derral Cheatwood, *The Geography of Execution: The Capital Punishment Quagmire in America,* Rowman and Littlefield, Lanham, MD, 1997; John Sorenson, Robert Wrinkle, Victoria Brewer, and James Marquart, "Capital Punishment and Deterrence: Examining the Effect of Executions on Murder in Texas," *Crime and Delinquency,* vol. 45, pp. 481–93 (1999).

49. Bush's support of the death penalty for the mentally retarded is described in Molly Ivins and Lou Dubose, *Shrub,* pp. 144–45. For the execution of Terry Washington, see Alan Berlow, "The Texas Clemency Memos," *The Atlantic,* July/August 2003. The Supreme Court stopped such executions in *Atkins v. Virginia* (008452) 536 U.S. 304 (2002).

50–52. The civilian toll in Afghanistan has been estimated at 1,000–1,300 while for Iraq (as of December 2003) estimates range from 3,200 to 9,766. (The lower figure does not include casualties that occurred after April 20, when major military combat operations ceased.) For Afghanistan, see: Craig Nelson, "U.S. Silence and Power of Weaponry Conceal Scale of Civilian Toll," *Sydney Morning Herald,* January 26, 2002; Ian Traynor, "Afghans Are Still Dying as Air Strikes Go On. But No One Is Counting," *The Guardian,* February 12, 2002; John Donnelly and Anthony Shadid, "Civilian Toll in U.S. Raids Put at 1,000. Bombing Flaws, Manhunt Cited," *The Boston Globe,* February 17, 2002; David Zucchino, "In the Taliban's Eyes, Bad News was Good," *Los Angeles Times,* June 3, 2002. See also Carl Conetta's careful assessment of civilian casualties: "Operation Enduring Freedom: Why a Higher Rate of Civilian Bombing Casualties," Project on Defense Alternatives, *Briefing Report #11,* The Commonwealth Institute, Cambridge, MA, 2002, *www.comw.org/pda/0201oef.html.* The estimate of 3,200 civilian casualties in Iraq from the war up to April 20, 2003, is the lowest estimate given by Carl Conetta in "The Wages of War: Iraqi Combatant and Noncombatant Fatalities in the 2003 Conflict," Project on Defense Alternatives, *Research Monograph #8, http://www.comw.org/pda/0310rm8exsum.html.* Conetta allows for a margin of error of 550, so his midpoint estimate is 3,750 and his upper estimate is 4,300. A less conservative estimate that continues to be updated as additional civilian casualties are reported puts the total, as of December 6, 2003, between 7,935 and 9,766. See *http://www.iraqbodycount.net*.

The accounts of episodes involving civilian casualties in Afghanistan are drawn from the articles by Donnelly and Shadid, Conetta, Nelson and Traynor, cited above, as well as from Carlotta Gall, "In Afghanistan, Violence Stalls Renewal Effort," *The New York Times,* April 26, 2003; Carlotta Gall, "Afghan Villagers Torn by Grief After U.S. Raid Kills Nine Children, *The New York Times,* December 8, 2003; Associated Press, "Six Children Killed in Afghan Raid, U.S. Military Says," *The New York Times,* December 10, 2003.

For Bush's statement about the care taken to avoid civilian casualties in Iraq, see "Remarks by the President in Commencement Address to United States Coast Guard Academy," May 21, 2003, *www.whitehouse.gov/news/releases/2003/05/20030521-2.html*. Rumsfeld's approval of raids likely to kill civilians is described in Michael Gordon, "U.S. Air Raids in '02 Prepared for War in Iraq," *The New York Times,* July 20, 2003. The account of the Iraqi family killed in the Basra raid is from Mark Santora, "For Family that Lost 10 to Bomb, Only Memories and Grief Remain," *The New York Times,* May 11, 2003. For confirmation that the raid missed its intended target, see Bill Brink, "Former Iraqi Official Known as 'Chemical Ali' Is Captured," *The New York Times,* August 21, 2003.

52. *The Challenge of Peace: God's Promise and Our Response,* published by the United States Conference of Catholic Bishops, Washington, D.C., 1983, is available at *www.osjspm.org/cst/cp.htm*.

53. Jean Bethke Elshtain is quoted from her *Just War against Terror: The Burden of American Power in a Violent World*, Basic Books, New York, 2003, p. 65.

53–54. Rumsfeld's claim is quoted by Craig Nelson, "Concern Grows over US Strategy, Tactics in Afghanistan," *Cox News Service,* October 29, 2001, and Franks's statement is in John Donnelly and Anthony Shadid, "Civilian Toll in U.S. Raids Put at 1,000,

Bombing Flaws, Manhunt Cited," *The Boston Globe,* February 17, 2002. For the comparison of civilian casualties in Kosovo and Afghanistan, see Carl Conetta, "Operation Enduring Freedom: Why a Higher Rate of Civilian Bombing Casualties."

54. The Pentagon spokesperson's remarks are quoted in John Donnelly and Anthony Shadid, "Civilian Toll in U.S. Raids Put at 1,000, Bombing Flaws, Manhunt Cited," *The Boston Globe,* February 17, 2002.

55–56. The casualties of the attempt to kill Saddam Hussein are referred to by Jane Perlez, "Continued Air Assaults on City Follow Attempt to Kill Hussein," *The New York Times,* April 8, 2003, and David Johnston, "Hussein Fate after Attack Still Unclear," *The New York Times,* April 9, 2003, p. B4. On the raid on the convoy on Syria's border, see Seymour Hersh, "The Syrian Bet," *The New Yorker,* July 28, 2003, and Hersh's interview with Amy Goodman, "How Bush Sacrificed the War on Al Qaeda for the War on Iraq," *www.democracynow.org/article.pl?sid=03/07/24/1513238*. Rutter's "five seconds" rule is quoted by Steven Lee Myers, "Anger and Warning After Suicide Bomb," *The New York Times,* March 31, 2003, p. A1, and the army's defense of this action is described in Brian Knowlton, "Army Defends Killing of Civilians at Checkpoint," *International Herald Tribune,* April 2, 2003, p. 6. Knickmeyer's report is quoted in the article by Jane Perlez cited above.

56–58. For Bush's "low collateral" order, see Bob Woodward, *Bush At War,* Simon & Schuster, New York, 2002, p. 208. Among the U.S. newspaper discussions of civilian casualties in Afghanistan were Edward Cody, "Taliban Claims Large Civilian Casualties; Afghan Rulers Increase Efforts to Win Support From Islamic World," *The Washington Post,* October 12, 2001, p. A23; Jonathan Weisman, "Civilian Death Count Disputed," *USA Today,* October 16, 2001, p. 3A; Edward Epstein, "U.S. Battles to Justify Bombings to Muslims; It Rejects Taliban Tab of Civilian Deaths," *San Francisco Chronicle,* October 16, 2001. Musharraf's plea for a halt was reported in John Burns, "Pakistan Leader Renews Plea for Early End to Raids, Fearing Muslim Unrest," *The New York Times,* October 24, 2001. Bush's concern with the public relations impact of civilian casualties in Afghanistan is described in *Bush At War,* pp. 272–73, and in respect of Iraq, in "Full Text of Brokaw's Interview with Bush" (An interview with Tom Brokaw of NBC News), *The New York Times,* April 25, 2003.

59. Michael Walzer's requirement that military forces be prepared to make sacrifices to avoid civilian casualties is defended in his *Just and Unjust Wars,* Penguin, Harmondsworth, 1980, p. 155.

60. Bush's United Nations speech of November 10, 2001, is available at *www.whitehouse.gov/news/releases/2001/11/20011103.html.* For bin Laden's interview with Tayseer Alouni, see CNN.com, "Transcript of Bin Laden's October interview," February 5, 2002, *www.cnn.com/2002/WORLD/asiapcf/south/02/05/binladen.transcript/*

Chapter 4: The Freest Nation in the World?

64. Bush's philosophy of trusting individuals to make the right decisions is taken from *A Charge to Keep,* p. 235.

65. "Texans can run Texas" is from *A Charge to Keep,* p. 44. For the comments from the presidential debates, see *www.newsminute.com/bushgoredebate2.htm* and *www.newsminute.com/bushgoredebate3.htm.* The remarks on gay marriage and the Confederate flag come from the debates between Republican candidates for the presidential nomination on the *Larry King Show,* February 15, 2000, and in West Columbia, South Carolina, January 7, 2000, while that on medical marijuana was reported in Susan Feeney, "Bush Backs States' Rights on Marijuana," *The Dallas Morning News,* October 20, 1999. The rejection of "big, exploding federal government" comes from the first presidential debate, *www.newsminute.com/bushgoredebate1.htm.*

66–67. For the number of people using Oregon's physician-assisted suicide law, see Office of Disease Prevention and Epidemiology, Department of Human Services, State of Oregon, *Fifth Annual Report on Oregon's Death with Dignity Act,* March 6, 2003, p. 4; available at *www.ohd.hr.state.or.us/chs/pas/02pasrpt.pdf.*

68. The court decision cited is *United States v. Moore*, 423 U.S. 122, 136 (1975); 21 U.S.C. § 801(3) (2001).

69. For the brief filed by bioethicists and lawyers, see *www.compassionindying.org/ashcroft_ruling/bioethicists_brief.pdf* Ari Fleischer's statement of the president's beliefs is from Associated Press's State and Local Wire Service, November 7, 2001.

70. See Nelson Lund, "Why Ashcroft is Wrong on Assisted Suicide," *Commentary,* 113 (2), February 2002, pp. 50–55.

70. See Conrad F. Meier "Ashcroft Rebuked in Oregon Court," *Health Care News,* June 2002, *www.heartland.org/health/jun02/suicide.htm.*

71–72. On the medical marijuana raids, see "Ashcroft's Other War," *Rolling Stone,* December 27, 2001, p. 34, *www.mapinc.org/drugnews/v01/n2128/a05.html/126;* Ethan Nadelman, "The Hospice Raid and the War on Drugs," *The San Diego Union Tribune,* September 19, 2002. Lockyer's comment is quoted in Heidi Lypps, "The Crackdown on Medical Marijuana," *CounterPunch,* September 17, 2002.

72. For the comment on the need to codify marriage as between a man and a woman, see "President Bush's Rose Garden News Conference," *The New York Times,* July 30, 2003. On the removal of federal controls from wetlands, see Douglas Jehl, "U.S. Plan Could Ease Limits on Wetlands Development," *The New York Times,* January 11, 2003.

73. On Gale Norton's rejection of the federal government veto over mining that causes irreparable damage to the environment, see: Editorial, "A Bad Law's Birthday," *The New York Times,* May 13, 2002, and Timothy Egan, "Norton Charts a Different Course for the Interior Department," *The New York Times,* August 19, 2001. On reviews of western landholdings, see Timothy Egan, "Bah, Wilderness! Reopening a Frontier to Development," and Editorial, "The End of Wilderness," both in *The New York Times,* May 4, 2003. Norton stated her position in "Helping Citizens

Conserve Their Own Land—and America's," *The New York Times,* April 20, 2002, a response to the editorial, "Nature Overrun," *The New York Times,* April 4, 2002, p. A22.

73–74. On the Bush administration's impact on the EPA, see Joan Lowy, "Administration Tweaks All Aspects of Environmental Policy," Scripps Howard News Service, December 19, 2002, and Eric Schaeffer, "Clearing the Air: Why I Quit Bush's EPA," *The Washington Monthly,* July/August 2002, *www.washingtonmonthly.com/features/2001/0207.schaeffer.html.*

75. The Paine quotation is from his *Dissertations on First Principles of Government* (1795).

75–76. On the Padilla case, see Timothy Edgar, "Interested Persons Memo on the Indefinite Detention Without Charge of American Citizens as 'Enemy Combatants'," ACLU, September 13, 2002, *www.aclu.org/SafeandFree/SafeandFree.cfm/ID=10673&c=206.* The *Milligan* case, *Ex parte Milligan,* 71 U.S. (4. Wall.) 2, 1866, at 120–21, is cited in the ACLU *Brief in the case of Jose Padilla, Donna R. Newman v. George W. Bush, Donald Rumsfeld, John Ashcroft and Commander M. A. Marr,* New York, September 26, 2002. On Congress's prohibition of the detention of American citizens, see 18 U.S.C. §4001 (a).

76. For Judge Mukasy's comments, and the remarks by the ACLU and Tribe, see Benjamin Weiser, "Judge Says Man Can Meet with Lawyer to Challenge Detention as Enemy Plotter," *The New York Times,* December 5, 2002, p. A24.

77. Judge Doumar's comments are quoted from Tom Jackman, "Judge Skewers U.S. Curbs on Detainee," *The Washington Post,* August 14, 2002, p. A10. See also Neil Lewis, "U.S. Is Allowed to Hold Citizen as Combatant," *The New York Times,* January 9, 2003, and Neil Lewis, "Sudden Shift on Detainee," *The New York Times,* December 4, 2003.

78. See Editorial, "Material Concerns," *The Washington Post,* November 27, 2002, and for the Justice Department's report, Eric

Lichtblau, "Justice Department Lists Use of New Power to Fight Terror," *The New York Times,* May 21, 2003.

78–80. America's "greatest export is freedom" is from *A Charge to Keep,* p. 240. Safire's comment is from his column "Kangaroo Courts," *The New York Times,* November 26, 2001, and the Spanish judge was cited by Ronald Dworkin, "The Threat to Patriotism," *The New York Review of Books,* February 28, 2002. For Bush's defense of the tribunals, see Mike Allen and Susan Schmidt, "Bush Defends Secret Tribunals for Terrorism Suspects," *The Washington Post,* November 30, 2001, p. A28, cited in Ronald Dworkin, "The Threat to Patriotism." Dworkin's own comment is from the same essay.

80–81. Mary Robinson is quoted in Anon., "UN Speaks Out on Afghan Detainees," *BBC News,* February 12, 2002, *http://news.bbc.co.uk/1/hi/world/americas/1816648.stm.* For the British Court of Appeal's opinion, see *The Times* (London), Anon., "Court Unable to Challenge Objectionable Detention," November 8, 2002, p. 49. On the Supreme Court's rebuff of Olsen's assertion, see Linda Greenhouse, "Analysis: Guantánamo Case About Federal Turf," *New York Times,* November 12, 2003.

81. For the solicitor general's report, see Eric Lichtblau, "U.S. Will Tighten Rules on Holding Terror Suspects," *The New York Times,* June 13, 2003.

82–83. On U.S. interrogation techniques, see Dana Priest and Barton Gellman, "U.S. Decries Abuse but Defends Interrogations," *The Washington Post,* December 26, 2002, p. A1. For the U.S. State Department report, see U.S. Department of State, Bureau of Democracy, Human Rights, and Labor, *Country Reports on Human Rights Practices—2002* (March 31, 2003). For Jordan, see *www.state.gov/g/drl/rls/hrrpt/2002/18279pf.htm* and for Azerbaijan, *www.state.gov/g/drl/rls/hrrpt/2002/18353.htm.*

83–84. The U.S. officials' comments are cited in Dana Priest and Barton Gellman, "U.S. Decries Abuse but Defends Interrogations." On the U.S. response to allegations of torture, see Alan

Cooperman, "CIA Interrogation Under Fire," *The Washington Post,* December 28, 2002, p. A9.

84. On the assassinations in Yemen, see Reuters, "Senators Support CIA Anti-Terror Effort," Reuters, December 15, 2002, *www.miami.com/mld/miami/news/4741736.htm.*

85–86. Dworkin is quoted from "The Threat to Patriotism," *The New York Review of Books,* February 28, 2002. On conditions in Guantánamo, see Carlotta Gall with Neil Lewis, "Tales of Despair from Guantánamo," *The New York Times,* June 17, 2003; Editorial, "The American Prison Camp," *The New York Times,* October 16, 2003.

88. For a comparison of end-of-life decisions in the Netherlands and in Australia, see Helga Kuhse, Peter Singer, Maurice Rickard, Malcolm Clark, and Peter Baume, "End-of-life decisions in Australian medical practice," *Medical Journal of Australia,* 166:4 (February 17, 1997) pp. 191–96.

Chapter 5: The Power of Faith

91. Sources for the statements about Bush's Christian practices and beliefs are, in the order in which they are mentioned: Richard Powellson, "Bush Says He Is at Peace with Decision on Iraq," Scripps Howard News Service, March 4, 2003; "Remarks by the President at the 20th Anniversary of the National Endowment for Democracy, Washington, D.C., November 6, 2003," *www.whitehouse .gov/news/releases/2003/11/20031106-2.html;* "President Bush Discusses Iraq in National News Conference," March 6, 2003, *www.white house.gov/news/releases/2003/03/print/20030306-8.html; A Charge to Keep,* p. 6; George W. Bush, "Duty of Hope" speech, Indianapolis, Indiana, July 22, 1999; David Frum, *The Right Man: The Surprise Presidency of George W. Bush,* Random House, New York, 2003, pp. 4–5; Bob Woodward, *Bush at War,* p. 65; Frum, *The Right Man,* p. 13; "Full Text of Brokaw's Interview with Bush," *The New York Times,* April 25, 2003; Elisabeth Bumiller, "Talk of

Religion Provokes Amens as Well as Anxiety," *The New York Times,* April 22, 2002; Mike Allen, "Comforting Words as a Matter of Faith," *The Washington Post,* February 3, 2003, p. A6.

92. On the religious beliefs of Americans, see Humphrey Taylor, Harris Poll #52, September 13, 2000, *www.harrisinteractive.com/harris_poll/index.asp?PID=112;* Richard Morin, "Keeping the Faith," *The Washington Post,* January 12, 1998; Richard Morin, "Do Americans Believe in God?" *The Washington Post,* April 24, 2000; "Among Wealthy Nations, U.S. Stands Alone in Its Embrace of Religion," Pew Global Attitudes Project, Pew Research Center for the People and the Press, December 19, 2002, *http://people press.org/reports/pdf/167.pdf;* Nicholas Kristof, "Believe It, or Not," *The New York Times,* August 15, 2003.

92–93. On Chancellor Schröder's refusal to say "so help me God," see Bill Keller, "God and George Bush," *The New York Times,* May 17, 2003. On American voters' unwillingness to vote for an atheist, see Peter Grier, "Voters Like Faith—But Not Theology," *Christian Science Monitor,* August 10, 2000, *www.csmonitor.com/durable/2000/08/10/fp1s4-csm.shtml.*

93–95. Bush's statements about his faith-based initiative are from "President Bush Implements Key Elements of his Faith-Based Initiative," Office of the Press Secretary, the White House, December 12, 2002, available at *www.whitehouse.gov/news/releases/2002/12/20021212-3.html.* On the plan to allow federal funds to be used for buildings where religious worship is held, see Eric Lichtblau, "Bush Plans to Let Religious Groups Get Building Aid," *The New York Times,* January 23, 2003. For evidence of selective acceptance of clients that makes the success of programs difficult to measure, see Melvin Olasky, *Compassionate Conservatism,* pp. 39–40. A skeptical view of the efficacy of faith-based programs is offered in Anna Greenberg, "Doing Whose Work? Faith-Based Organizations and Government Partnerships," in Mary Jo Bane, Brent Coffin, and Ronald Thiemann, eds., *Who Will Provide? The Changing Role of Religion in American Social Welfare,* Westview, Boulder, CO, 2000, pp. 191–92.

96–97. Clifford's views are taken from William K. Clifford, "The Ethics of Belief," in John Burr and Milton Goldinger, eds., *Philosophy and Contemporary Issues,* 9th ed., Prentice Hall, Upper Saddle River, N.J., 2004, pp. 148–49. Reprinted from William K. Clifford, *Lectures and Essays,* Macmillan, London, 1879. The quotes from Bush are from, in order of appearance, *A Charge to Keep,* p. 136 (two quotes), p. 138 (two quotes), p. 139 and p. 6.

For Bush's belief that only Christians have a place in heaven, see Molly Ivins and Lou Dubose, *Shrub: The Short But Happy Political Life of George W. Bush,* p. 58, quoting Sam Howe Verhovek. "Is There Room on a Republican Ticket for Another Bush?" *The New York Times Sunday Magazine,* September 13, 1998.

98. For Luke's reference to the location of the Sermon on the "Mount," see The Gospel According to Luke, 6:17–49. For scholarly views of the origin of the "sermon," see Robert Guelich, "Sermon on the Mount," *The Oxford Companion to the Bible,* New York: Oxford University Press, 1993, pp. 686–89; Harvey K. McArthur, *Understanding the Sermon on the Mount,* Harper and Brothers, New York, 1960. For Popper's view of the difference between science and religion, see his *The Logic of Scientific Discovery,* Routledge, London, 1977.

99. Bush's statement that he is "here for a reason" is cited by Bob Woodward, *Bush at War,* p. 205. For the description of him as "God's chosen man," see Interfaith Alliance, "President Plays the Christian Trump Card," February 26, 2003, *www.interfaithalliance.org/About/About.cfm?ID=4668&c=6.* Howard Fineman's "Bush and God" appeared in *Newsweek,* March 10, 2003.

100–101. For William K. Clifford, see "The Ethics of Belief," in John Burr and Milton Goldinger, eds., *Philosophy and Contemporary Issues,* p. 152. For Greg Thielmann, see David Sanger and James Risen, "CIA Chief Takes Blame in Assertion on Iraqi Uranium," *The New York Times,* July 12, 2003. Al Gore's "Remarks to MoveOn.org," were given on August 7, 2003, and are available at *www.moveon.org/gore-speech.html.*

102. The Bush quotes, and the appreciative comments from the audience about his "preaching" are from "President Bush Implements Key Elements of His Faith-Based Initiative," December 12, 2002, available at *www.whitehouse.gov/news/releases/2002/12/20021212-3.html.*

103. On "public reason," see Stephen Macedo, *Liberal Virtues,* Clarendon Press, Oxford, 1990, Chapter 2; John Rawls, "The Idea of Public Reason Revisited," *The University of Chicago Law Review* 64 (1997) p. 799; and John Horton, ed., *Liberalism, Multiculturalism and Toleration,* Macmillan, London, 1993.

104–105. On the "gag rule," see *www.whitehouse.gov/news/releases/20010123-5.html.* I owe this reference to International Women's Health Coalition, "Factsheet: Bush's Other War," *www.iwhc.org/index.cfm?fuseaction=page&pageID=468.*

The IWHC notes that although Bush says "It is my conviction that taxpayer funds should not be used to pay for abortions . . ." Federal law has prohibited the use of federal funds to pay for abortions since 1973. For Bush's comment on the source of the right to life, see "President Bush Signs Partial Birth Abortion Ban Act of 2003," November 5, 2003, *www.whitehouse.gov/news/releases/2003/11/20031105-1.html.*

105. Bush described marriage as "sacred" in the second presidential debate, available at *www.newsminute.com/bushgore debate2.htm.* On his lack of support for gays and lesbians, see Sheryl Stolberg, "Vocal Gay Republicans Upsetting Conservatives," *The New York Times,* June 1, 2003. On Bush's support for Santorum, see Reuters, "Bush Sees Embattled Santorum as 'Inclusive Man,' " April 25, 2003, *www.publicbroadcasting.net/wbur/news.newsmain?action=article&ARTICLE_ID=488030.* On the Supreme Court's decision, see CNN, "Supreme Court Strikes Down Texas Sodomy Law," June 27, 2003, *http://us.cnn.com/2003/LAW/06/26/scotus.sodomy/.*

105–106. On abstinence, the CDC Web site referred to is at *www.cdc.gov/nccdphp/dash/rtc/.* On condoms, see Laura Meckler, "President Bush says NO to Condoms," Associated Press,

September 30, 2002; *http://am-i-pregnant.com/aip.data/article/show/contraception/0/191680.shtml.* On both these issues, see also "Politics and Science," a Web site of Representative Henry Waxman, *www.house.gov/reform/min/politicsandscience/.* On the actions of the U.S. delegation at the Fifth Asian and Pacific Population Conference, see the speech made by Assistant Secretary of State Arthur E. Dewey, December 16, 2002, and the U.S. conditional proposal, December 14, 2002, available at *www. iwhc. org/index.cfm?fuseaction=page&pageID=487.* See also "U.S. Stance on Abortion and Condom Use Rejected at Population Conference," Associated Press, December 17, 2002. Again, these references are from the International Women's Health Coalition, "Factsheet: Bush's Other War," *www.iwhc.org/index.cfm?fuseaction=page&pageID=468.* See also Editorial, "The War Against Women," *The New York Times,* January 12, 2003.

106–107. On the HIV/AIDS initiative, see Elisabeth Bumiller, "Bush Pushes AIDS Plan Criticized by Some Conservatives," *The New York Times,* April 30, 2003, p. A22; Sheryl Stolberg, "$15 Billion AIDS Plan Wins Final Approval in Congress," *The New York Times,* May 22, 2003.

107. For opposition to the idea that "public reason" should exclude appeals to religious faith, see Richard John Neuhaus, *The Naked Public Square: Religion and Democracy in America,* Grand Rapids, MI: William B. Eerdmans Publishing Co., 2nd ed., 1996.

110–111. For DeLay's statements, see Paul Krugman, "Gotta Have Faith," *The New York Times,* December 17, 2002, and Alan Cooperman, "DeLay Criticized for 'Only Christianity' Remarks," *The Washington Post,* April 20, 2002, p. A5. Paige and the Baptist Joint Committee are cited by Brent Staples, "To Worship Freely, Americans Need a Little Elbow Room," *The New York Times,* April 27, 2003. Bush is quoted by Elisabeth Bumiller, "White House Letter: Talk of Religion Provokes Amens as Well as Anxiety" *New York Times,* April 22, 2002.

Chapter 6: Sharing the World

117. Condoleezza Rice is quoted from "Campaign 2000—Promoting the National Interest," *Foreign Affairs*, January–February 2000, *www.foreignpolicy2000.org/library/issuebriefs/readingnotes/fa_rice.html.*

118. Alexander Downer's statement, of May 2, 2002, can be found at *www.australianpolitics.com/news/2002/05/02-05-07a.shtml.* Robert Goodin is quoted from his "What Is So Special about Our Fellow Countrymen?" *Ethics*, 98 (1988) pp. 663–86, reprinted in Robert Goodin, *Utilitarianism as a Public Philosophy*, Cambridge University Press, Cambridge, 1995, p. 286.

120–21. On Gates's challenge and the initially inadequate U.S. proposal, see "Annan Issues Global AIDS Fund Plea," *CNN.com*, *www.cnn.com/2001/WORLD/africa/04/26/nigeria.annan.02/;* and Sheryl Gay Stolberg, "AIDS Fund Falls Short of Goal and U.S. Is Given Some Blame," *The New York Times*, February 13, 2002. For the Frist-Helms initiative, see "Frist and Helms Seek $500 Million Increase for AIDS," March 24, 2002; *www.senate.gov/~frist/Press/NewsReleases/02-047/02-047.html,* and for Bush's response, Associated Press, "Bush Proposes Spending $500 Million on AIDS," *The New York Times*, June 19, 2002; Jim Lobe, "Activists Slam Bush AIDS Initiative," Inter Press Service, June 20, 2002; *www.commondreams.org/headlines02/0620-02.htm.*

121. For details of Bush's AIDS bill, see Amy Goldstein and Dan Morgan, "Bush Signs $15 Billion AIDS Bill; Funding Questioned," *The Washington Post*, May 28, 2003, p. A02. *www.washingtonpost.com/ac2/wp-dyn/A46237-2003May27.*

122–24. On the Bush administration's projected increase in foreign aid, see the testimony of Andrew Natsios, Administrator, U.S. Agency for International Development, on the Millennium Challenge Account before the Senate Foreign Relations Committee, March 4, 2003, *http://foreign.senate.gov/hearings/NatsiosTestimony030304.pdf.* For comparative figures on foreign aid, see OECD, "Net ODA in 2001—as a Percentage of GNI," *www.oecd.org/pdf/M00037000/*

M00037873.pdf; OECD "Aid at a Glance Chart, United States" *www.oecd.org/gif/M000000000/M00000299.gif;* OECD "Aid at a Glance Chart, Denmark" *www.oecd.org/gif/M000000000/M00000278.gif.* On U.S. private aid, see World Bank, *World Development Indicators 2001,* table 6.8, *www.worldbank.org/data/wdi2001/.* For the comparison with earlier U.S. levels of foreign aid, see Isaac Shapiro and Nancy Birdsall, "How Does the Proposed Level of Foreign Economic Aid under the Bush Budget Compare with Historical Levels?" Center for Global Development and Center on Budget and Policy Priorities, March 20, 2002, *www.cbpp.org/3-14-02foreignaid.htm.* The amount Bush sought for the war with Iraq and its reconstruction can be found in: Executive Office of the President, "President Submits $74.7 Billion Supplemental Appropriations Request for Funding War on Terrorism," March 25, 2003, *www.whitehouse.gov/omb/pubpress/2003-06.pdf;* Thom Shanker, "Rumsfeld Doubles Estimate for Cost of Troops in Iraq, *The New York Times,* July 10, 2003; Elisabeth Bumiller, "Bush Seeks $87 billion and UN Aid for War Effort," *The New York Times,* September 8, 2003.

125–26. Jeffrey Sachs is quoted in Nicholas Kristof, "When Prudery Kills," *The New York Times,* October 8, 2003. For doubts about whether the funding for the AIDS initiative would be provided, see Amy Goldstein and Dan Morgan, "Bush Signs $15 Billion AIDS Bill; Funding Questioned," *The Washington Post,* May 28, 2003, p. A02. Andrew Natsios was testifying before the Senate Foreign Relations Committee, as cited above.

126–27. Bush's comments in support of free trade come from the following sources: *A Charge to Keep,* p. 235; George W. Bush, "A Distinctly American Internationalism," speech delivered at the Ronald Reagan Presidential Library, Simi Valley, California, November 19, 1999; *www.ransac.org/new-web-site/related/govt/testimony/bush-111999.html;* "Remarks by the President in Press Conference at Conclusion of the Summit of the Americas," April 22, 2001, *www.whitehouse.gov/news/releases/2001/04/2001042311*

.html; "President Bush Addresses Council of the Americas," May 7, 2001, *www.usemb.gov.do/IRC/speeches/bush8.htm;* "President Signs Trade Act of 2002," August 6, 2002; *www.whitehouse.gov/news/releases/2002/08/20020806-4.html;* and "President Delivers Commencement Address at Coast Guard," May 21, 2003; *www.whitehouse.gov/news/releases/2003/05/20030521-2.html*

127. On the cost of trade barriers against exports from poor nations to rich ones, see Oxfam, *Rigged Rules and Double Standards: Trade, Globalisation, and the Fight against Poverty,* 2002, p. 5; available at *www.maketradefair.com.* Oxfam's evaluation of U.S. policies can be found in Chapter 4. Bush supported AGOA in his "Remarks to the African Growth and Opportunity Act Summit," January 15, 2003, available at *www.whitehouse.gov/news/releases/2003/01/20030115.html.* But the fall in overall U.S. imports from sub-Saharan nations is documented in *2003 Comprehensive Report on U.S. Trade and Investment Policy Toward Sub-Saharan Africa and Implementation of the African Growth and Opportunity Act: A Report Submitted by the President of the United States to the United States Congress, May 2003*, p. 18. *www.ustr.gov/reports/2003agoa.pdf.*

128–29. Bush's remark about the confident demolishing trade barriers is from his Candidacy Announcement Speech, Cedar Rapids, Iowa, June 12, 1999; cited on *www.issues2000.org/Celeb/George_W__Bush_Free_Trade.htm.* Shi Guangsheng is quoted in Paul Magnusson, "Bush Trade Policy: Crazy-Quilt Like a Fox," *BusinessWeek online,* April 15, 2002; *www.businessweek.com/magazine/content/02_15/b3778058.htm.* For the *Weekly Standard* comment, see David Brooks, for the Editors, "The Problem with K Street Conservatism," *Weekly Standard,* June 24, 2002; and for George Will's view, see his "Bending for Steel," *The Washington Post,* March 3, 2002, p. A21. On the outcome, see Elizabeth Becker, "U.S. Tariffs on Steel are Illegal, World Trade Organization Says," *The New York Times,* November 11, 2003, and Richard Stevenson and Elizabeth Becker, "Bush Avoids a Trade War by Lifting Steel Tariffs," *The New York Times,* December 5, 2003.

129–130. For the *The Wall Street Journal*'s comment on the farm bill, see Editorial, "The Farm State Pig-Out," *The Wall Street Journal,* May 2, 2002. Bush's comment was reported in Elizabeth Becker, "House Passes the Farm Bill, Which Bush Says He'll Sign," *The New York Times,* May 3, 2002. On the international impact of the bill, see Elizabeth Becker, "Raising Farm Subsidies, U.S. Widens International Rift," *The New York Times,* June 15, 2002, p. A3; John Boehner and Cal Dooley, "This Terrible Farm Bill," *The Washington Post,* May 2, 2002, p. A23; and T. Randall Fortenbery and Bill Dobson, "Analysis of Key Non-Dairy Provisions of the Farm Security and Rural Investment Act of 2002," *Marketing and Policy Briefing Paper No. 77,* Department of Agricultural and Applied Economics, College of Agricultural and Life Sciences, University of Wisconsin, Madison, May 2002, pp. 16–17. For Pascal Lamy's comment, see Senator John McCain, "Farm Bill 'Appalling Breach' of Federal Spending Responsibility," press release, May 7, 2002, *www.senate.gov/~mccain/index.cfm?fuse action=Newscenter.Viewpork&Content_id=508.* James Wolfensohn's comparison of the size of the subsidies with the amount of foreign aid is from his "A Partnership for Development and Peace," keynote address delivered at the Woodrow Wilson International Center, March 6, 2002; *www.worldbank.org/html/extdr/extme/jdwsp030602.htm.* The Brazilian claim is discussed in Randall Fortenbery and Bill Dobson, "Analysis of Key Non-Dairy Provisions of the Farm Security and Rural Investment Act of 2002," pp. 17–18. On subsidies for cotton growers and their impact on poor African farmers, see Peter Beinart, "Grain of Salt," *The New Republic,* June 9, 2003; Center for International Development at Harvard University, "WTO Public Symposium 2003: Developing Countries and the WTO," *www.cid.harvard.edu/cidtrade/geneva/cotton.html;* "United States Dumping on World Agricultural Markets: Can Trade Rules Help Farmers?" Institute for Agriculture and Trade Policy, Minneapolis, MN, no date, Cancun Series Paper No. 1; *www.tradeobservatory.org/library/uploadedfiles/United_States_Dumping_on_World_Agricultural_Ma.pdf.*

132–34. On the Bush administration's rejection of the ICC, see Neil Lewis, "U.S. Rejects All Support for New Court on Atrocities," *The New York Times,* May 7, 2002. The reaction evoked by this rejection is described in Felicity Barringer, "U.S. Resolution on World Court Revives Hostility," *The New York Times,* June 11, 2003. Richard Dicker is quoted in Elizabeth Becker, "U.S. Suspends Aid to 35 Countries over New International Court," *The New York Times,* July 2, 2003, and the EU's support for the court is reported in "EU Backs New International Court," *Sify News,* June 22, 2003, *http://sify.com/news/international/fullstory.php?id=13177817*. On Australian objections to the standards of justice to be applied by the U.S. to those captured in Afghanistan, see Annabel Crabb, "U.S. lashed over 'double standards' on Hicks trial," and Robert McClelland, "Hicks' trial will not be justice as we know it," both in *The Age* (Melbourne) July 10, 2003.

135. Bush's "first things first" statement is reported in Edmund Andrews, "Bush Angers Europe by Eroding Pact on Warming," *The New York Times,* April 1, 2001, p. A1. Ari Fleischer's comment is from his press briefing, May 7, 2001, *www.whitehouse.gov/news/briefings/20010507.html.* U.S. emission levels are given in U.S. Department of State, *U.S. Climate Action Report 2002,* Washington, D.C., May 2002, Chapter 3, *www.epa.gov/globalwarming/publications/car/index.html.*

136. For the censoring of the EPA report on global warming, see Andrew Revkin with Karen Seelye, "Report by the EPA Leaves out Data on Climate Change," *The New York Times,* June 19, 2003; editorial, "Emissions Omissions," *The Boston Globe,* June 21, 2003, p. A14.

137. On the administration's argument that global warming is too uncertain to warrant costly preventative measures, see Andrew Revkin, "U.S. Sees Problems in Climate Change," *The New York Times,* June 3, 2002, p. A1; Office of the Press Secretary, White House, press release: "President Bush Discusses Global Climate Change," June 11, 2001, *www.whitehouse.gov/news/releases/2001/06/20010611-2.html;* John Heilprin, "Bush Global Warming Re-

search Plan Ripped," Associated Press, February 26, 2003, *www.nrdc.org/news/newsDetails.asp?nID=898.* On the precautionary principle and climate change, see Samuel Loewenberg, "Precaution is for Europeans," *The New York Times,* May 18, 2003, Sec. 4, p. 14; see also Cass Sunstein, "Beyond the Precautionary Principle," *University of Pennsylvania Law Review,* 151:3 (January 2003) 1003–1058.

138. For Bush's comment on the Kyoto Protocol, see *www.newsminute.com/bushgoredebate2.htm.*

138–39. On the relative contributions to global warming of the U.S. and developing countries, see Duncan Austin, José Goldemberg, and Gwen Parker, "Contributions to Climate Change: Are Conventional Metrics Misleading the Debate?" World Resource Institute Climate Protection Initiative, Climate Notes, *www.igc.org/wri/cpi/notes/metrics.html,* and G. Marland, T. A. Boden, R. J. Andres, 2000. "Global, Regional, and National CO_2 Emissions," in *Trends: A Compendium of Data on Global Change*, Carbon Dioxide Information Analysis Center, Oak Ridge National Laboratory, U.S. Department of Energy, Oak Ridge, TN, *http://cdiac.esd.ornl.gov/trends/emis/em_cont.htm.*

140. The figures on emissions are from 1996. See G. Marland, T. A. Boden, and R. J. Andres, "Global, Regional, and National Fossil Fuel CO_2 Emissions," *http://cdiac.esd.ornl.gov/trends/emis/top96.cap.*

142. The CIA figures on emissions efficiency are from Andrew Revkin, "Sliced Another Way: Per Capita Emissions," *The New York Times,* June 17, 2001. On China's improvement, see G. Marland, T. A. Boden, R. J. Andres, 2000. "Global, Regional, and National CO_2 Emissions," *http://cdiac.esd.ornl.gov/trends/emis/em_cont.htm.*

Chapter 7: War: Afghanistan

143. For Bush's September 11 remarks, see "Statement by the President in His Address to the Nation," September 11, 2001, *www.whitehouse.gov/news/releases/2001/09/20010911-16.html.*

144. Bush has often claimed that America is a peace-loving nation. See, for example Ron Fournier, "President Honors Veterans, Heads to Power-Short California," Associated Press, May 28, 2001; and "Remarks by the President in Commencement Address to United States Coast Guard Academy," May 21, 2003, *www.whitehouse.gov/news/releases/2003/05/20030521-2.html.* Bob Woodward, in *Bush at War*, p. 30, reveals that it was Bush and Rice who made the decision to draw no distinction between terrorists and those who harbor them.

145. On Cuban terrorists in Miami, see Juan Tomayo, "Anti-Castro Plots Seldom Lead to Jail in U.S.," *The Miami Herald,* July 23, 1998.

145–46. On Austria-Hungary's ultimatum to Serbia, and reactions to it, see G. P. Gooch and H. Temperley, eds., *British Documents on the Origins of the War, 1898–1914,* London, 1926–38, vol. XI, No. 91; cited in Zara Steiner, *Britain and the Origins of the First World War,* St. Martin's Press, New York, 1977, pp. 221–22; and Charles Horne, ed., *Source Records of the Great War,* vol. I, The American Legion, Indianapolis 1931, p. 285. Bush outlined his ultimatum to Afghanistan in his "Address to a Joint Session of Congress and the American People," Washington, D.C., September 20, 2001. *www.whitehouse.gov/news/releases/2001/09/20010920-8.html.*

146. Cardinal Francis George is quoted from Catholic News Service, "Response Called Necessary," *The Catholic Free Press,* October 12, 2001, p. 1.

147–48. *The Challenge of Peace: God's Promise and Our Response,* published by the United States Conference of Catholic Bishops, Washington, D.C., 1983. I have summarized relevant points from paragraphs 85–97.

149. The suggestion that the terrorist operations of September 11 depended less on the Afghanistan bases than on flight schools in Florida comes from Carl Conetta, "Strange Victory: A Critical Appraisal of Operation Enduring Freedom and the Afghanistan War," Project on Defense Alternatives, *Research Monograph #6,* The Com-

monwealth Institute, Cambridge, MA, 2002, p. 32; *www.comw.org/pda/0201strangevic.html*. The FBI counterterrorism expert is quoted by Walter Pincus, "Al Qaeda to Survive bin Laden, Panel Told," *The Washington Post,* December 19, 2001; cited in Conetta, p. 5.

151–52. For "bombers coming from all directions" see *Bush at War*, pp. 98, 107. Woodward describes Bush's impatience on pp. 63, 99, 113, 151–2, 157–8, 168. On the Taliban's interest in negotiating a solution, see John Burns, "Taliban Refuse Quick Decision over bin Laden," *The New York Times,* September 18, 2001, p. A1; Amir Shah, "Islamic Clerics Ask Osama bin Laden to Leave Afghanistan; U.S. Rejects Proposal," *The New York Times,* September 20, 2001; John Burns, "Clerics Answer 'No, No, No!' and Invoke Fates of Past Foes," *The New York Times,* September 22, 2001, p. B3. The Bush administration's contempt for "pounding sand" is described by Woodward in *Bush at War*, pp. 38, 123. For the decision to oust the Taliban, see *Bush at War*, pp. 167, 174. For a detailed critique of the switch to this goal, see Carl Conetta, "Strange Victory: A Critical Appraisal of Operation Enduring Freedom and the Afghanistan War."

Chapter 8: War With Iraq

157. On the understanding that Resolution 1441 required further authorization for the use of force, see United Nations, Press Release SC 7564, November 8, 2002, "Security Council Holds Iraq in 'Material Breach' of Disarmament Obligations, Offers Final Chance to Comply, Unanimously Adopting Resolution 1441 (2002)" *www.un.org/News/Press/docs/2002/SC7564.doc.htm*.

158. For the speech in which Bush gave his ultimatum to Saddam Hussein, see "President Says Saddam Hussein Must Leave Iraq Within 48 Hours," *www.whitehouse.gov/news/releases/2003/03/iraq/20030317-7.html*. For references to many other speeches making the same point, see *http://uggabugga.blogspot.com/2003_04_13_uggabugga_archive.html#92763368*. For the State of the Union address, January 28, 2003, see *www.whitehouse.gov/news/*

releases/2003/01/20030128-19.html. For the evidence before the war began that the evidence regarding Iraq's attempted purchase of uranium in Africa was based on a forgery, see John Donnelly and Elizabeth Neuffer, "Intelligence? Dubious Claims Erode U.S. Credibility," *The Boston Globe,* March 16, 2003; David Ensor, "Fake Documents 'embarrassing' for U.S." *www.cnn.com/2003/US/03/14/sprj.irq.documents/,* posted March 14, 2003. On the doubts about the aluminum tubes, see Joby Warrick, "U.S. Claim on Iraqi Nuclear Program Is Called into Question," *The Washington Post,* January 24, 2003, p. A1.

160. Cook explained the reasons for his resignation in "Why I Had to Leave the Cabinet," *Guardian,* March 18, 2003. On the legality of the war, see Lord Goldsmith, "Legal Basis for the Use of Force Against Iraq," *http://open.gov.uk/NewsRoom/NRArticle/0,1169,223412%7E801b22%7Efs%7Een,00.html.* For Vaughan Lowe's view, see Crimes of War Project, "Would War be Lawful Without Another UN Resolution?" March 10, 2003, *www.crimesofwar.org/special/Iraq/news-iraq2.html* and Professor Vaughan Lowe, Professor James Crawford, and others, "War Would Be illegal," *Guardian,* March 7, 2003, letters. A critique of the Australian government's legal justification for participating in the war is Andrew Byrnes and Hilary Charlesworth, "The Illegality of the War Against Iraq," *Dialogue,* published by the Academy of the Social Sciences in Australia, vol. 22, no. 1 (2003) pp. 4–9.

161. Moseley's admission is quoted in Michael Gordon, "U.S. Air Raids in '02 Prepared for War in Iraq," *The New York Times,* July 20, 2003.

162. For Bush's response to Knoller, see "President George Bush Discusses Iraq in National Press Conference," March 6, 2003, *www.whitehouse.gov/news/releases/2003/03/20030306-8.html.* Bush's reference to Saddam's "vast arsenal" comes from his Radio Address to the Nation, February 8, 2003, U.S. Department of State International Information Programs, *http://usinfo.state.gov/regional/nea/iraq/text2003/0208bush.htm.* He used similar language on many other occasions, including his speech in Cincinnati on Octo-

ber 7, 2002 (see "President Bush's Speech on the Use of Force, *The New York Times,* October 8, 2002).

162–63. Powell's statement that Saddam has not developed weapons of mass destruction was made at a press briefing in Cairo on February 24, 2001, after he had met with the Egyptian president and foreign minister. See John Pilger, "The Big Lie," *Daily Mirror,* September 22, 2003, *http://www.mirror.co.uk/news/allnews/page.cfm?objectid=13434081&method=full&siteid=50143*. The transcript of the press briefing is available at *www.usis.it/file2001_02/alia/a1022304.htm*. For Richard Haass's account of what Rice told him, see Nicholas Lemann, "How it Came to War: When Did Bush Decide that He Had to Fight Saddam?" *The New Yorker,* March 31, 2003. Joseph Wilson describes his trip to Niger in Joseph Wilson, "What I Didn't Find in Africa," *The New York Times,* July 6, 2003.

163. For the contents of the October 2002 National Intelligence Estimate on Iraq, see "Text of Statement by George J. Tenet," *The New York Times,* July 12, 2003. On Tenet's call to Hadley, see Dana Milbank and Walter Pincus, "Bush Aides Disclose Warnings from CIA," *The Washington Post,* July 23, 2003, p. A1.

164. On the grounds for doubting the African uranium story, see Walter Pincus, "CIA Asked Britain to Drop Iraq Claim," *Washington Post,* July 11, 2003, p. A1. For the repetition of the story by Rice, Rumsfeld, and Wolfowitz, see Walter Pincus, "Bush Team Kept Airing Iraq Allegation," *The Washington Post,* August 8, 2003, p. A10.

164–65. On Bush's use of the "forty-five-minutes notice" claim see Dana Milbank, "White House Didn't Gain CIA Nod for Claim on Iraqi Strikes," *The Washington Post,* July 20, 2003, p. A1. Bush repeatedly claimed that Saddam had links with Al Qaeda. For example, in just eight days, between October 28 and November 4, 2002, he made this claim in eleven separate speeches. For details, see *http://uggabugga.blogspot.com/2002_11_03_uggabugga_archive.html#84038908*. He continued to make this claim in September 2003, although he then admitted that there was no evidence linking

Saddam Hussein to the September 11 attacks. See David Sanger, "Bush Reports No Evidence of Hussein Tie to 9/11," *The New York Times,* September 18, 2003. For repudiation of the claims about links between Al Qaeda and Iraq, see James Risen, "Captives Deny Qaeda Worked with Baghdad," *The New York Times,* June 9, 2003; Robert Scheer, "Bad Iraq Data from Start to Finish," *Los Angeles Times,* June 10, 2003; and Anne E. Kornblut and Bryan Bender, "Cheney Link of Iraq, 9/11 Challenged," *The Boston Globe,* September 16, 2003. For a contrary view, see Stephen Hayes, "Case Closed," *The Weekly Standard,* November 24, 2003, and for commentary on this article, see Michael Isikoff and Mark Hosenball, "Case Decidedly Not Closed," *Newsweek Web Exclusive,* November 19, 2003, *www.msnbc.com/news/995706.asp/0cv =KB10* For a devastating exposé of the intelligence on which the Bush administration based its case for war with Iraq, see Seymour Hersh, "Selective Intelligence," *The New Yorker,* May 12, 2003, pp. 44–51. On the general issue of stretching the evidence about Iraq's weapons of mass destruction, see Evan Thomas, Richard Wolffe, and Michael Isikoff, "Where are Iraq's WMDs?" *Newsweek,* June 9, 2003, *www.msnbc.com/news/919753.asp #BODY;* and Barton Gellman, "Frustrated U.S. Arms Team to Leave Iraq: Task Force Unable to Find Any Weapons," *The Washington Post,* May 11, 2003, p. A1. Iraq's attempt to negotiate with the U.S. is described in James Risen, "Iraq Said to Have Tried to Reach Last-Minute Deal to Avert War," *The New York Times,* November 6, 2003.

167. Bush's account of the orders he gave to Franks can be found in "Full Text of Brokaw's Interview with Bush" (An interview with Tom Brokaw of NBC News), *The New York Times,* April 25, 2003. The passage quoted from the UN Charter is from Article 2(7), available at *www.un.org/aboutun/charter*. The resolutions referred to are Security Council Resolution 688 (April 5, 1991) *http://srch0.un.org:80/Docs/scres/1991/688e.pdf*, and Security Council Resolution 841 (June 16, 1993) *http://srch0.un.org:80/ Docs/scres/1993/841e.pdf*. I am indebted here to Gregory Fox, "The Right to Political Participation in International Law," in

Cecelia Lynch and Michael Loriaux, eds, *Law and Moral Action in World Politics,* University of Minnesota Press, Minneapolis, 1999, p. 91. For further discussion of the ethics and law of humanitarian intervention, see my *One World,* Yale University Press, New Haven, 2002, ch. 4.

168. The quote from Con Coughlin is from his *Saddam, King of Terror*, Ecco, New York, 2002, p. 315.

169. For Bush's statement that the U.S. was right not to send troops into Rwanda, see the second presidential debate, *www.newsminute.com/bushgoredebate2.htm.* Rice's statement ignoring the president's stance is quoted in Philip Gourevitch, "The Congo Test," *The New Yorker,* June 2, 2003, p. 33. See also James Bennett, "Clinton Declares U.S. and the World Failed Rwandans," *The New York Times,* March 26, 1998.

170. On the resolution in Congress authorizing the use of force against Iraq, see Alison Mitchell and Carla Hulse, "Threats and Responses: The Vote: Congress Authorizes Bush to Use Force Against Iraq, Creating a Broad Mandate," *The New York Times,* October 11, 2002, p. A1; "Congress Passes Iraq Use of Force Resolution," *http://usgovinfo.about.com/library/weekly/aa101102a.htm.*

171–72. For descriptions of conditions in hospitals in Iraq during the war, see Paul McGeough, "Descent into a Charnel-House Hospital Hell," *Sydney Morning Herald,* April 10, 2003, p.1. For the killing of Mazen Dana, see "Cameraman Killed By U.S. Troops," *CNN.com,* August 17, 2003, *www.cnn.com/2003/WORLD/meast/08/17/sprj.irq.cameraman.reut/* and for that of the al-Kerim family, see Justin Huggler, "Family Shot Dead By Panicking U.S. Troops," *The Independent,* August 10, 2003.

172–74. For an estimate of Iraqi deaths, civilian and combatant, see Carl Conetta, "The Wages of War: Iraqi Combatant and Noncombatant Fatalities in the 2003 Conflict," Project on Defense Alternatives, *Research Monograph #8, http://www.comw.org/pda/0310rm8exsum.html.* The death toll among U.S. military forces and those of its supporters is given in Associated Press, "U.S. Soldier Killed in Bombing is 400th to Die in Iraq," *The Washington*

Post, November 15, 2003. For the number of Americans injured, and personal accounts of the impact of those injuries, see Neela Banerjee, "Rebuilding Bodies, and Lives, Maimed by War," *The New York Times,* November 16, 2003. On the use of napalm, see Andrew Buncombe, "U.S. Admits It Used Napalm Bombs in Iraq," *The Independent,* August 10, 2003. On the environmental problems caused by the war and its aftermath, see United Nations Environment Programme, *Environment in Iraq: UNEP Progress Report,* Geneva, October 20, 2003. *http://postconflict.unep.ch/publications/Iraq_PR.pdf.* For Iraq's cultural losses, see Adam Goodheart, "Missing: A Vase, a Book, a Bird and 10,000 Years of History," *The New York Times,* April 20, 2003; Alberto Manguel, "Our First Words, Written in Clay, in an Accountant's Hand," *The New York Times,* April 20, 2003; David Mehegan, "Burned Libraries Make Iraq's History a War Casualty," *The Boston Globe,* April 21, 2003, p. B7; Eleanor Robson, "Iraq's Museums: What Really Happened," *The Guardian,* 18 June 2003; U.S. Department of State, Bureau of Educational and Cultural Affairs, "Iraq Cultural Property Image Collection," *http://exchanges.state.gov/culprop/imfact.html.* The figures on violent deaths in Baghdad are taken from Iraq Body Count, Press Release PR5, "Over 1,500 Violent Civilian Deaths in Occupied Baghdad," September 23, 2003, *www.iraqbodycount.net/press.htm.*

174–75. For Kofi Annan's dilemma, see "Secretary-General presents his annual report to General Assembly" [Sept. 20, 1999] SG/SM/7136 GA/9596; *http://srch0.un.org:80/Docs/SG/index.html.*

175–76. See Human Rights Watch, "Briefing to the 59th Session of the UN Commission on Human Rights: Democratic Republic of the Congo," February 27, 2003, *www.hrw.org/un/chr59/drc.htm;* Human Rights Watch, "D.R. Congo: Civilians at Risk of Revenge Killings in Ituri," *Human Rights News,* March 11, 2003, *http://hrw.org/press/2003/03/congo031103.htm;* Philip Gourevitch, "The Congo Test," *The New Yorker,* June 2, 2003, p. 33. On the final UN deployment, see Reuters, "UN Approves Troop Deployment in Congo," *New York Times,* May 30, 2003.

Chapter 9: Pax Americana

180–81. For Webster's view, see Daniel Webster, secretary of state, to Lord Ashburton, August 6, 1842, reprinted in John Bassett Moore, *A Digest of International Law* 409, 412 (1906). For discussion, see Michael Byers, "Letting the Exception Prove the Rule," *Ethics and International Affairs,* 17:1 (2003) pp. 9–24. The relevant section of the United Nations Charter is Chapter VII, Article 51, available at *www.un.org/aboutun/charter*.

182. For U.S. threats and actions regarding North Korea, see Barbara Starr and Suzanne Malvaux, "Officials: U.S. Reviews Military Options amid Korea Tensions," CNN, January 18, 2003, *http://edition.cnn.com/2003/WORLD/asiapcf/east/01/18/korea.war/;* Martin Nesirky, "U.S. Bombers Sent to Deter North Korea," Reuters, March 6, 2003, *http://uk.news.yahoo.com/030306/80/dusz5.html;* "Full Text of Brokaw's Interview With Bush" (An interview by Tom Brokaw of NBC News), *New York Times,* April 25, 2003.

183. For Bush's comment on what Chirac needed to be told, see Fox News, "Raw Data: Text of Bush Interview" [with Brit Hume] Monday, September 22, 2003, *http://www.foxnews.com/story/0,2933,98006,00.html.*

183–84. See "U.S. Documents Show Embrace of Saddam Hussein in Early 1980s Despite Chemical Weapons, External Aggression, Human Rights Abuses." National Security Archive, George Washington University, *www.gwu.edu/~nsarchiv/NSAEBB/NSAEBB82/press.htm*. On international law on the legitimacy of governments, see Brad Roth, *Governmental Illegitimacy in International Law,* Clarendon Press, Oxford, 1999, pp. 162–63.

185. The thesis that democracies are less likely to be aggressors goes back to Kant's *Perpetual Peace,* section II, and is also associated with Joseph Schumpeter. See Michael Doyle, "Liberal Institutions and International Ethics," in Kenneth Kipnis and Diana Meyers, eds., *Political Realism and International Morality,* Westview, Boulder, CO, 1987, pp. 185–211; first published as

"Liberalism and World Politics," *American Political Science Review,* 80:4 (1986) 1152-69. See Matthew White's assessment at *http://users.erols.com/mwhite28/demowar.htm.* This site also has links to other Web discussions of the thesis.

185–86. See U.S. Department of Defense, *Quadrennial Review Report,* September 30, 2001, *www.defenselink.mil/pubs/qdr2001.pdf.* For the quote from Richard Betts, see his *Surprise Attack: Lessons for Defense Planning,* Brookings Institution, Washington, D.C., 1982, pp. 14, 43, cited by Neta Crawford, "The Slippery Slope to Preventive War," *Ethics and International Affairs,* 17:1 (2003) p. 32. Hobbes's classic work is *Leviathan,* (1651). The quotes here and below come from chapters 13 and 17.

188. For the second presidential debate, see *www.newsminute.com/bushgoredebate2.htm.* The "strong and humble" statement was in "President Bush Addresses Council of the Americas," May 7, 2001, *www.usemb.gov.do/IRC/speeches/bush8.htm.*

For Project for the New American Century's "Statement of Principles," see *www.newamericancentury.org/statementofprinciples.htm*

The signatories include the following appointees in the Bush–Cheney administration: Elliot Abrams, who has served as Bush's director of the National Security Council's Office for Democracy, Human Rights and International Operations, and as Special Assistant to the President for a region that includes the Middle East; Paula Dobriansky, undersecretary, Global Affairs, U.S. Department of State; Aaron Friedberg, deputy national security adviser and director of Planning to Vice President Cheney; Lewis Libby, chief of staff to Vice President Cheney; and Peter W. Rodman, assistant secretary of defense for International Security Affairs.

189. For the "Letter to President Clinton on Iraq," see *www.newamericancentury.org/iraqclintonletter.htm*

189. On Shulsky's role in the Iraq intelligence debacle, see Seymour Hersh, "Selective Intelligence," *The New Yorker,* May 12, 2003, p. 44.

191. Rumsfeld's reference to stopping Hitler is from *Fox Special Report with Brit Hume,* August 19, 2002, as cited in

Lawrence F. Kaplan and William Kristol, *The War Over Iraq: Saddam's Tyranny and America's Mission,* Encounter Books, San Francisco, 2003, p. 115. On America as the world's policeman, see pp. 120–121.

192. For the Truman quote, see Harry S. Truman, address in San Francisco at the Closing Session of the United Nations Conference, June 26, 1945, Truman Presidential Museum and Library, *www.trumanlibrary.org/trumanpapers/pppus/1945/66.htm*. For Bush's challenge to the Security Council, see "President George Bush Discusses Iraq in National Press Conference," March 6, 2003, *www.whitehouse.gov/news/releases/2003/03/20030306-8.html*

193–94. See Richard Perle, "United They Fall," *The Spectator,* March 22, 2003, *www.spectator.co.uk/article.php3?table=old§ion=current&issue=2003-05-10&id=2909*. See also Richard Perle, "Who Says the United Nations Is Better than NATO?" *International Herald Tribune,* November 28, 2002, *www.iht.com/ihtsearch.php?id=78361&owner=(IHT)&date=20021129130235;* see also Yahoo/Reuters, "Perle: War Against Terror is Not Over," April 25, 2003, ***http://story.news.yahoo.com/news?tmpl=story&u=/nm/20030425/pl_nm/iraq_perle_dc_1***. For Kaplan and Kristol's assertion that there is no higher authority than America, see *The War Over Iraq,* p. 120.

194–95. On the U.S. contribution to the UN, see United Nations Secretariat, "Status of Contributions as at 31 December 2002," ST/ADM/SER.B/600, January 23, 2003. Annex II. For "Ranking the Rich," see *Foreign Policy*, no. 136 (May–June 2003); *www.foreignpolicy.com/story/story.php?storyID=13656*.

195. For Blair's readiness to disregard a veto, see BBC News, "Clearing the Decks for War," February 24, 2003, ***http://news.bbc.co.uk/2/hi/middle_east/2769839.stm;*** BBC News, "Russia Ready for Iraq Veto," March 10, 2003, ***http://news.bbc.co.uk/2/hi/middle_east/2835241.stm;*** Diego Ibarguen, Daniel Rubin, and Martin Merzer, "France, Russia Prepared to Veto War Resolution," *Mercury News,* March 10, 2003, *www.bayarea.com/mld/bayarea/news/5361001.htm*.

195–96. For Bush's speech to the UN, see "President Addresses United Nations General Assembly," September 23, 2003, *http://www.whitehouse.gov/news/releases/2003/09/20030923-4.html.* For Kofi Annan's speech, see Press Release SG/SM/8891/GA/10157, "Adoption of Policy of Preemption Could Result in Proliferation of Unilateral, Lawless Use of Force, Secretary-General Tells General Assembly," September 23, 2003, *http://www.un.org/News/Press/docs/2003/sgsm8891.doc.htm.*

197. "What's wrong with dominance?" is asked by Kaplan and Kristol on p. 112 of *The War Over Iraq*.

198. On the response to Bush's "first things first" statement, see Edmund Andrews, "Bush Angers Europe by Eroding Pact on Warming," *The New York Times,* April 1, 2001, p. A1. For Glover's views, see his essay, "Can We Justify Killing the Children of Iraq?" *The Guardian,* February 5, 2003.

199. For the *Bulletin of Atomic Scientists* report on the dangers posed by the smuggling of radioactive materials, see its issue of February 27, 2002, *www.thebulletin.org/media/current.html.*

199–200. On NATO's unity, see NATO, "September 11, One Year On," *www.nato.int/terrorism/,* and for the UN Security Council Resolution 1373 (2001), see United Nations Press Release SC/7158, September 28, 2001, *www.un.org/News/Press/docs/2001/sc7158.doc.htm.* Kiesling's letter is quoted in Matthew Rothschild, "Bush Trashes the United Nations," *The Progressive,* April 2003.

Chapter 10: The Ethics of George W. Bush

203. See Robert Nozick, *Anarchy, State, and Utopia,* Basic Books, 1977, p. ix.

204. "President Outlines His Agenda for U.S.–African Relations," June 26, 2003, *www.whitehouse.gov/news/releases/2003/06/20030626-2.html.*

206. See *A Charge to Keep*, pp. 10, 147; and press release, "President Signs Born Alive Infants Protection Act," Office of the

Press Secretary, August 5, 2002, *www.whitehouse.gov/news/releases/2002/08/20020805-6.html*. The reference to Exodus is 21:22–23.

207. For Jesus on turning the other cheek, see Matthew 5:39, and for Paul, Romans 12:17–21. For the views of religious leaders on the war with Iraq, see Peter Steinfels, "Deaf Ears on Iraq," *The New York Times*, September 28, 2002; Laurie Goodstein, "Diverse Denominations Oppose the Call to Arms," *The New York Times*, March 6, 2003; Laurie Goodstein, "Conservative Catholics' Wrenching Debate Over Whether to Back President or Pope," *The New York Times*, March 6, 2003.

208. For the *Time* poll, see "Beyond the Year 2000: What to Expect in the New Millennium," a special issue of *Time* (Fall, 1992), cited by Robert Fuller, *Naming the Antichrist: The History of an American Obsession*, Oxford University Press, New York, 1995. The quote about liberty being God's gift is from Ann McFeatters, "Religious Leaders Uneasy With Bush's Rhetoric," *Pittsburgh Post-Gazette*, February 12, 2003. For the significance of Bush's use of the term "evil ones," see David Frum, *The Right Man*, p. 140. Frum's comment on the phrase "axis of evil" is on pp. 238–40. The comment from Don Evans is quoted by Howard Fineman, "Bush and God," *Newsweek*, March 10, 2003, p. 25.

209. Walter Lippmann's remark is from his *A Preface to Politics*, University of Michigan Press, Ann Arbor 1962, p. 7 and is quoted by Andrew Delbanco, *The Death of Satan: How Americans Have Lost the Sense of Evil*, Farrar, Straus and Giroux, New York, 1996.

209–10. On Bush's instinctive responses, see Bob Woodward, *Bush at War*, pp. 340–42. Frum's comment is from *The Right Man*, pp. 273–74.

210. John DiIulio's letter to Ron Suskind, dated October 24, 2002, was a source for Ron Suskind's "Why Are These Men Laughing?" *Esquire*, vol. 139 no. 1, January 2003. The text of the letter is available at *www.esquire.com/features/articles/2002/021202_mfe_diiulio_1.html*.

211. The comment from Nicholas Kristof is in his "In Blair We Trust," *The New York Times,* July 8, 2003, and the one from Howard Fineman is from "Bush and God," *Newsweek,* March 10, 2003, p. 30.

212–13. For the quote from DiIulio, see the letter cited above. Frum's anecdotes about his use of "damn" and Bush's understanding of being truthful are on pp. 13–17 of *The Right Man*. Frum's praise of Bush is on p. 272 of that work.

213–14. For an account of Lawrence Kohlberg's views, see his *The Philosophy of Moral Development: Moral Stages and the Idea of Justice*, Harper and Row, San Francisco, 1981, pp. 18–19, 24. Kohlberg's sequence of stages has been criticized on various grounds, including that it is based on studies of boys only. (See Carol Gilligan, *In a Different Voice,* Harvard University Press, Cambridge, MA, 1982.) Though some of these criticisms are valid, Kohlberg's view of moral development may nevertheless provide a helpful way of understanding Bush's moral judgments. Frum's statement that the country could trust the Bush administration not to lie or cheat is on p. 20 of *The Right Man.*

214–16. Rice and Rumsfeld are quoted in James Risen, "Bush Aides Now Say Claim on Uranium Was Accurate," *The New York Times,* July 14, 2003. Bush's initial evasion of the issue is described in David Sanger and Carl Hulse, "Republicans Dismiss Questions over Banned Weapons in Iraq," *The New York Times,* June 18, 2003. Rice admitted responsibility in her interview on *The NewsHour with Jim Lehrer*, as quoted in Richard Stevenson, "Bush Denies Claim He Oversold Case for War with Iraq," *The New York Times,* July 31, 2003. Bush "absolutely" took responsibility in his news conference, reported in "President Bush's Rose Garden News Conference," *The New York Times,* July 30, 2003.

216–17. On Bush's failure to support an independent inquiry, see Richard Stevenson, "President Asserts He Still Has Faith in Tenet and CIA," *The New York Times,* July 13, 2003, and Carl Hulse, "Senate Rejects Panel on Prewar Iraq Data," *The New York Times,* July 17, 2003. On Scott McClellan's repeated evasion of the question about why Bush made an inaccurate statement on when doubts were raised about the uranium claim, see press briefing by Scott McClellan, July 15, 2003, *www.whitehouse.gov/news/releases/2003/07/20030715-2.html.*

See also Roy Eccleston, "President's Answers Raise Questions," *The Australian,* July 6, 2003, p. 6.

217. See John DiIulio's letter to Ron Suskind, referred to above. On DiIulio's subsequent apology, see "Ex-Bush Aide Offers Apology for Remarks," *The New York Times,* December 3, 2002.

218. For the events involving President Hugo Chávez, see Christopher Marquis, "Bush Officials Met with Venezuelans Who Ousted Leader," *The New York Times,* April 16, 2002. On the cut to the budget for enforcing corporate standards, see Anne Kornblut, "For Bush Team, Getting Reelected Is Constant Theme," *The Boston Globe,* December 29, 2002. The voting figures for those who rated honesty important are from Frum, *The Right Man,* p. 9.

219. On the convenient timing of Bush's conversion, see Howard Fineman, "Bush and God," *Newsweek,* March 10, 2003, p. 27.

For Krugman's statements, in the order quoted, see his *New York Times* columns as follows: "Gotta Have Faith," December 17, 2002; "The Rove Doctrine," June 11, 2002; "Rejecting the World," April 18, 2003; "A Touch of Class," January 21, 2003; "Threats, Promises and Lies," February 25, 2003; and "Steps to Wealth," July 16, 2002. For a collection of Krugman's columns, see his *The Great Unraveling*, W. W. Norton, New York, 2003.

221–22. The quote from Strauss about religion is from his *Thoughts on Machiavelli*, Free Press, Glencoe, IL, 1958, pp. 230–31; see also "On a Forgotten Kind of Writing," *Independent Journal of Philosophy* 2, 1978, p. 27. I am grateful to David Luban for these citations. Thomas Fleming is quoted by Jeet Heer, "The Philosopher," *The Boston Globe,* May 11, 2003, p. H1. Robert Locke's essay on Strauss is "Leo Strauss, Conservative Mastermind," *FrontPageMagazine.com,* May 31, 2002, *www.frontpagemag.com/Articles/ReadArticle*

.asp?ID=1233. The "no higher duty" quote is from Peter Berkowitz, "Misreading a Political Philosopher," *Weekly Standard,* June 2, 2003, *www.weeklystandard.com/Content/Public/Articles/000/000/002/717acusr.asp*. For Miles Burnyeat's essay, see "Sphinx without a Secret." *The New York Review of Books,* vol. 32, no. 9, May 30, 1985.

222. On who is a Straussian, see James Atlas, "A Classicist's Legacy: New Empire Builders," *The New York Times,* May 4, 2003; Jeet Heer, "The Philosopher," *The Boston Globe,* May 11, 2003, p. H1; and see Seymour Hersh, "Selective Intelligence," *The New Yorker,* May 12, 2003. Atlas includes Richard Perle among the Straussians, a claim forcefully rejected by Joshua Muravchik in "The Neoconservative Cabal," *Commentary,* September 2003, p. 28.

223. For Bush's extraordinary statement about the reasons for attacking Iraq, see "President Reaffirms Strong Position on Liberia: Remarks by the President and United Nations Secretary-General Kofi Annan in Photo Opportunity, the Oval Office," *www.whitehouse.gov/news/releases/2003/07/20030714-3.html;* Ken Fireman, "The 'Right Decision': Bush Defends Intelligence that Led the U.S. to War," *Newsday,* July 15, 2003; Dana Priest and Dana Milbank, "Bush Defends Allegation On Iraq," *The Washington Post,* July 15, 2003, p. A1.

223–24. The statement about Rove's power, and Rove's admission about his use of the war on terror for political advantage, are both to be found in James Carney, "General Karl Rove, Reporting for Duty," *Time,* September 29, 2002. For Daschle's comments accusing Rove of making partisan use of the national security debate, see "Bush and Daschle Comments on National Security," *The New York Times,* September 26, 2002.

Acknowledgments

I thank George W. Bush for making this book possible. Had he not given ethics such prominence in his presidency, there would have been nothing to write about. Beyond that prerequisite, however, there are many others who have contributed to the book. Campbell Goodloe Hackett and Diego von Vacano provided excellent research assistance. I couldn't wish for a better critic than Brent Howard, who read the draft with great care and suggested numerous improvements, as well as additional sources of information. Simon Keller, Jeff McMahan, and Agata Sagan also gave me valuable suggestions. For taking the time to answer specific queries, I thank Jim Grote, Dale Jamieson, Paul Kurtz, and David Luban.

I have discussed questions about the sanctity of human life with my students at Princeton University, and have learned from many of them, but from none as much as from Michael Kimberly, who researched these issues with a thoroughness that is rare in undergraduate work, even at Princeton. The faculty and 2003–4 visiting fellows of the Center for Human Values gave me further useful feedback when I presented part of the book at one of our center's seminars. I am particularly grateful to Anthony Appiah, who presented a critical response on that occasion. I also drew on the book for my 2003 Lewis Burke Frumkes Lecture at New York University, and again benefited from the ensuing discussion.

My sources are listed in the preceding section, and they include many who have worked hard to construct informative Web sites about the Bush presidency, from whitehouse.gov down. But I must mention "Jerry Politix" of bushwatch.org whose daily e-mails notify me of articles about Bush appearing in the media. Carl Conetta, whose studies for the Project on Defense Alternatives have been particularly valuable, Iraqbodycount.org, and Representative Henry Waxman's Politics and Science page. Thanks, all of you, for the free public service you are providing.

I thank Princeton University for providing me with the leave during which this book was written. During part of this leave I had congenial working conditions in the Centre for Applied Philosophy and Public Ethics at the University of Melbourne, and I am grateful to Tony Coady and Graham Priest for making this possible.

I owe a special debt to Kathy Robbins, my agent, for encouraging me to proceed with this book, and finding the right publisher for it. And finally, I thank my editor at Dutton, Ryan Harbage, who has always been wonderfully enthusiastic about the book, while retaining sufficient detachment to keep a keen eye on ways in which it can be improved.

Index

INDEX

INDEX

INDEX

INDEX

Also by Peter Singer and available from Granta Books
www.granta.com

PUSHING TIME AWAY

My Grandfather and the Tragedy of Jewish Vienna

'What binds us pushes time away' wrote David Oppenheim to his future wife, Amalie Pollak, on March 24, 1905. Oppenheim, classical scholar, collaborator, then critic of Sigmund Freud, and friend and supporter of Alfred Adler, lived through the height and depths of Vienna's twentieth-century intellectual and cultural history. He perished in obscurity at a Nazi concentration camp in 1943, separated from family and friends. Almost fifty years later, Peter Singer set out to explore the life of the grandfather he never knew and made some startling discoveries.

'A beautifully written and deeply moving personal document by one of our pre-eminent contemporary philosophers' Joyce Carol Oates